THE OTHER BUDDHISM

AMIDA COMES WEST

CAROLINE BRAZIER

First published by O Books, 2007
O Books is an imprint of John Hunt Publishing Ltd.,
The Bothy, Deershot Lodge, Park Lane, Ropley, Hants, SO24 0BE, UK
office1@o-books.net
www.o-books.net

Distribution in:

UK and Europe
Orca Book Services
orders@orcabookservices.co.uk
Tel: 01202 665432 Fax: 01202 666219 Int. code (44)

USA and Canada
NBN
custserv@nbnbooks.com
Tel: 1 800 462 6420 Fax: 1 800 338 4550

Australia and New Zealand
Brumby Books
sales@brumbybooks.com.au
Tel: 61 3 9761 5535 Fax: 61 3 9761 7095

Far East (offices in Singapore, Thailand, Hong Kong, Taiwan)
Pansing Distribution Pte Ltd
kemal@pansing.com
Tel: 65 6319 9939 Fax: 65 6462 5761

South Africa
Alternative Books
altbook@peterhyde.co.za
Tel: 021 447 5300 Fax: 021 447 1430

Text copyright Caroline Brazier 2007

Design: Stuart Davies

ISBN: 978 1 84694 052 1

A CIP catalogue record for this book is available from the British Library.

Printed in the US by Maple Vail

THE OTHER BUDDHISM

AMIDA COMES WEST

CAROLINE BRAZIER

BOOKS

Winchester, UK
Washington, USA

Previous publications:

Buddhist Psychology

(published May 2003, Constable Robinson)

Dedication

To my Father
Jim Bates
Methodist minister
On his 81st Birthday

CONTENTS

PREFACE

Writing this preface, I am far from home. It has become a pattern in our lives that January sees my husband, David, and I travelling in North America. Next week we will be joining members of our organisation in Vancouver for a series of lectures, workshops and retreats, but this week we are in Hawaii.

Hawaii seems a fitting place to begin writing the preface for this book. A small island, set in a large ocean, it has long been seen as providing both a contained environment in which particular species have established themselves apart from the rest of the world, but also as a microcosm of the larger systems found elsewhere on the planet. In this space, many of the issues which face us all, living on this small planet, become apparent. These limited perspectives provide a mirror for many of the issues which this book explores, the issues that face humanity today at the dawn of the twenty-first century.

There are other reasons, though, why it feels appropriate to begin this preface here on Hawaii. After all, Amida Buddha promised to build a Pure Land in the West where all would quickly become enlightened. Hawaii is about as far West as you can go on this planet before plummeting over the artificial edge of the dateline and into the Far East. Beyond the sunset of my home skies, this island paradise is set deep in the jewel blue Pacific Ocean.

The mythologies which hold our lives give them shape and meaning. The spiritual edge is so often in the mists of the tales we tell. This is a place of stories.

It is fitting too, that this place, more than any other in the West, has been the home of Pureland Buddhism for many years. Everywhere one goes there are little Pureland temples and churches. The Honganji Mission, the

Jodoshu Church, each village has its small, clapperboard chapel set back amid the banana trees and plumeria. Here we feel very much at home as we talk with Pureland priests and find that, despite our different cultures, there is so much that need not be explained. Yes, yes, we say, as they ask us about our views of this doctrine or that. Yes, yes, we bow, grateful to find people steeped from birth in the practice we have come to love.

Yet in reality, I am a long way from home. Back in England, Pureland is hardly known. Time and again Western Buddhists question us with curiosity and even suspicion. Can this really be Buddhism? It is so different, so strange. This isn't what the Dalai Lama teaches, is it? Yet the Pureland spirit is at the core of Buddhism right across the East. In Japan, members of the different Pureland schools make up the largest denomination in the Buddhist population, there are many more Pureland practitioners, for example, than Zen practitioners. Pureland is popular. It has long been the Buddhism of ordinary people. Pureland Buddhism came to Hawaii with immigrant workers from China and Japan. They came to work on the sugar plantations from the late nineteenth century. Despite harsh conditions, these workers brought with them many things from their native culture and particularly they brought their religion. The Japanese community in particular grew strong and aspects of Japanese life became well established on the islands. Japanese Buddhism flourished here and soon each plantation had its chapel, many with resident priests. Pureland, being the religion of the people, was the most widespread, but other traditions also established temples. There are Zen, Tendai and Shingon temples too.

In The Buddhist House, our centre in England, we have a small shrine. It is shaped like a wooden cupboard, darkly lacquered, with two layers of opening doors at the front. The outer doors are solid and close with a sliding bolt. The inner ones consist of an open framework with gauze stretched across it. Through these one glimpses the standing figure of the Buddha Amida, set back in a niche beneath an arch of carved flying birds. These inner doors are usually left closed. There is a little shelf that can be pulled out below them on which incense may be offered, and a small cupboard space beneath the shrine in which family photos and other mementos can be stored.

This shrine was given to us by a Japanese friend who has done much to support the Japanese elders on the island here. She has re-housed a number of similar shrines over the years, as families here move away from their religious roots, often taking on the faith of their adopted country, the United States, be it Christianity or consumerism. The younger generation no longer have space for these antiquated pieces of furniture in their homes, yet are keen for the family shrines to be used by those who respect their religious origins. So this old wooden shrine was shipped back to England for us by friends in Hawaii as a token of our connection with the island. Pureland has come a long journey. It still has far to go.

I often think of the faith of those Japanese workers. Perhaps the shrine was brought all the way from Japan by a family. Maybe it was the only item from their old life to accompany them. Those must have been hard times, and to set out into such an uncertain future in search of employment must have been a big step. Much grief must have been involved in leaving the family village, with little hope of ever returning.

Maybe, on the other hand, the shrine was bought on the island. It would have been an important focus for the family life, the place where photographs and letters might be stowed, the ancestors honoured and the unfolding collective story recorded. It was probably the best item of furniture the family possessed. In all the uncertainties of an impoverished life, it sustained faith.

I was talking the other day with a Japanese friend who remembered as a child seeing his grandmother bowed before her shrine, chanting; the smell of incense and the rhythmic tones of nembutsu, the call to Amida.

Faith holds us in uncertain times. It transforms the mundane and the arduous. It sharpens our awareness of the bitter-sweet beauty of life.

It is not only the Pureland roots which make Hawaii a fitting setting to write this preface. Hawaii is also a place which has its own rich traditions of native spirituality. These embrace the natural world with deep respect. Through this relationship with nature, it touches other unseen dimensions. In Hawaiian spirituality the veil between the mundane world and the spiritual is very thin. A land where oceans and mountains are never far away and gulches brim over with verdant tropical foliage, filled with the melodic calls of minah, and the bright scarlet flashes of cardinals, there are easy echoes of the Pureland expression of spirituality through natural images.

Here also there is a respect for the forces that, greater and more mysterious than we can know, shape our lives in unpredictable ways. A volcanic island, the fires that rise from the earth are ever present. Respect for the power of the elements is always implicit. When a lava stream engulfs that road in which you live, you cannot resist its force. Such experiences make us humble.

But change is not always to be feared. A recent earthquake here threw many people's agendas into confusion, but for our group, it brought unexpected benefits in the human warmth and support it released. People rallied around, as often in times of trouble, and in the process discovered new levels of community. We were not the only ones. I heard from a good friend in the Jodoshu temple how people had come over from a neighbouring town to straighten their tombstones, knocked over by the quake. The little community of the temple were full of gratitude and appreciation for this help.

Being on an island in mid-ocean, it is easy to feel cut off from the world's troubles. The air is warm and balmy. The pace of life is gentle and governed by the forces of nature far more than it is elsewhere. Timber buildings succumb to voracious wood boring insects at a far faster rate even than those at our centre in France. Small rodents find their ways into even the most modern kitchen unless one is willing to use a great deal of poison and traps. At night, in this part of the island, I am lulled to sleep by the chirruping of the coqui frogs. It is sad to hear that these little tree frogs are the subject of a harsh war at present in which large areas of countryside are sprayed with acid, killing not only the frogs, but also many other species of insect and animal that live there. A recently arrived species, people find the nightly chorus of the coqui irritating. They forget that on a volcanic island all species are introduced. They will go to considerable lengths to preserve their illusion of paradise.

This place is not immune from the effects of modern life. Air travel is one of the most polluting forms of transport we have. To get to these islands and visit our Buddhist communities here I have travelled just over 7000 miles on two planes. My carbon foot print is alarming. Living here, unless one stays on the same island all the time, though, one inevitably flies. There are no ferries between the islands, and introducing them would create its own environmental problems, threatening whale routes and transmitting plant species and disease from island to island. The island has little public transport, so cars run bumper to bumper through the more populated areas of its Western side. Vast quantities of consumer goods are transported here from the mainland two and a half thousand miles away. Every vehicle, most building materials, food, furniture, household goods all arrive in great containers at the islands' docks. The military have long used these islands for bases, their location providing a convenient jumping off point for operations in Asia and a far away training ground for troops. There are social problems, drug use and child abuse here as in most other corners of the world. Poorer people struggle to find affordable housing whilst the rich build multi-million pound dwellings fronting onto the ocean. As engaged Buddhists we are not short of work here.

In the longer run, the islands will be profoundly affected by changes in the earth's climate. A microcosm of our planet, they will experience the same rising temperatures, changes in sea levels and alterations of weather pattern that the rest of the planet anticipates. Water supplies are vulnerable to drought and the life of the seas to changing water temperatures. Coral reefs may die and unhealthy levels of toxic algae create the notorious "red tides" which kill other marine life and endanger human health.

And yet, this afternoon I can still swim in the tide pools, floating easefully in the salty water among the myriad brightly coloured fish. Privileged to join this strange world, my mask allowing me to see what otherwise I might so easily miss. A shoal of golden butterfly fish include me in their number, a needle fish passes me, watching me sideways with his strangely intelligent eye. A vivid purple and yellow clearer wrasse follows close. Life is infinitely surprising and beautiful.

A reappraisal of the values which underpin our modern lives is called for. For aeons people lived much closer to the soil. Although past civilisations have played their part in transforming environments, none has been so detached or so destructive as we. We have moved away from the times when we lived within the natural order of the year. Now we expect produce when we want it, not when it is in season. We do not put on extra clothing in cold weather, we adjust our central heating. We cannot go back, but we need to find a different way to live in the present. Such behaviours are contributing to the disaster which lies ahead.

The shift that has occurred has to a large degree come out of the human attempt to create a more comfortable lifestyle. It is ironic that the search to control our environments and create better conditions for ourselves has resulted in such a backlash. It has thrown the very systems that sustain life as we know it out of balance, forcing them towards a new equilibrium which may be much less conducive to comfortable living. There is a need for people to find a new way of being that is more harmonious with the order of things, to find a way that respects our situation and our planet. This is not an easy task. It requires faith.

Pureland Buddhism is new to the West. Beyond the Japanese and Chinese communities, it has made little headway with Westerners in either Europe or the United States. Yet this approach to the teachings of Shakyamuni Buddha has much to offer us in the West. In its devotional practices, this approach embodies the teachings of non-self, shifting us from an ego-centric perspective into a way of thinking that is exploratory, relational and faith based. Freeing us from the confining pressures of guilt and achievement oriented religion, it liberates us to live more naturally.

This book offers a simple exploration of Pureland Buddhism. It is an attempt to convey something of the flavour of this rich tradition and to offer a way to practice in the Western context. The central message is one of hope that comes from an approach to faith which is both open and joyous. The core values of gratitude, humility and wonder, community and love speak to our condition.

In Pureland the recognition of context and ancestry as the conditions which have enabled our lives is very important. This book is dedicated to my father in expression of such feeling. My father has been an inspiration to me in many ways. It is with some amusement that I see how much my own life owes to his example. (Do we ever intend to follow in our parents' footsteps?) A Methodist minister, he is still a powerful and intelligent preacher, and actively involved in many groups in his community in North Devon, having retired many years ago after twenty seven years as chaplain at Southlands College in London. Much of my childhood was spent at the college, where I saw his work with students and in various socially based projects. I also saw his involvement with the anti-war movement and his socialist concerns. His father before him was a missionary in China and my father's early childhood took place in a mission compound. I often quip that I am redressing the balance.

In truth though, we have all engaged in our own ways in the same process, that of exploring faith and its religious expression in the context of our respective eras. The world is not so big and East and West need equally to find new faith in the times to come.

Having dedicated this book to my father, I would also like to acknowledge the role my mother has played in introducing me to the natural world from a very early age, teaching me the names of plants, animals and birds as we walked in the countryside. Also she introduced me to poetry, which she read to me, often at night before I went to sleep, the rhythms of the poems would fill my dreams. The love of words that comes from this is part of my pleasure in writing.

When I wrote *Buddhist Psychology* a number of people asked if I would write a sequel giving more emphasis to the Pureland approach which we practice in the Amida-shu tradition. This book is certainly informed by my years working as a therapist. Through this work I have met many inspiring people and heard many stories that have touched me deeply. This book will, I hope, be of interest to those for whom *Buddhist Psychology* has guided therapeutic practice.

In my experience, however, what is therapeutic cannot be divorced from the spiritual underpinnings of a life. Psychology has much to answer for in the current world and Western models have been influential in creating a climate of individualism. The fear of creating repression has contributed to a surge of indulgence. As this book suggests, such trends have serious social implications. I hope therefore that this book will provoke discussion about the underpinning values of many fields including the psychotherapeutic.

Such discussion is not idle debate. Most importantly I hope that this book will contribute to the growing voices that call for a reconsideration of our basic social values. I hope it will join those voices which question the status quo of our society and will invite an exploration of what is beautiful, what is unknown. Buddhism has a rich heritage of wisdom. So far in the West our experience of this has only been partial. The time is perhaps now ripe for *The Other Buddhism*.

Caroline Brazier

Amida Order

The Buddhist House

12 Coventry Rd

Narborough

LE19 2GR

UK

www.amidatrust.com

CHAPTER ONE

A BITTER SWEET WORLD

When Irene died, the bees came.

It was three o'clock one Saturday morning in May when Irene died, in those wee, dark hours before the dawn when nature draws breath, when babies cry their first and when the frail slip away.

A small group of us from the community were gathered around her bed. As it became evident that her breathing pattern was changing and that she was sliding into the last moments of her life, we began to chant the Buddha's name. We held hands, David, my husband holding his mother's hand in his. She took a last breath as we held ours, and then, almost imperceptibly, she stopped. It was a peaceful death.

We had slept little for several nights, sitting vigil in Irene's room. Now as the first bird began to sing its dawn song, the room became quiet. We stayed, sitting, with her body in our midst for a little while. Slowly the sun began to come up.

Then, getting up and walking through to the sitting room next door, David told me that he wanted to go out into the garden to be close to the plants that Irene had tended with so much love and care. I went with him, feeling the proximity of his sadness like chill breeze across my skin.

David walked on ahead, down to the greenhouse where Irene had spent so much time. I followed at a distance, hearing his tears across the clear air. Both intimate and solitary, the moment hung in unscheduled space.

A scent of blossom from the huge lime tree that Irene had so loved shrouded the air. She had watched it dancing in the breeze as she lay in bed during those last days. In front of me, the gravel path was wet and glistening with dew, catching the light of a street lamp at the end of the garden. In the half-light, indeterminate shapes of foliage overhung its edges.

Suddenly as I started to walk down the garden, I became aware of a loud droning noise.

What was it?

I looked around, expecting to see something mechanical approaching: perhaps a helicopter overhead, perhaps some large vehicle on the road. The noise was so loud, so intrusive. If it were a helicopter surely it would land any moment here on the lawn.

Then, looking up, I saw what was causing it. A huge cloud of bees was circling above me, looking for all the world like a tornado. The sky was all but blotted out, and the droning noise drowned out the other sounds of early morning. Alone and held by the noise, I watched as the swarm funnelled its way up the front of the house, right against the tall bay windows, and hovered just outside Irene's bedroom. The sound was overwhelming, almost otherworldly in its intensity. In the air there hung the heavy smell of honey.

Out of this noise, I called to David to come and witness what was happening, and after some little while he came back from the green house to stand beside me.

"Look up"

We stood together, watching and marvelling at this happening.

Eventually the bees settled, forming a mass on the wall just beside Irene's window. Then, gradually, they moved into the roof space above the lintel. The bees had returned to an old haunt.

When we had moved into The Buddhist House in Leicestershire three years earlier, in the summer of 2001, we noticed that large numbers of bees were entering and leaving the eaves above Irene's bedroom window. As we were having building work done at the time and since the builders needed access to that area, high up near the roof, we needed to do something about these resident bees. Understandably, the builders wanted to avoid getting stung while working on the high scaffolding. They wanted the nest removed.

After some searching of directories and a few phone calls, we discovered a local beekeeper, who agreed to come and move the swarm to a new location. He had hives some distance away to the north of the city, so the bees could safely be transported without risk of their finding their way home.

Over the course of a few days, the beekeeper spent a lot of time high on the builder's scaffolding, painstakingly removing the bees' nest into a travelling box. It was fascinating to watch the care with which he made sure that each small creature found its way into the wooden crate. He left the crate on top of the scaffolding for a couple of days to ensure that the last stragglers would catch up and not be left behind. Then on the third evening, after the swarm had settled for the night, he took the box away to the place where he kept his hives.

We saw nothing more of the bees until the Friday afternoon, three years later, which was the day before Irene died. Irene was lying in her bed, very sick and in her last full day of life, looking out towards her beloved lime tree with eyes that no longer seemed to see this world. Following her gaze, we started to notice that a few bees were buzzing at the window. All afternoon one or two bees hovered around outside her room, but we hardly registered their presence as we went about the necessary and intimate tasks of caring for a very sick person.

We did not know the portentous quality of their arrival.

To grieve is to live

The experience of being with a dying person is one of deep engagement.

Things seem to run at a different pace and the quality of each moment to extend into a timeless dance. While ordinary life continues on the street outside, the house of the dying exists in an abyss of extraordinary time and space. It can be a time of great beauty and peace.

At the same time, the experience of caring for the dying is firmly grounded in day to day details of human process. The managing of a body that has ceased to function brings us face to face with the less aesthetic aspects of our nature. There is a lot of cleaning up, lifting, rearranging and cleaning up again to be done.

Some Buddhist monks were trained to meditate on the loathsomeness of the body, hoping to jettison lingering worldly aspirations, and in particular to dispel any residual longing for the female form, by scrutinising the decaying remains of corpses at the charnel ground. Most of us, however, exude enough unpleasant substance and odour prior to our final demise to make this last step in the study of the dying process unnecessary.

This said, there is a strange beauty too in the body at the point of letting go of life. It is in the touch of skin, so frail and translucent that it looks as if it could be damaged at any rough handling, and in the little expressions of love that pass between us in the performance of simple acts of caring, when self-consciousness and modesty have dropped away. It is in the poignant and the startlingly earthy, as we are haunted by an uneasy anticipation of grief, yet find ourselves sharply alive. The time of death is a time of great pathos. We live on a knife-edge between joy and despair. We are bathed in love and we touch profound aloneness. The moment is tender in the certain knowledge that it will not last.

In this moment we experience the bitter-sweet quality of being fully alive. This quality touches both the heights and the depths simultaneously with a presence, gentle as the brush of gossamer. We touch the inexpressible in the ordinary.

Yugen

During the twelfth century in Japan a genre of creative expression emerged that was described as *Yugen*. This was mostly, but not entirely, found in poetic writing. To understand the meaning of *yugen*, one can delve into the cultural roots which created the context for this style to emerge. *Yugen* is sometimes described as an allegorical form of writing. However, it differs considerably from the allegorical style of Western medieval writing. The quality of description which *yugen* offers is at once simple and understated, and at the same time is multi-layered.

The effect of a *yugen* poem upon the reader has been compared to the quality of *shikantaza* meditation. This is the meditation in which one simply sits and in the sitting observes thoughts pass across the surface of the mind like clouds across a summer sky. The reader of the poem is drawn, through the quiet tone of the writing, into an experience akin to that of sitting in stillness, whilst the images of the poem arise, like the mental objects in the mind of the meditator. The reader observes each image but does not follow. The objects are not grasped, but nevertheless touch the heart.

The imagery of a *yugen* poem tends to draw one's attention into the far distance. Often the perspective described is open, a somewhat featureless landscape in which the eye is drawn to objects a way off: the view out over the sea at sunset, an expanse of marshland, a mountain landscape. The tenor of the poem is quiet. The scene may be misted or in the half-light of dawn or dusk. There is a stillness. One feels one can breathe the air and smell the scent of blossom or the brine of the sea. Understated to a point that approaches neutrality, the images of *Yugen* express the subtle experience of life.

In writing about poetry there is both gain and loss. The writer can help the reader to gain understanding by explaining imagery and unpacking the layers of meaning implicit in a few words. At the same time, the analysis of the poem cannot convey the poet's meaning as eloquently or forcefully as the poet did in the original. It is the very complexity of poetry that enables it to touch our minds and hearts simultaneously, compounding layers of imagery into forms that break open to yield their concealed wisdom. Whilst an understanding of what is meant by the *yugen* quality and its roots can give us insight into what we might be expected to experience in hearing a *yugen* poem, it is no substitute for allowing the poem itself to move us.

One such poem was written by the twelfth century poet-priest Saigyo, here in a translation by Burton Watson (Watson 1991)

> Even a person free of passion
> would be moved
> to sadness:
> autumn evening
> in a marsh where snipes fly up

As we read this poem, we perceive its wistful quality. The melancholy atmosphere of an autumn evening creates a stage on which the flight of birds stirs a response in the observer. We feel our breath clouding in the evening air, hear the silence of the marshes, smell their dank wateriness and see the long vista of reeds and sallows. We stand beside the poet in mutual aloneness.

In the first part of the poem we see the figure of the writer, a monk, who might think himself free of passion and yet is touched by the scene. Typical of its type, the poem juxtaposes this image of the solitary, static human, with the ascent of snipes in the second part. There is a sense of separation between the elements, but also of their relationship.

First the viewer looks to the monk and sees both his effort to overcome the passions and the inevitable slippage into feelings. Then the view point shifts, the monk sees the snipes. We, as readers, are invited to move from one perspective to the other. We take in both aspects of the scene and in them see our own responses reflected. We see the stasis and the movement; the isolation and the relationship. We feel our emotions rise with the birds. We feel our heart pulled to connect.

Thus with great economy of words the poem conveys an experience of complex emotional tenor. William LaFleur writes of this poem:

> *The tranquillity that is so clearly a part of this poem contravenes any attempt to classify the poem according to conventional rubrics; the twilight and death that are present are a twilight and death that refuse to be bound by our customary ways of understanding and reacting to them. Thus even in the emotions engendered by a poem expressive of yugen there is an indeterminacy* (LaFleur, in Sanford J, LaFleur, W and Nagatomi, M, 1992)

The complexity of view, exemplified in this poem, expresses the feeling of yugen. It expresses the bitter-sweet nature of life. The image of a marsh in the autumn evening seems suggestive of death. It is the end of the day, the end of the year. There is a feeling of closure. Yet, in its midst, not separated, but part of the environment, life springs up. In the midst of death, life arises. The snipe fly from the reeds. Life, death; the elements are not independent of one another but in relationship.

The quality of *yugen* puts us in touch with a dimension of experience beyond the ordinary. In the everyday scene, we experience the universal. The feeling of *Yugen* bring us into contact with something beyond the mundane. It involves all our faculties, whilst at the same time keeping the object of that relationship misted from view. We long for something, but the true nature of the object of our longing is hidden in imagery; it is beyond our view.

Yugen poetry uses allusion rather than direct description of this other dimension. In its portrayal of the everyday world, it speaks the simple truth about the nature of real things, and, through this, points to universal truth. It expresses things that are beyond conceptualisation, in the realm of the immeasurable, yet it rests in concrete representations of the natural world.

As we experience the scene reflected in the poem we are put into direct relationship with something we feel to be present, but cannot name. This feeling of an intangible presence is both unsettling and a source of great peace. In the imagery, we sense the reliability of the universe. We are shaken out of our commonplace assumptions and see the ordinary through new eyes.

Today we visit Irene's grave. It is winter and squalls of snow bluster round us as we walk up the hill at the natural burial ground where she was interred. The wet grass looks forlorn and dishevelled, not yet ready to foster the new growth of spring. Last year's teasels and docks stand above the field, the life colour drained out of them. Pine trees in the copse at the lower edge of the ground hang dark and uneasy.

The grave has settled so the soil is lower than ground level. At one end a rabbit has been digging, almost uprooting the rose bush. There are dwarf daffodils flowering amongst the stones and the tulip bulbs that we begged from the waste heap at the botanical gardens in Sheffield last summer are growing strong, red-flecked leaves.

Life and death; Irene is returning to the soil. Winter is turning into spring. Snow, rain, sun, the seasons continue to unfold.

A blackbird settles in the hawthorn, singing.

A psychology of loss

The experience of reading Saigyo's poetry evokes a feeling of emotional sensitivity. On the one hand there is the indeterminacy in the *yugen* quality that LaFleur identifies, but on the other, the feeling evoked is one that is so precise, that every hair on the neck is raised and the sparse landscapes of imagery seem to touch every pore of our skin. There is profound silence and stillness against which every pin-drop movement becomes precious. The very complexity of the emotional environment creates calm and brings us to life. Like the times when we accompany the dying, time expands languidly to embrace every tiny sound or movement in the rich colouration of our experience.

Thus, undoubtedly, within this emotional space, the experience of loss and sadness plays a significant role. But even this experience of grief is complex. When we read the poems of Saigyo we cannot miss the constant presence of death and loneliness in his imagery, alluded to in so many of his works. It pervades the landscape. Scenes are so beautifully depicted, but pervaded with melancholic colours and tones. The awareness of impermanence hovers, and yet, in the presence of this sadness and death, we are also brought to feel an intense peace. Saigyo's message is clear as the wintry air he portrays. Beauty and life are to be found in death and sadness.

We do not know a great deal about Saigyo's early life. What we do know is that he was of a warrior family and began his career as a member of the Emperor's elite guard. This was a prestigious role, but at the age of twenty two he left it to become a Buddhist priest. What led to this change is a matter of speculation, but it has been suggested that he may have had an unhappy love affair, or experienced the loss of a loved one. Were this so, it would suggest that there were parallels between Saigyo's early life and the Buddha's own story. The Buddha, after all, had an early life of comfort and personal success, but this was transformed by an encounter with the realities of pain and death. Both men turned in response to the spiritual path.

The encounter with death and painful separation brings us to the heart of the Buddhist understanding of human process. It is seen to be both the source of spiritual motivation and the underpinning to psychological difficulties. In *Buddhist Psychology* I showed how the central teaching of the Four Noble Truths arose from the Buddha's own search for meaning after his encounters with sickness, old age and death. You can read a much fuller account of these central teachings in that book. Here I will offer a brief summary so that we may take the matter further. For the sake of clarity for the reader, I will use English translations of the original terms, including Sanskrit originals in brackets. Some of these translations are open to discussion but I will not re-enter this here as I have dealt with the matter elsewhere.

The teaching of the Four Noble Truths, which was one of the first given by the Buddha after his enlightenment, shows how we react to afflictions (*dukkha*). When we are faced with loss or affliction, feelings arise in us (*samudaya*) which are uncomfortable. Our immediate reaction is to seek ways in which we can distract ourselves from this feeling. We develop craving for distraction (*trishna*). Craving initially leads us into finding sensual distractions (*kama*) to take our minds off the problem. Maybe we drink or eat or watch television or go jogging.

As we repeatedly turn to sensual distractions to alleviate the feelings arising in us, we start to identify with the behavioural pattern associated with the distraction. At this point we are not just having our favourite drink. The process of drinking our favourite drink gives us a sense of identity. Humans are very good at appropriating things for themselves. We talk of being a "real ale girl" or a "Guiness man" or maybe even a "G and T person" or perhaps we simply feel our world in incomplete without our nightly cocoa. The band plays "our tune" and we go to "our local" to relax. In such ways we build a sense of self, or as the teaching expresses it, we become (*bhava*). We create a comfortable world of the familiar around ourselves. So we dull down the sharper aspects of life.

If painful life events continue to unfold, however, our sense of identity is no longer sufficient to sustain us. We start to become self-destructive, and to long for oblivion or non-becoming (*abhava*). This is the final stage of craving. In one sense it is the point at which a person is most cut off from their feeling reactions. At the same time it is the most distressing point a person can reach.

Much of the theory base of Buddhist psychology explains the steps involved in this process of the creation and sustaining of self. There is much detail. The teachings on the *Skandhas* and on *Dependent Origination*, both key teachings in the Buddhist tradition, can be mapped onto this basic understanding of how the self is created. They build on the teaching on the Second Noble Truth, (*samudaya*,) elaborating the route of attachment, of senses, self-building and destruction; *kama*, *bhava* and *abhava*. They describe the process whereby we try to escape from our feeling response and insulate ourselves from the possibility of grief by creating a sense of identity. The teachings on the *Skandhas* and on *Dependent Origination* give detailed analysis of the self-perpetuating nature of these processes and the way they condition our minds to respond in predictable ways, reinforcing our sense of self through our involvement with a world that is also created and viewed through a personalised, and thus limited, window.

According to Buddhist psychology, the sense of self can be seen as a way in which we attempt to control an apparently uncontrollable universe. In building our identities, we attempt to hold onto a feeling of permanence and continuity in the face of constant flux. The self-creating activities, however, are themselves seen to be sources of further pain and affliction, thus making the process of self-building, the cycle of *samsara,* into a self-amplifying cycle. If building an unassailable sense of self is our aim, its constant erosion by reality creates distress and fear and this in turn drives us to want to create a more secure and rigid sense of self.

The processes of escape, however, are not seen as an inevitable consequence of exposure to affliction. There is another way.

In the teaching of the Four Noble Truths, the Buddha suggests that a person can unhook themselves from the object of their craving. They can unhook from the processes of sensual attachment, self-building and self-destructiveness. They need not attempt to disperse the discomfort and psychological pain that comes from life's afflictions by distractions.

Having unhooked from the impulse to escape, though, the person is left with a lot of energy. This can be an uncomfortable feeling, and we are used to finding ways to dissipate it.

Even in quite ordinary circumstances it can be hard to simply sit with feelings of agitation or distress. A teenage daughter fails to return at the hour agreed and the last bus has now gone past. A letter from the Inland Revenue seems to suggest that a large amount of tax is due that had not been anticipated. Our partner is angry with us, in our view without justification. Small day to day events can leave us feeling unsettled, and often we will find ourselves making small distractions for ourselves to dissipate that agitation, without even realising what we are doing. We make a cup of tea, walk up and down, read the newspaper, switch on the television.

Of course, behind each small incident may lie fears of greater losses, however apparently irrational. Dreadful things do happen. Some teenage daughters are the victims of drink drive accidents or date rapes. Some tax demands herald bankruptcy and lead to a decline into homeless poverty. Some marital disagreements are the first sign that the partner has decided to end the marriage. Mostly these calamities do not occur. Rationally we dismiss thoughts that dwell on the worst possibilities, but nevertheless, as we read the newspapers or hear of the experiences of friends and acquaintances we are constantly reminded of the fragility of our lives. The possibility of loss surrounds us. Loss is often unpredictable and is usually out of our control.

The teaching of the Four Noble Truths suggests that having unhooked ourselves from the objects of escape, we apply the energy in a focused way. If we are able to interrupt the cravings that are taking over our lives, then the energy embedded in the feeling responses that arise in us can be harnessed (*nirodha*) for the spiritual path (*marga*). Our grief can become the fuel for our spiritual life. Once harnessed, we will naturally live in a way that is in tune with that way of being.

This is the basic model that Buddhist psychology offers for personal transformation. It is universally accepted by Buddhists of different schools, although the exact interpretation of the teaching varies. Its suggestion is that change comes about when we are able to unhook ourselves from the distractions in which we habitually indulge and invest out energy in authentic ways.

This all sounds good in theory, but the difficulty arises when we ask ourselves how we should go about putting it into practice. Habit patterns are hard to break and we cling to our sense of who we are for a reason. Stepping off the cycle of *samsara* is like taking a leap into the abyss.

Facing grief, either our own or other people's, is not easy. I do not have a formula to offer you. Recently I was running a course and midway through a student got a message that he should go home because his mother was dying. I sat with him that evening before he set out to drive the long journey home, but though I felt deep sorrow for his situation, I felt completely at a loss for words to comfort him. Despite my concern and my longing to reach out to him, nothing I could think of to say seemed adequate to the circumstance. What could one say? Here was a young man, facing the loss of his mother relatively early in his life; she not so old, but had struggled with illness for many years. It is just a very, very sad situation. I felt a lot of love, but felt nowhere to place it. I felt clumsy.

As one goes through life, particularly working in a profession where one is expected to offer a suitable response to such situations, one tends to become more adept at finding something to say. Phrases that express "I am here" or "it's OK to cry" slip off the tongue more easily. But really they seem very inadequate to the enormity of what is being faced. At best they convey a sense of fellow feeling. At worst they create a gloss that leaves the grief unheard. The presence of death leaves us all naked.

Responding from our nakedness takes courage. To recognise the reality of another's grief and not fall into platitudes, however well constructed, requires us to enter the unknown with the other person. We have to be willing to shed our own defensive clothing and reach out in the darkness.

Yugen and the expression of loss

In responding to another's grief, in my experience, one of two things can happen.

Either I feel deeply affected, touched by many emotions that seem to change and flow with the story that is unfolding. The atmosphere can be electric. My skin feels thin and sensitive. My body tuned to every nuance of the others' experience. The moment by moment ebb and flow of tears, eye contact, softly spoken words, the holding of a hand, each take on that special quality of transmission we feel when we are truly accompanying another human being.

Alternatively, nothing happens. I hear the story but in the depths of my being, I feel more or less unmoved, although I know I should be. I do not meet the other. Or maybe he or she does not meet me. I may try to say the right thing, even seem to succeed in offering comfort, but somehow the encounter slips through my hands. I am at some level playing an artificial role.

What makes the difference? I can have theories about what I should do to make myself really available to the other person, but at the end of the day, after more than twenty years working in caring and psychotherapeutic professions, I cannot say I have an answer. The meeting of two people is an act of grace.

The touching of grief that happens when we really encounter another person, as in the first example has something of the quality of *yugen*. It is both poignant and unknowable. The words they utter, the unspoken images, all form a shifting scene of light and dark against a backdrop of empty spaces. In the melancholy and sadness we find both the extremity of aliveness and, alongside it, certain knowledge of impermanence and impotence. This process has a quality of tranquillity that might seem strange in concept, yet feels completely natural to both of us.

In the nuances of feeling, a tenderness of quite exquisite delicacy can arise. At the same time, the simplicity and ordinariness of the daily details that we become aware of in this heightened state touch the heart with their humanity. Like the reeds and the birds of the marsh, everyday objects and events become the containers for the inexpressible. A poetry of interchanges unfolds in such ways.

It is the ordinary things of life that offer most pathos. Irene's gardening shoes still sit on the shelf in the greenhouse, gathering cobwebs. Their toes are scuffed and are somewhat misshapen. The insoles curl a little, shaped by the tread of her feet over the years. We do not move them. A fitting memorial, we notice them when we go to care for the new seedlings.

The primrose on my window sill reminds me of Easters of childhood when I stayed with my grandmother in Devon. There were so many primroses growing wild in those days. We would walk to the ruined chapel at Spraecombe, buried in ivy, or to the aptly named Eastercott Farm, and return with bunches of the flowers. And she would smile. I look at the primrose in the pot, pale yellow and cheerful, and I smile too.

Treasuring these moments, we breathe the bitter-sweetness of life.

To experience *yugen* qualities as we sit with someone who has been bereaved is to experience not only the sadness and grief of impermanence. It is also to open to something beyond the experience of either of us. Beyond the everyday detail of the loved one's life, the universal quality of life hovers. Beyond the experience of love that grows in the listening, the universal love emerges.

Faith and the Four Noble Truths

The teaching of the Four Noble Truths offers a model of the spiritual life. In this model loss and grief become the fuel for the spiritual journey. Unhooking from distraction creates the key to transformation. If we can step out of the habit patterns of avoidance and cease from comforting ourselves with sense based diversions, we will be on the path. The problem is that life is rarely so simple.

The patterns of distraction and self-creation are long established. Relinquishing them is not the easy assignment it might seem. From the moment of our birth (another instance of *dukkha* according to the teaching of the Four Noble Truths) we have been accumulating strategies for distracting ourselves from affliction. By the time we reach adulthood these have become firmly set into patterns of thought, interest and behaviour that we have come to identify with. We have created a sense of self. In all probability, this sense of self has become complex and multi-faceted. The Buddhist teachings give plenty of explanation of the process. Different circumstances trigger different patterns of response. Each becomes a self-perpetuating cycle of perception and behaviour. We are invested in seeing ourselves in particular ways and seeing the world in particular ways. In all events, we are very reluctant to give up our sense of self.

Of our own ability, it seems, we are not able to shift the layers of conditioned thought. These patterns grow out of our fears and insecurities. Added to this, the thought of losing control of our personalised world through changing our perceptions itself creates further fear that becomes what seems like an insurmountable obstacle to our spiritual journey. To change our patterns of behaviour through our own efforts is very difficult. Yet, without our bidding, an experience of loss turns our personal world upside down. We have no choice in the matter. It can bring us into the awe-inspiring space in which our previous ways of reacting no longer function. At least for a moment, habitual responses drop away.

The time of grief or trauma is often a time when psychological opportunity arises. I recall working with a young man who had been in a car accident. He came to me for a few therapy sessions because he was experiencing panic attacks. As we talked about his situation, it soon became clear that, on the one hand, he was experiencing extreme anxiety to the level where he was no longer able to go to work. On the other hand, the accident had led him to re-evaluate his life and realise that many of the things he was currently doing, including his present employment, now felt empty and pointless. Although he had not been physically injured, the accident had made him painfully aware of how easily his life could have been destroyed. It could have been so different. Only by chance, it seemed, had he survived. Before the accident he had been intent on achieving success in his career and settling down in a comfortable house. He wanted to become successful. Now these goals seemed empty and a lot less important. Through the experience of the accident, his self-image had changed, and he started to think about other things he might do in life. Through counselling, his plans began to evolve, and new creative energy emerged that led him to enrol for a new course at college with a view to becoming a teacher.

This example illustrates a situation that is relatively commonplace. An experience in which death becomes a real possibility rather than a distant concept unsettles a person's life track and brings them to reconsider their priorities. This may be a superficial change, but often the process of transformation is profound. When grief touches us, something inside us stops, and at that point we may experience something of the spirit of *yugen*. We may see beyond the mundane.

The impetus for change does not come from our own decision to change. The encounter with the reality of our mortal state which brings us up short is not something that we can will ourselves to experience. The opportunity for change is a gift. Our change of heart comes through our meeting with external factors which are not under our control. It is our contact with that which is other, with the world that is not our personally constructed view, which creates psychological and spiritual transformation.

Spiritual change arises from our encounter with the world of the other. In Buddhism we talk of non-self. Reality breaks through the shell of delusion. This may happen through the experience of a death or of some other major loss. Such occurrences create shock waves that shatter our world-view and create the possibility of change.

On the other hand, positive and enjoyable experiences can also shake us out of our dormancy. An inspirational experience may awaken us to the limitations of our mental constructions. For example, sometimes such a window is created through a meeting with someone exceptional or through a novel experience. The birth of a child, a breathtaking view, a poem, may all inspire us and take us out of our selves. To change our way of being in the world, something external to ourselves is required. We cannot find it in ourselves to make the leap out of our patterns of avoidance without help.

The interruption of habit which an encounter creates can take many forms. Sometimes pain and inspiration work together. It was, after all, the sight of a holy man walking across the market place that inspired the Buddha to set out on his spiritual quest, but this meeting happened in the wake of his encounters with sickness, old age and death.

Mystery and faith

Why did the bees come? What brought them to Irene's window that morning? Why did we go into the garden? Why did I look up? The questions bring further questions. Answers do not come. And if they do, perhaps something is lost.

No answers.

In their arrival, the bees help me to touch something beyond expression. I cannot say why they arrived at that point. I have no metaphysic or natural explanation to fall back on. The timing seemed to belie coincidence, and yet my practical mind finds no reason for their coming. They speak to my being in a different language. Their presence resonates with ancient stories of portentous occurrences. It connects me to feelings and intuitions that go beyond words. Like the rising of a snipe, the bees are as messengers of the gods.

Stepping onto a different path we go beyond our rational minds into another kind of knowing. Despite the limitations of intellectual frameworks which we are so good at creating, our senses recognise the truth of our perceptions. We feel held by a deep bodily knowledge of truth, without having words to ascribe to the process of knowing. This is the foundation of faith, and faith is the starting point and the end of the spiritual journey. To go beyond the simple goals of our habit based lives and live more freely requires an act of faith and faith is grounded in a sense of something beyond the ordinary context of our lives. Left to our own devices, we tend to circle round our habitual routes, keeping to safe territory, but when we meet the extraordinary and the shocking, something breaks through this wall of resistance letting new light flood into our lives.

Beyond the ordinary is the unseen. Beyond the extra-ordinary the unseen becomes a little more visible, but yet remains shrouded in its own mystery. Faith involves the recognition of a world beyond self. It involves being willing to trust that there is an unknown and an unacknowledged reality beyond our personal certainties. It is the acceptance that forces shape our lives which we do not and cannot understand. Faith is the willingness to step into the mystery of life and death, despite our fear. It is the force which invites us into a moment of full aliveness. Through allowing ourselves to open up to such experiences we feel the inexpressible. We touch the measureless.

CONCEPTS INTRODUCED IN THIS CHAPTER
- Yugen: the expressing the inexpressible
- The Four Noble Truths
- Faith as a route to change

CHAPTER TWO

SNAKES, DRAGONS AND FATHOMLESS DEPTHS

Ant hill mind scheming

Dreaming air filled castles

Nembutsu drawbridge

At the bottom of the Ant Hill lies the naga serpent. Its sleek coils stir. Does it wake or sleep?

The Ant Hill Sutra (MN23) tells the story of a dream. In this dream a Buddhist monk, or *Bhikshu*, discovers the serpent of spiritual energy buried under the layers of human delusion signified by the image of an ant hill. You can read more about this wonderful sutra in my previous book, *Buddhist Psychology*, but for now, we only require a rudimentary outline.

As the monk digs into the ant hill in his dream, he discovers a series of objects. Each represents a different layer of his conditioned nature. The dream progresses. Each time he extracts an object, the monk is instructed to discard it. Throw out the bar, throw out the toad, throw out the fork, throw out the sieve, throw out the tortoise, throw out the axe and block, throw out the piece of meat. One after another, all the objects are rejected. With them conditioned nature dissolves. The Ant Hill is empty. Only the naga serpent remains at the very bottom, a symbol of spiritual vitality.

This is the dream; the ideal. This is the perfected human. This too is the image of Buddhism that prevails in the West.

But we do not inhabit dreams. As humans we are complex, layered with a rich patina of delusions. Some are charming and benign, others pernicious, vicious and downright unpleasant. Ah, such is our folly. We dream of the cosmic detox, cleansing our systems of these uninvited intrusions, but the reality is that most of us can no more easily throw out our tortoises, sieves or the bloodied steaks of our psyche than control our irritation when the driver in front takes a crazy turn across our path. We just don't have it in us.

Pureland Buddhism offers a different view. Less well known in the West, in the East its teaching is widespread. Yet it has an important place in the spectrum of Buddhist traditions. Its message in a nutshell: we are not of the nature to save ourselves through our own efforts. The more we try, the more we encounter the complexity of our deluded state. The great Pureland sages learned the hard way. Salvation must come from without, from encounter, from meeting what is other. Only in connection with the mea-sureless, unknowable mystery of the other do we transcend the limits of our nature.

The pursuit of perfection

Encountering Buddhist teachings can seem like a euphoric extravaganza of human potential. Initially, in the first flush of convert fervour, we strive for perfection. Enlightenment is, after all, but a night of sheer determination under the bodhi tree away. Absolute refusal to budge until enlightenment strikes is bound to yield success. Wasn't this what our founder discovered? It is simply a matter of making sufficient effort. We sit, and sit and sit.... and sit.

For a while we seem to make some progress in taming the wayward passions. The mind is getting quieter. Could that glimmer of something at the edge of our awareness be... might it be... a spiritual experience? We waver between pride and self righteousness (no problem; after all, spiritual pride is the last defilement to be given up before enlightenment is reached, so maybe this dawning pride is a herald of imminent awakening). Then, sadly, we get distracted and fall into irritation or criticism or wayward fantasies and realise that we have blown our chance of enlightenment at this attempt and must start the whole process over again. With such realisation, we descend into self-pity and despair. This is not going to be so easy.

After a few vicissitudes between pride and despair, all but the most intrepid practitioners have to admit that maybe the whole enlightenment business is not quite as easy as they had first thought. Perhaps as a lesser human being, it is all going to take a bit longer... or maybe a bit more effort. At such a point we probably become more moderate in our expectations and recognise that at the current rate of progress, enlightenment is going to take a long time.

The practitioner seeks a new rationale. Returning to the texts, further guidelines are required. Ah, yes, *there is a middle way*. Perhaps this well trodden path can lift us out of this particular cycle of samsara and take us into the higher realms. Middle is taken to be moderation. Who can expect to do it all in one short lifetime? After all, we have infinite aeons and many rebirths in which to complete the task. Let's not get too hung up on perfection.

There is a Tibetan game, used to teach young *Tulkus,* reincarnated lamas, the facts of spiritual life. It is a bit like "snakes and ladders" and involves throwing dice to determine ones next birth as one moves around a board marked with squares representing the different possible lifetimes into which one is being reborn. In its Western incarnation, the game is accompanied by a book, which contains graphic descriptions of the different destinations in which the player is being reborn. Judging by these descriptions, especially as they dwell on the numerous hell realms, young Tibetan monks have just as blood thirsty imaginations as modern Western video-trained youngsters. My experience of playing this game is that it can go on for day after compulsive day, and that most of the early stages involve numerous return trips to the hell realms; cold, hot, black rope and crushing or whatever. Enlightenment is certainly not a speedy process.

Westerners, with our legacy of aversion to the whole topic of hells, tend to prefer a more benign, but equally slow, model of progress. We embark on a slow plod up the hill of the spiritual life. Moderate expectation is the key to spiritual contentment and the antidote to pride or ambition. Thus the "good enough" Buddhist is born. A few good books and a more or less daily practice create a benign ambience. Comforted by omnipresent Buddha-nature, the practitioner is now in danger of settling into a comfortable liberality, verging on the complacent. Without challenge, such a spiritual life degenerates into a dulled process of seeking personal fulfilment through universalist pleasantries.

For many of us the spiritual path to perfection becomes a frustrating encounter with the lesser nature of humankind. Whether we settle for increased effort or for unselfcritical mediocrity, the destination remains distant. Striving for perfection is often more revealing of our failings. As we discover more and more aspects to our delusion, the high goalpost inevitably moves further away into the distance. The slow path meanwhile can lead to interminable states of stagnation. At some stage the practitioner starts to ask him or herself "What is it all for anyway?" and to feel dissatisfied with the answer.

Self-perfection: the modern disease?

Modern society, as societies in the past, sets its own ideals of perfection. Within this ideal, individuals weave their personal tapestries of aspirations. Each age creates its own pressures. Each person internalises these in their own translation.

Individualism is a distinctive feature of modern Western society that lies very close to the self-perfection project. If one had to characterise the twentieth and twenty first century social ideals, the pursuit of individual achievement in its many manifestations would be bound to lie high upon the list. This pursuit takes many forms and is evidenced in many ways.

On the one hand it leads to a splitting up of community as each person engages in their own personal journey. We see a move towards smaller and smaller living units. More houses are owned by single occupiers than ever before. Family sizes are getting smaller, and the extended family less significant as people move away from their geographic roots to live and work. Relationships are often more transient. Although marriage remains ever popular, serial monogamy is becoming the predominating pattern, reflecting a prevailing philosophy that values personal fulfilment in relationship above social continuity. Career development often requires individuals to be willing to move in order to find the right job, contributing to the unsettled nature of society. People go through life much more alone than in past ages.

Of course such fragmentation has its down side. In the summer of 2003, French society was shocked when *la canicule*, an extreme heat wave, took the lives of thousands of elderly people in Paris and other large cities. This experience was a loss of innocence. Whereas French people had previously thought of themselves as having a caring, family based society, which indeed they had until recent times, the situation had now changed. Many elderly people had been left to face the extreme conditions alone or in nursing homes where inadequate or impersonal care had led to deaths from dehydration and other effects of the heat.

In the climate of individualism, self-perfection becomes the activity of choice. Industries for aiding this process proliferate. Beauty aids and cosmetics, business and career coaching, exercise regimes, educational monitoring and goal setting, personal fulfilment trainings, courses in spiritual cultivation can all be seen as adjuncts of this phenomenon. Of course the therapy industry itself can be seen as providing a significant piece in this jigsaw, the image of the fully actualised person being one popular blue print for perfection.

Such self-perfection is, however, just as much a mirage in these social contexts as it is in the spiritual arena. When success, in whatever form an individual pursues it, becomes the goal, and that success is measured in a person's ability to achieve perfection, its achievement is bound to remain elusive. Just as with spiritual perfection, our responses to the drive for social perfection fall into two extremes. In modern society some are led to follow a lifestyle driven by the ever more distant yet entrancing phantom of achievement, while others to settle for complacency and immediate comfort.

Such states of unmitigated striving or of retreat into undemanding mediocrity provide a measure of insulation against the more uncomfortable aspects of life. They occupy and distract us. Only rarely do we become aware of the way our lives have been taken over by such pursuits. It sometimes takes a *canicule* to break us out of our complacency. Only the peril of such a circumstance shakes us out of the numbing obsession with the self-project and throws us into consideration of our real position. In such situations, psychological change becomes possible at a more than cosmetic level. Our spirit is engaged.

Opportunity in failure

Just as at times of loss or grief a reorganisation of our mental structure can take place and deeper connection with others can occur, so too at the point of failure is the point at which spiritual opportunity arises. When things break down and spiritual ambition falters, we see our pretences and delusions more clearly. We come face to face with our imperfect nature and drop our façade of competence. The despair that accompanies such an experience is the spring board for a more solid approach to life.

Despair is often seen as a negative force to be avoided, but the kind of despair which arises when we honestly face our inability to fulfil the ideal which we have set up for ourselves can be productive. It is not the despair of self-pity. It is an encounter with the real nature of our lives. At such a point the futility of reliance upon personal effort is faced. Such experience opens the door to profound awareness of the need for something, anything, beyond our self as a source of support.

The connection with what is not self is the central message of the Buddha's teaching. According to Buddhist doctrine, the self is an illusory trap, and not something we can rely upon for our salvation. The nature of all things is non-self. As it states in one of the fundamental Buddhist teachings, the teaching on the three signs of being, *sarva dharma anatma;* all things are non-self. Understanding the process of failure and the futility of pursuing self- perfection, we naturally turn to that which is beyond self. Yet many of us still unwittingly seek the spiritual path through the route of the perfection of the self.

Honen, the great Pureland master and founder of a tradition that has now given rise to several modern schools of Japanese Pureland Buddhism, came to such a point of desperation in his own spiritual practice. This crisis led to his great spiritual breakthrough. Having begun his Buddhist studies as a young boy, Seishi-maru, as he was known prior to his final ordination, proved a brilliant scholar, and was sent to Mount Hiei, which was the centre of Buddhist academia in the twelfth century. There he was eventually given his ordination name, Honen.

Honen devoted himself to the spiritual life for a number of years, and achieved an impressive reputation. But he himself was the first to recognise that spiritual fame and glory were not to be equated with spiritual perfection. Although he was to all intents and purposes successful, his achievements did not satisfy his spiritual longing. They did not provide the means for him to achieve the spiritual states that he was seeking. Tempting as the accolades of junior and even senior members of the religious circle might be, what they offered was merely distraction and a spiritual trap.

Honen's search continued. Feeling that, in the institutions of his day, the main point of the spiritual life was still evading him, at the age of 24, he moved on to Nara, the ancient Japanese capital. There he studied with more great teachers. His search took him from temple to temple. He learned much, but never felt satisfied.

Eventually, returning to Mount Hiei, Honen immersed himself in studying the Buddhist texts, or sutras in the library of Kurodani monastery. Feverishly he explored the writings of the sages of the past, hoping that within them he would find some clue about how to proceed. He was never content to rest on his achievements. All that he read confirmed his sense that he, and indeed most others, were incapable of the level of spiritual achievement which the texts seemed to demand. He struggled with his inability to vanquish self-centred thoughts and actions. He could not even conceptualise how it would be to reach such a state.

At the age of 43, Honen hit rock bottom. Despairing of his capacity to accomplish spiritual perfection, he felt engulfed by his spiritual incapacities. Of this time, he wrote

"Upon introspection, I realise that I have not observed a single precept or succeeded in the practice of meditation. A master once said, "One will not enter samadhi unless one becomes pure in body and mind through observation of the precepts". Further the mind of the common man is easily distracted by conditions around it. It is like the monkey which flits from branch to branch, confused, vacillating and unable to

concentrate. In which way does undefiled wisdom emerge? Without the sword of undefiled wisdom, how will we extricate ourselves from the fetters of unwholesome karma and evil passions? Unable to sever ourselves from the fetters, how will we deliver ourselves from the bondage of transmigration through birth and death in the delusive worlds in order to realise emancipation? This is indeed lamentable and disheartening.

We here do not have the potential to observe the Three Ways of Learning, namely precepts, meditation and wisdom. Although I have asked various wise and learned men if there be teaching and practice more attuned to myself other than the Three Ways of Learning, no one was able to teach or provide me guidance.

In despair I entered the repository of Buddhist scriptures, in grief gazed upon holy texts there and took a volume into my hands. It was the "Commentary on the meditation Sutra authored by Master Zendo (Shan Tao)" (Honen Shonin Gyojo-ezu chapter 32, from a translation by Atone and Hayashi)

Honen's despair was born of profound honesty. Although there is no doubt that he was already a well respected scholar and recognised as a saintly figure, he was not seduced by the accolades that came with this religious success. Rather, he knew in his heart, that despite all the years of study and practice, perfection was still a long way off.

This was the point when he reached his spiritual breakthrough. It was a breakthrough that took him, not to an experience of his own perfection, but to knowledge that, imperfect as he was, the spiritual realm was always available to him. In particular it led him to embrace the Pureland practice of Amida Buddha which we will explore in this book. This practice involved reliance upon the measureless grace of Amida, which transcends the personal and the created world of delusion.

For Honen, spiritual maturity lay in recognising and embracing his dark side, not in the futile attempt to rid himself of it. It came from recognising the limitations of his own capacities and letting slip the struggle to overcome all obstacles through his own effort to perfect himself. Only after such release was he able to see the truth of the spiritual situation.

Chasing ideals

Modern people long for perfection. It is understandable that people tend to seek role models who appear to demonstrate the achievement of such perfection in their own lives. We want to look at another and to believe that perfection is possible. We want our dreams of our own potential confirmed. That person is enlightened, we think, so there is hope for me. That person lives the ideal life, we imagine, so I can have faith that one day I will too.

Perfection is demanded, but at the same time, the path of the perfected is perilous. The religious leader who claims perfection for him or herself, or even who is willing to have others make such claims on his or her behalf, is in danger of falling into a trap of egotism and grandiosity of the kind that their religious path is intended to overcome. When a teacher is ready to make such claims, the stakes are heightened. Cynicism or adulation follows, often in equal measure. Some will flock, and others criticise or mock. This is, after all, the age of the anti-hero. Only in the mythic realms of the long dead is religious perfection really safe.

The myth of perfection is slippery though. It can creep in in unexpected places. Recently I was talking about Honen's life with a group of people who were new to Buddhism. Having described Honen's experience of recognising the inadequacy of his accomplishment in his own search for spiritual perfection, emphasising as I did so the ubiquitous human situation in which our aspirations are confounded by the realities of our day to day lives, I imagined that others would be inspired by Honen's honesty and insight. During the subsequent discussion session, I was rather taken aback when a member of the group commented. "So Honen realised he wasn't going to make it". The tone of voice of the speaker suggested a growing lack of interest. If Pureland Buddhism is based on the teachings of a failure, who even admitted his inability to deliver the goods, how could it be worth pursuing? Surely Honen had settled for second best.

For a moment I was caught off balance. Why was this person missing the point? Didn't they see that Honen's realisation was not simply about his own imperfection, but said something profoundly important about the imperfection of every human? Wasn't it obvious that all those teachers, who were heralded as examples of perfection, were in Honen's shadow? Surely they were just caught in the delusion of their own or someone else's self-perfection project? Only Honen saw the truth. How could anyone not see the truth of Honen's real saintliness? But of course, therein lay the paradox.

Oh dear! How we humans want our religious leaders, or at least the founders of our religious traditions, to be perfect. We want to know that our chosen religious system works. We look to our founders for evidence.

Religious founders live different lives to the rest of us, moving in the higher echelons of spiritual space, and we look to them to offer dreams of what we could become. In such a way, in my responses to these comments, I had also become caught up in elevating the founder of my tradition to a kind of perfected status. In my own mind I was engaged in defending this status, at least to myself, by subtly translating Honen's words in my own mind into a kind of saintly modesty. I was simply asserting a different model of perfection. I had created the perfect imperfect person. Other teachers might claim to be, or be acclaimed as being, enlightened. He had the humility and wisdom to realise that this is not a human design factor.

This insight in a strange way had elevated him in my mind, had made him even more perfect....

Honen's insight however remains simple. Salvation does not arise through pursuit of our own salvation or enlightenment. We cannot become perfect. However much we try, there will always be more layers of shortcomings to be discovered. This does not mean we should not try, and Honen was consistent in his attempt to live the ethical rigours of the religious life, but spiritual investigation, if it is honestly undertaken, reveals more and more subtle levels of dubious thought and action. In our deluded state we may happily assume that we are kind generous people most of the time. The occasional angry outburst or selfish action could soon be overcome through a little more self-control. We believe that, once trained, the mind will behave like a docile sheepdog, which has learned to jump through an obstacle course of life experiences, and head straight for the finish line of *nirvana*. But minds are more akin to monkeys than to sheep-dogs, and training the mind is consequently a formidable task.

The monkey is cunning and so the monkey mind is well named. Frequently we trick ourselves into believing in our own capabilities, but a few early successes in the taming process do not necessarily herald continuing success. Usually as soon as we think our minds are becoming docile and controlled, something happens that reveals our thoughts and motivations as complex and devious. The mind becomes quieter and less reactive, but then satisfaction creeps in. Satisfaction becomes pride and leaves us vulnerable to some chance happening which disrupts our equilibrium. At this, we react with a burst of irritation far stronger than we would have had before. This is not surprising since the disturbance is twofold. Not only have we been disturbed in our peaceful state, but also the disturbance has demonstrated the fragility of our recent spiritual progress. We feel aggrieved. The mind has shown its lack of metal. Our motivations have been shown to be mixed.

The flawed helper

As one involved in the training of counsellors, I am often struck by the maxim commonly offered in the profession that the student's motivation should primarily be for the benefit of their clients rather than for their own personal gain. Of course such a qualified statement provides useful guidance for rejecting the most unsuitable applicants for the profession, but nevertheless, it plays into a belief that motivation can be clean and detached from self-interest. It seems to suggest a profession that can only be practiced by actualised beings who have already achieved the state of self-perfection which their clients are looking for and are now able to impart the wisdom they have acquired to others.

In fact, identifying the qualities desirable in the trainee counsellor, and discussing the type of motivation that might lead a person to this kind of work, raises ever more complex questions. The harder one looks into the matter, the more uncertain the ideal becomes. Humans are complex and we often prefer not to see too deeply into our mental processes. The person who simply expresses altruistic motivation probably lacks awareness of their own process.

When a counsellor feels empathy for the client, how much is based on truly seeing the client as they are, and how much is muddied with identification? It is all too common to mistake a feeling of personal resonance for empathy. If we empathise most easily with those who are like ourselves rather than those who are very different, it is probably because we are mistaking the feeling of recognition and familiarity that comes from our own experience for empathy rather than really hearing the other person's experience as it is. True empathy means feeling how it is to walk in the other's shoes for a while. It means getting out of our assumptions and hearing their experience in a way that is fresh enough to startle.

Discussing the nature of empathy is an exploration of our encounter with others. We will return to it from time to time in this book. If encountering others is a spiritual activity, entering into an empathic relationship becomes a spiritual exercise. Yet here too, our incapacity is evident. The intrusive nature of self-interest is ever present. There are many questions. Does the counsellor want the client to change? If so, in what way does she want them to change? Is this fired by an entirely altruistic motive? Or does the counsellor displace her values, desires and dreams onto the client without realising it? Does she have pride invested in the outcome, albeit subtly? Or is the investment in reducing her own discomfort? Does the client's story in some way mirror a current life dilemma the counsellor would personally like to solve? If so, what will happen if the client concludes that there is no answer?

Looking more closely, every caring response can be found, at least in part, to be fuelled by self-interest and in part by altruism. Although I give the example of the counsellor, the same is true in any other helping profession. The helper and the helped are intertwined as deeply as any humans are with one another when they start to care. The more we care, the more we are touched. The more we are touched, the more we bring our flawed nature into relationship. The more we connect with one another, the more we import our failings into the encounter. The more we progress upon the path of personal honesty, the more confusion of motivation we discover. Self-awareness brings dilemmas never imagined by the naïve practitioner.

And yet, it is that very humanity of response, confused as it is, that creates the real possibility of helping. It is the fact that we bring who we are, and not a sanitised version of the truth, that allows a deeper truth to emerge and the other to change. If we are aware of our own nature, we meet one another not in the act of one, the helper, dispensing wisdom to the other, the helped, but in an attitude of *fellow feeling*. We are all imperfect and capable of making a mess of our lives.

When I was a student I visited a counsellor for a few sessions. I don't remember much of what we talked about, but I do remember the woman was quite young herself. I now imagine she was quite inexperienced. At the time, however, she seemed to me to be very competent. I felt quite intimidated by her, although, looking back, there seems no real reason why I should have felt this. Each visit I would look at my counsellor and feel completely inadequate. I imagined she listened to my troubles and found it hard to believe my naivety. She was always immaculately dressed and looked as if she had her life completely in order. I, by contrast, smarted with the indignity of my various problems. I felt disabled by shame.

Then one week, our last session by chance, I noticed that she had a ladder in her tights. She seemed unaware of this and carried on responding to me as confidently as she had before, but that ladder left more impression on me than any of the words she used. Suddenly she became a fellow human being for me. She no longer represented an impossible ideal. She was less than perfect and didn't even know it. Her presence no longer highlighted my failings. I felt warm towards her.

Not by our own effort

Seeking perfection is a common human goal, but the process often becomes self-defeating. In the sixth form I remember spending many free periods discussing the problem of selfishness with my friends. In the idealism of youth, we sought to find a way of being that did not involve selfish motivation. Although we did not name it so, we were in effect embarked upon a spiritual journey which held the ideal of spiritual perfection as its goal. We were not successful. As Honen had, though with much less spiritual devotion behind us, we found that although altruism was our ideal, try as we might, in every action that we undertook, self-interest and other dubious motivations could be uncovered. Mostly it didn't even take much introspection. Any fool could see that we were riddled with pride, jealousy, laziness, pettiness, ambition and greed. In vain we hoped that recognising these miserable motivations might lead us to improvement, but as our consciousness of these failings increased, it only seemed to serve to make matters worse. Where we had any success, we soon found ourselves caught in smugness and feelings of superiority over our more worldly classmates. Mostly, though, even this level of success was hard to come by. Eventually we gave up and got interested in environmentalism instead. Saving the world seemed a better bet than saving ourselves.

Perhaps the raw idealism of such enterprises is most apparent in the young. In her book *Through the Narrow Gate*, Karen Armstrong writes of her experiences as a young nun. During the seven years she was in the Catholic convent in the early sixties, she struggled to overcome every aspect of her mind and body and bring them to a point of emptiness. She sought to rid herself of any elements of self-interest and to be completely open to God. This struggle drove her to her mental and physical limit, as her body rebelled more and more against the mental straight jacket she tried to impose on it. Eventually she left. Reflecting back ten years later, she wrote:

The ideal of the religious life is still, I think, a beautiful one. But only a few of those who undertake it are capable of it. My most crucial mistake was the overvaluing of will. Rebecca and I were both ill in the Order, but such was the strength of belief in the sovereignty of will power that it never occurred to the nuns until too late that we ought to see a doctor. How lovely it would be if the will really were supreme; if the mass of emotion, bodily impulses and disorders and the murky subconscious could all be controlled by a strong act of will. In the Order I discovered that we are complex beings, mind, heart, soul, and body engaged in a continuous bloody battle. Indeed, one of the most important things I learned from the religious life was the relative impotence of will. It is a good, though humbling, thing to realise. It brings a kind of peace with it. (Armstrong 1981 p 280)

Time makes most of us more sanguine. Enlightenment is not common these days. Ask any practitioner intent on nirvana through his own effort: have you ever met someone who achieved enlightenment? Perhaps you will be luckier than I. If you hear of a fully enlightened teacher, check them out. In my experience, the response is usually to speak of a teacher of a teacher living in a remote part of the world, beyond immediate scrutiny.

But don't get me wrong. This is not in any way to devalue the wisdom and saintliness of many good practitioners and teachers. There are and have been many inspirational people whose lives present us with examples of the best human beings can be. But perfection, no. Indeed, perfection would be to miss the point. It is the humanity a person exhibits in their imperfection that is inspiring; the person who flies to the other side of the world to be with their dying relative despite feeling overwhelmed by their crippling fear of flying; the person who brings aid to a shattered community of refugees achieving massive practical improvements in living conditions, despite being impossible to live with due to their erratic temper and complete lack of concern for social norms; the musician who plays and sings beautiful ballads, despite agonising self-consciousness and stage fright that sometimes leads them to interrupt the performance mid-way and have to be coaxed back on stage.

Honen's concern was partly for his own spiritual journey, but far more it was for the lot of others. If he, with all the advantages on a monastic education and the best teachers of his time could still find flaws in every area of his life that he put under the spiritual microscope, how much chance did ordinary people stand? Any religious system had, in his mind, to be accessible to ordinary people. The discovery that he made in the writings of the seventh century Chinese master Shan Tao was that the spiritual life was indeed accessible to such common people. In Shan Tao's view, anyone could achieve salvation, but this did not come through personal effort. It came through something greater.

This understanding did not avoid the search for perfection. It simply recognised the reality that most of us are incapable of achieving perfection ourselves. The source of spiritual nourishment is beyond us. The expectation is not of self-perfection, but rather of salvation through relationship. Put simply, what Honen came to understand was that enlightenment was not something that can be achieved through massive personal effort. Although he was not against effort in spiritual practice, and indeed encouraged it, such effort was not the route to salvation. Self-perfection was not the goal. Spiritual consummation was a gift that came from outside the self. Specifically it came through the relationship with Amida Buddha, growing out of the measureless power of the Buddha's love. What was required to receive salvation in this way is not a matter of effort. It was a matter of faith. Such an approach is often referred to as "*other-power*", and in the chapters that follow we will return to this concept. We will explore the nature of the connection with Amida, the measureless, which is central to the Pureland path.

Foolish beings of wayward passion

Pureland is the Buddhism of ordinary people. Whether or not perfection is ultimately possible, Honen recognised the folly inherent in pursuing it as a spiritual end. Self-perfection becomes a trap in which deeper delusion is often the only possible outcome. As ordinary people we fall all too easily into such follies.

The more deeply he looked into his own behaviour and thoughts, the more Honen saw the pervasive nature of ambition, personal intent and all the other factors that cloud pure motivation. In his futile attempts to gain control over mental process, he recognised how, as fast as one intruding thought was eliminated, another slipped in. He saw how, despite his earnest endeavour to achieve pure mind, at more and more subtle levels, every effort sank into failure. His spiritual breakthrough came through giving up the attempt to find perfection. When this happens, another path arises.

Honen's spiritual realisation was radical. It was also important in spreading Buddhism to the ordinary people of his day. It opened up the possibility for the common working people of medieval Japan to engage with the religious life, despite the limitations of their circumstances. It introduced a form of Buddhism that was simple enough for all, both conceptually and in terms of the practice it involved.

This practice of Pureland Buddhism involved calling on Amida Buddha through the six syllable phrase known as the nembutsu, and so it was suitable for lay people who could not easily visit the great temples. Previously Buddhist teachings had been largely limited to the sphere of monastic and courtly life, but Honen's approach offered them to the people in the villages and towns. Honen taught to fisher folk and stock raisers, to people whose assigned profession left no room for precepts and meditation, and he taught them that spiritual salvation was still available to them. However poor their actions might be deemed, they could live lives of faith. The Pureland tradition thus began with a political act of democratisation. No longer was Buddhist practice the province of the elite.

Pureland Buddhism describes humans as *bombu.* This term literally means a "foolish" or "common" person. The word derives from the Chinese, and in normal usage has a rather derogatory tone. In Pureland Buddhism the word was adopted to assert the value of ordinariness as a basis for entering the spiritual life. Thus the term has taken on a more technical meaning.

> *The common meaning (of bombu) comes from a more relative, social stance, while the Pure Land meaning comes from a more subjective and personally religious one. In Pure Land Buddhism, it is an extremely important notion in that it describes the situation of the sincere practitioner who nevertheless finds him or herself totally incapable of avoiding the acts prohibited by the Buddha. (Jodo-Shu Research Institute website)*

In other words, this term is used to describe the person who deeply recognises their personal failure in the self-perfection project. Knowing that one is *bombu* is a fundamental of Pureland faith.

The term *bombu*, commonly used by Japanese writers, is a short version of the phrase *zai-aku sho-ji no bon-bu*. Commonly in English we translate this phrase as *"a foolish being of wayward passion"*. What a wonderful terminology! This phrase contains both description and medicament. To recognise the position of the fool is to recognise our humanity. The wise fool has a rich pedigree, how much more so the foolish one. Knowing our inability to escape from the cycle of the passions, we open to change.

Building the Ant Hill

The Ant Hill sutra describes the layers of the conditioned mind. It shows the complexity of our deluded state and the way that one delusion rests upon another. Let us look again at some of the items it identifies. The greatest delusion is our belief in our own perfection and our refusal to face the reality of our nature. The first thing that the bhikshu encounters as he digs into the ant hill mound is a bar. This bar represents a complete denial of the problem. The image is of the wooden pole which lay across the road going into a village, intended to keep out unwanted visitors. This is the mentality which avoids difficult questions and criticism in the attempt to preserve an illusion of sanctity. When we are in the grip of self-deception, we are not willing to look at our own nature. We imagine our perfection and do not want to discover evidence that things may be otherwise.

In this model, the highest levels of the psyche, represented by the first three objects taken from the ant hill, are associated with social conformity. The second object pulled out of the ant hill is the toad. The toad represents resentful anger. When a person becomes obsessed with the achievement of a spiritual goal, there is a great danger that they will simply create more layers of self-delusion. If we are reminded of our faults when we are in such a frame of mind, we tend to become irritable. This is what is being suggested by the toad. Frequently a person who is heavily invested in appearing spiritually advanced will manage to keep their irritation hidden, but their anger will seep out through indirect remarks or unhelpful actions. Such indirectly expressed anger may not be immediately apparent but creates a negative force field around the person. We might think of it as a passive-aggressive response.

I remember once talking with a non-Buddhist therapist friend who had been working with a group of people that included a number of Buddhists. She commented that she had never met so many passive-aggressive people as she met in Buddhist circles. This made me think. From what she said, the people concerned were serious practitioners, who spoke a great deal about developing compassion, loving kindness and calm. They set high store on mindfulness and observing the minutiae of their reactions. I suspected that what had happened was that they had learned to suppress any behaviour that was overtly aggressive or negative, but that the feelings which might underlie such behaviour had not gone away. As a result of this many small confrontations and differences in the group were probably being avoided. The group members were presenting themselves as nice people to be with, but their feelings of irritation did not necessarily go away. In a social situation, such a presentation could persist unchecked, but in the group situation where they were interacting intensively with other people, conflicts were bound to crop up. These did not fit with the ideal of calm and loving kindness. As a consequence such feelings were repressed, only to emerge later as indirect remarks and unpleasantness. The context of the group, with its more intensive inter-personal environment, created a backlog of negativity, and indeed probably unleashed pre-existing resentments that its members were carrying. Although behaviour can be trained, negative emotions are not so easily discarded. "Saints" are often hard to live with in private.

The third object to be taken from the Ant Hill is the fork. The fork represents the horns of a dilemma, the process of prevarication between two possibilities. When the attempt to suppress negative behaviours and thoughts becomes untenable, the practitioner begins to get an inkling of the enormity of the spiritual task ahead. At this point there is a crisis. Not sure where to go next, a person who is still convinced of the need to seek personal perfection may fall into strategies that effectively buy time. This is a kind of avoidance. It happens when a person plays around with different possibilities but does not really commit to any of them in a serious way. The person engages in intellectual debate with no real end in view or wavers between different life options without really engaging in a meaningful process or making an actual change in direction. Such a person might move from spiritual practice centre to spiritual practice centre, never staying long enough to really be challenged by the lifestyle or teachings. There are many people caught in this pattern of constant mobility who spend years on end circulating round different religious establishments. It is a sort of spiritual tourism: always the holiday, never real life.

Taking the ant hill as a model of the conditioned mind, these three upper levels can be seen as forming a set. They can be correlated with the levels of non-becoming (*abhava*). Conflict is avoided by destructive processes, the deadening of experience. These levels are all about processes of denial. A person who is caught in these behavioural patterns skims over the surface of life, and avoids engagement with the real situation. Such a person may believe that he or she is living a spiritually fulfilled life, but may in fact never face the life dilemmas that will bring about real spiritual maturity. Conflicted feelings manifest, but, being products of complacency, they are, relatively easy to avoid. The person who is operating at these levels may assume there is little further personal work to be done.

What is not apparent to the practitioner, though may be evident to those who know her, is that these layers of denial rest upon the layers of self building represented by subsequent objects in the sutra. The next objects to emerge from the heap are the tortoise and the sieve, which represent the *skandhas* and the *five hindrances*. These are the components of the self, the processes by which identity is created and maintained. Far from being the final elements in a process of higher spiritual development, the upper layers represent the compounding of the process of delusion.

The bottom of the ant hill

At the heart of the ant hill, lies the naga serpent, the symbol of spiritual energy. This spiritual energy sleeps surrounded by the objects of passion. Far below the objects of denial, the bar, the toad and the fork, the images of the last objects to be removed from the heap point to rather more potent energies. Our spiritual nature is embedded in our wayward nature. We are creatures of the earth, and our capacity to grapple with the spiritual dimension is closely related to our capacity to recognise the ordinary nature of our being, and more deeply, our seemingly infinite capacity to get it wrong. Most proximate to the serpent in the imagery of the Ant Hill Sutra are the piece of meat and the axe and block. These are the representations of raw lust and of sensual attachment. It is out of the presence of these wayward passions, our most primitive responses, that our spiritual energy is forged. At this most profound level we are inseparable from our animal nature.

The Ant Hill Sutra shows us our deluded state and the way in which the *bombu* nature is constructed. In the sutra the *bhikshu* is instructed to throw out all the layers of conditioned nature. This image presents an ideal. The achievement of the state of perfection seems simply a matter of eradicating each layer of conditioning in turn until the naga serpent is left, pristine and guarded, but as we have seen, the attempt to throw out the layers of conditioning is generally destined for failure. Paradoxically, though, in letting go our attempt to appear perfect, some of the outer layers of the construction may be diminished. As we let go of our struggle with spiritual attainment, the compounded delusions are more likely to drop away and we are more likely to be left facing our more basic nature as beings driven by raw emotions and drives.

Although Honen's teachings did not eliminate the possibility that some might succeed in overcoming these obstacles by steady practice and saintly quality, his realisation was that for himself and for the vast majority of human kind, the path of purity was not a practical option. Entangled in our passions, the drive to perfection creates only further layers of delusion. Perhaps we are not destined to throw away our tortoises and toads. Perhaps in trying to do so, we merely create new layers in the ant hill.

These layers are manifestations of *bombu* nature. The processes of attachment and accumulation, these elements build our defences against the world we would embrace. To engage in Pureland practice is to acknowledge our *bombu* nature, to practice profound honesty. Through this honesty we perhaps diminish our tendency to compound our self delusion with layers of denial and pretence. Exploring our *bombu* nature, brings us closer to the heart territory of spiritual practice. As we recognise the unfathomable depth of our corrupting scripts, we see the power of the undesirable forces within us. We can fight the *dragons of anger and ogres of greed* but it is not in our capacity to conquer them. To fight dragons, in the words of the hymn, requires faith and joy.

CONCEPTS INTRODUCED IN THIS CHAPTER
- The conditioned nature of mind
- Problems of seeking perfection
- Honen's insights into the futility of self-perfection
- The Foolish Being

CHAPTER THREE

DEPENDENCE AND GRATITUDE

We plough the fields and scatter
The good seed on the land
But it is fed and watered
By God's almighty hand
(harvest hymn, Matthias Claudius)

What do we do by ourselves, and what is done for us? What do we accomplish through our own effort and what unfolds through grace?

The unfolding of a life remains a mystery. Existing within the circle of human experience, our actions and even our thoughts are far from original. Every word we breathe has been breathed by others before us. The thoughts that press against the limits of our brains are not new. They are the recycled images of others' ideas. How else could humanity progress in such phases and fashions, but through the progression of our shared story? What we hold dear has been held dear by others before us. What we discover is already in someone else's mind.

Nothing new

As humans, we can have a rather over-inflated view of our own uniqueness. We are fascinated with ourselves and devote much time and energy to refining our credentials. Who doesn't in his heart of hearts see himself as a special case and an exceptional human being? But we do not function alone. We do not create from originality. We are the containers of a heritage that continues from before our birth and into an undetermined future. We are collectors and re-assemblers, reprocessing ideas and passing them on.

We contribute to the spiral of ideas that unfold over generations to mark the development of cultures and civilisations, but each of us individually is simply a cog in a bigger process. We are less important than we think.

Yesterday, sitting in a park, I watched two small girls playing. The older one, who was about four years old, had a beach ball; the younger, scarcely bigger than a toddler stood opposite her, hands clasped excitedly in front of her.

"I'll throw the ball to you" the older girl said.

Her voice was confident, instructive, and tinged with parental concern for her younger sibling. She sounded like a teacher or nanny, or maybe her own mother, despite her young age.

The younger girl looked back coyly, "please" she said, looking out from under long eyelashes. Her tone and manner were simultaneously charming, slightly affected, to a degree that could have been older than her years.

The older girl threw the ball. Being light, it caught in the wind and blew away to the side.

Immediately the mood changed.

"Oh no!" the elder sister exclaimed in panic, and for an instant looked to her mother for help. Her mother, however, was preoccupied with feeding a new baby. The child stood transfixed, the small misfortune having undermined completely the image of maturity that she had previously embodied. A moment of indecision, then she ran, jumping down a small wall, sure footed as a young goat, to retrieve the ball.

It was an ordinary sort of exchange; a normal part of growing up. Yet, something about that interchange struck and fascinated me.

The two girls were so lively. Their expressions, however, conveyed moods and manners that seemed beyond their years. There was something unreal about the interaction. It was in the precision of tone in which they spoke, which appeared to indicate an inappropriate level of maturity and poise. Yet the apparent maturity dissipated immediately when things went awry. Such responses amuse us. Children mirror adult mannerisms, and we see ourselves reflected in their expressions. The unknowingly parody our modes of speaking that seem so individual and personal. In the playground one can see children "playing school" or "mummies and daddies", acting out the roles of adults, and often doing so in ways that mimic strictest tone of voice and most authoritarian mannerisms.

Children's games bring home to us our own worst aspects in ways we might prefer to avoid, but also they show us the universality and unoriginality of so much of how we are. After all, here was I, an adult from a completely different part of the country, recognising the language of behaviour of these two small girls and enjoying its nuances. This was only possible because human communication, and particularly communication within a culture such as "England", has a limited range of possibilities.

Children learn this complex language of gesture. Despite their young age, these two girls had already assimilated a whole range of responses, not just by learning through their own trial and error efforts to overcome life's hurdles, but also through observing and absorbing the actions of their parents. Such learning brings with it feelings of greater security. The child learns to master her environment. Soon she will learn how to behave with decorum even when a beach ball rolls off target. She will learn to avoid embarrassment. But not all learned behaviours are concerned with defence. To reduce all behaviours to defensive mechanisms seems to miss the creative and joyful aspects of the process.

Some gesture is instinctive. We do not even have to learn it. Patterns of aggression and submission for example are common to many animals. Some human gesture is of this type, arising from our genetically determined drives for reproduction, territoriality and survival. Behaviours that are in part instinctively programmed are often rehearsed by young animals, whose play is an important part of integrating the ability to assert and to defend. Observing young humans with the eye of the zoologist, we notice behaviour that is not so different from that of other young animals.

A few years ago we adopted two abandoned boy kittens at our centre in France. They were charming and lively and endeared themselves to everyone. Watching them at play became a favourite distraction in the community, for we all enjoyed their energy and exuberance. But also, for those of us who had had children of our own, part of the fascination arose from the fact that they reminded us of our own youngsters when they were growing up. If they walked across the yard together, they would never make the whole distance without one of them being tempted to cuff the other. The ensuing fight would leave them rolling together in the dust until they exhausted themselves. This behaviour reminded me of my son and his friends at around the age of eight or nine. They would never seem able to walk along the street together without starting a play fight and would constantly be engaged in rough and tumble, carrying on in just the same way as the kittens. Boys will be boys. Whether kittens or human, despite our attempts to avoid thinking in gender stereotypes, some behaviour differences seem to be inborn.

Other behaviour is learned. Children copy from others. They learn ways of interacting from the sources around them. They embody characteristics of family members and teachers, the television presenter and the woman at the sweet shop. The word embody is particularly apt here, for such experience is learned more readily through our bodies. We catch habits of action and gesture from one another, often without any cognitive process intervening. Friends and acquaintances mirror each other's body language and create common vocabulary of responses. Watch a group of teenagers together, or mothers congregating at the school gates and see how similar their modes of gesture are. Couples grow more alike with time, developing a similar set of face and manerisms.

We inherit the body patterns of our families and with it take on the behavioural habits of our parents. What mother has not at times caught herself scolding her children in just the same tone of voice which she herself heard as a child from her own mother.

"Goodness, I sound just like my mother" she says.

But even the remark is not original. She is the typical daughter becoming the mother and recognising the process of transmission between the generations. As we recognise these trends we protest to ourselves; we assert that we are now and they were then. We seek solidarity with other daughters who have become like their mothers. We attempt to demonstrate our independence, but in practice we simply demonstrate our conformity. We are about as original as the teenager in blue-jeans with the pierced belly button.

The two girls I met in the park have learned parts already. Some of their gesture may be instinctive, but most is far too English to be inborn. They have learned their roles. Not only can they speak their parts, the one the teacher and carer, the other the coy recipient, but also now they are already able to adapt to different roles as circumstances demand. The elder child, whilst being the elder, speaks with the confidence of authority. She knows she must, in this circumstance, take care. The younger, free of responsibility, is grateful for the attention. She has learned to be cute in order to play her part. She rewards the elder with her devoted looks and willing participation in the game. It is a common human strategy. Unless a younger sibling takes her place, the youngest child may well still be doing cute at thirty-something, and looking for a world that will play ball with her.

We think that we direct our lives, but the reality is different. Far from exerting control as we imagined, we mostly run our lives along predictable lines, coasting on autopilot. Often we struggle to even notice the patterns of response that have us in their grip. Our awareness is deadened. In Buddhist terms, we might say we are in the grip of Mara. Delusion and death amount to much the same in this respect. Our habitual behaviour dulls our consciousness so that we hardly inhabit our lives. Foolish beings! We are empty vessels in the sea of life.

Navigating the seas

Thus, whilst so often we are caught up in seeking our individuality and perfecting our bodies and our minds, most of what we do and are is not of our own making. We do not choose our birth circumstances, unless indeed these are determined through our karmic accumulation. We make resolutions that we break. We find ourselves acting in ways that surprise us. We say things unguardedly and then regret them. We catch each other's moods, each other's mannerisms.

If, when in conversation, I scratch my nose, in all probability your nose will itch. If I cross my legs, you may well do likewise. Try it. If you watch people talking you will notice that, without realising it, they often mirror one another's body language. Therapists know that if they pay attention to their own body sensation, they may learn something of the client's unexpressed feelings. Even at a micro level, a cellular level, we replicate each other's patterns of response. We unconsciously absorb another's tensions. If you have ever comforted someone who is in a high state of anxiety, you will probably have noticed how knotted your shoulders became in the process, how on leaving the room you had the impulse to shake off the body tensions which you had picked up without realising it.

Observing someone who is talking to a friend on the phone, and you will notice their voice subtly mirroring that of the person at the other end. Their accent may shift. Commonly a person speaking with childhood friends will slip back into their hometown dialect. Watch a person leaving a meeting and see how their walk, how their stance has been influenced by the mood of the group. If the meeting was tense, notice the taut expression on the face, the clenched jaw line. If it was positive, notice the upright posture and smiling face.

Our thoughts and actions are shaped by others. We are extremely prone to automatically taking our cues from the people around us. Much of what we think of as intentional behaviour is actually determined by such factors. The explanations we give ourselves are rationalisations.

If a hypnotist implants a suggestion, say to draw the curtains at a certain cue, the person who follows that suggestion is likely, if questioned, to say that he drew the curtains because it was getting dark outside, or for some other logical reason. In other words, even when the behaviour is known to be unconsciously programmed, the person finds a rational explanation for having done it. It is part of the way that people typically reassure themselves that they are in charge of their lives. We like to believe that we act of our own free will. Much of our behaviour is like this. We go about our lives entranced, behaving in ways which we have learned from others, that we have internalised through our own repeated actions, and yet we think of ourselves as autonomous and as exercising free choices.

So much is programmed, yet our lives are not predetermined. Buddhism has never suggested it so. On the one hand our histories, encounters and circumstances have made us who we are. On the other hand, within the parameters that they set, we do make choices. From our stock of possible responses we choose. Sometimes we draw out wiser responses, other times unwise ones. To this degree, we are authors of our actions, but we do not have much ability to determine the range from which these possibilities are drawn.

Humans are a strange mixture of motivations and instincts. Mostly we run along pre-worn tracks with little thought of the implications, but occasionally we act decisively and even heroically. Often our choices are driven by dubious and unconscious motivations, but yet we are capable of deep concern for others. Frequently we take the easy path, the less courageous and in doing so condition our minds to further dulling, diminishing our ability to live well.

If we develop some insight, we can start to imagine that we are in control of our lives. Perceiving some of the layers of thought and action that make up our responses, it is easy to believe we understand ourselves. We think we can break out of our bad habits, or even that we could become enlightened. But such insights are not enough. Awareness is not sufficient to break through all our patterns. So much of what we are is not even ours to change. It is programmed in. This is *bombu* nature

And even where it seems it may be possible for us to change, the undercurrents of unconscious processes, of unrecognised manifestations of greed, hate and delusion, the three poisons that lie at the core of all mental afflictions according to Buddhist theory, pull us back into old habits. Our minds have unfathomable depths. We are as leaves on the surface of a pond, drifting with the currents that the wind whips up.

Some of our life's determinants come from within, but many come from without. We can only grasp what is proffered, and if it is good, accept it with gratitude. We overestimate our capabilities. This is our arrogance. To accept that we have a vast accumulation of personal baggage, and recognise that we have much less power of self-determination than we might have liked to think is, however, surprisingly freeing. On the one hand we are full of all sorts of negative impulses and driven by all manner of dubious motivations, and on the other hand, what we are is a product of our experiences, relationships and histories and hardly of our making at all. It has come from others with whom we have had dealings. Pureland invites us to see our common nature with others and to appreciate our shared fallibility through a sense of fellow feeling.

Pureland also invites the practitioner to let go of striving for individual goals and personal perfection. Such projects are built of sand. More though, such striving traps us in that very delusion that Buddhist teaching would have us relinquish. It binds us to the cycle of self-creation. To accept our complexities and our messy natures is a great relief.

Recognising the other as real

In Pureland the attention is not on developing our own faculties. Of course, we try to do something about our grosser habits, but this is seen as a secondary practice. We recognise that even in this we are bound to have many failures and confused motivations. Primarily, though, the practice focuses our attention beyond ourselves. This looking beyond self is not about using the features we see in others as a subtle way to build the sense of identity (though being bombu, inevitably such mixed motivations creep in again and again). It is, rather, an attempt to acknowledge and appreciate what is truly other.

Despite all our limitations and failures, we are still wonderfully looked after. Despite our incompetence and lack of imagination, bigger processes of life go on. Beyond the messy realities of our individual lives, the great stories of history unfold. Despite all the problems of humanity, the sun still rises, and often the world is a beautiful place.

All this we take for granted. Yet on it we ground our lives. Even the most secular amongst us wakes each morning, confident that most of what is needed for the day's existence will be there.

And thus, we take for granted that which is beyond our self world. The human tendency is toward grandiosity. We have a great capacity to divert and incorporate experience into our personal projects. We create personal worlds that reinforce our sense of substantiality, but it is, in fact, the things that surround us that are real, and not our internal fantasy world. We use each other as props to our psychological structures. In doing so, we do not respect others or recognise them as having existence in their own right. We incorporate them into our agendas and viewpoints. Doing this we subtly undermine the integrity of life.

Pureland Buddhism points us towards a deep appreciation for what is other. Put technically, it looks to the *non-self* reality of other people and things. In other words, as with other Buddhist traditions, it is concerned with helping us to become less caught up in the personal perspective and to recognise our limitations of view. It centres on a relationship with the quality of otherness both on the human and the transcendental levels. Thus the perspective it offers can be seen as *other-centred*.

For the reader who has previously encountered Buddhism as it is mostly taught in the West, there may be conceptual struggles with these ideas. Although Pureland Buddhism is grounded in the same understanding of the human predicament as all Buddhism is (though it is less optimistic about our ability to achieve salvation through our own efforts), its emphasis is different. Pureland emphasises our *bombu* nature, our dependency. It sees the person as caught in a morass of deluded thoughts and perceptions. It sees how we are rescued time and again by the others in our lives. We are held and supported by our environment. We are cared for by other people. We live through grace.

Gratitude

Most of what we have, we take for granted. We do not acknowledge our debt to others. Most of the time, we do not even recognise the limitations of our own originality. We assume that we have been the engineers of our lives, even though they are so patently shaped by others. We over estimate our own efforts and underestimate the input that others make.

Yet our effort is a small part of what it takes to sustain our lives. Even if we grow our own food and haul logs back from the woods, as we do at our centre in France, we depend greatly on the work of others. In its natural state, that area would probably be impenetrable forest. We rely upon the generations of farmers who have cleared and tilled the soil before us. We rely on paths cut by previous occupants of the site. We rely on tools; saws, spades, garden forks. Mostly we rely on buying seeds, developed by seed manufacturers and packaged in printed paper envelopes, though sometimes we collect our own. In summer we rely on water supplies to keep our crops alive. In winter we rely on freezers or other preserving methods to store the produce. These of course use electricity and bottled gas, and sometimes other ingredients bought from the shops. We rely on cars to transport us to the shops (the nearest place to buy a spade is six miles away). These rely on all the mass transportation systems of the modern commercial infrastructure. It is a tiny example, but it brings home our reliance on others. If such simple things as growing ones own food and collecting one's own firewood, carried out in a rural, "back to nature" setting, is so interlinked with the support of others, how much more so are our activities in urban life.

This catalogue is simply a reflection of the human effort which goes into daily life. If we reflect on our reliance on natural processes, the list becomes even longer. Plants only grow with sun and rain and soil, with the nutrients that come into that soil through organic processes of growth and decay. They rely on insects or wind to pollinate them, on temperature variations and levels of humidity. The complexity of eco-systems is something at which we can only wonder.

In our pride we produce pumpkins and leeks, carrots and tomatoes, strawberries and beans, and we happily take the credit.

The harvest thanksgiving is a traditional part of country life. Those who live the whole of their lives close to the soil know all too well the impotence of the farmer and the gardener when rains fail or frosts come at the wrong times. Each year the harvest is a miracle, given by the grace of God. Modern farming methods prise back some control for the farmer with mechanised watering systems, chemicals that prevent diseases and give nutrients, and methods of crop protection for inclement weather, but these systems come at a cost, often creating larger scale problems as they disrupt the natural order of things. Drawing water from rivers which are already reduced by drought or polluting the land with the over-use of artificial substances creates environmental problems which upset other aspects of our ecosystem.

At the end of the day, too, these methods do not ward off the most extreme effects of climate and other hazards. In the summer of 2003, the extreme drought in France left fields of crops withered and unharvested, and, despite the lorries that drove south from northern Europe full of hay, many livestock were slaughtered prematurely. As conditions worsen over the coming years, and effects of climate change impact more deeply, we can expect increasingly to see our powerlessness over nature. At such times, too, we may feel gratitude and appreciation for what we have previously taken for granted. Once more we may feel the impulse to give thanks.

Although many Buddhists speak of inter-dependence as our basic state, the truth is that we are in a position of great dependency. We need food in order to stay alive, but the crops do not need us. We need sunlight, but the sun does not need us. We need air to breathe, but the atmosphere is not dependant on human activity to maintain its' oxygen levels. As Lovelock tells us in his recent book, *Revenge of Gaia* (Lovelock 2006), the planetary system may be a lot better off without its human occupancy.

Inter-dependency is a relatively rare condition, just one of the twenty four *pratyayas* or conditions listed in the seventh book of the Abhidharma. (see Brazier 1995) In the narrow sense, the pratyayas are the conditions on which different mental states arise, but, taken more generally, they can be seen as the conditions for all things. Inter-dependence implies mutuality, a situation in which factors support one another and the removal of either would lead to the destruction or impairment of both. In most aspects of our lives, this is not our situation, much as we, in our pride, would like to think it so. Dependence is common. We need many things to stay alive and to live functioning lives. We need other people for our practical and emotional wellbeing.

Gratitude is a fundamental aspect of Pureland Buddhism. It is also the antidote to the grandiosity so endemic in our modern society. Ultimately too, it creates a happier situation. Individualism and self-sufficiency create loneliness. They lock us into isolation. Gratitude opens us up to the presence of a supportive net of others, with whom we are deeply and unavoidably connected. It brings with it appreciation and even wonderment at the beauty of life around us and the kindness and courage of the ordinary people whom we encounter.

Opening up to gratitude, however, also involves facing our pride and letting go of some of the defensive structures which we have created in order to protect us from knowing our vulnerability and dependence. In this, it can be frightening and even painful. It also goes against a life-time of habit. In his book, *River of Water, River of Fire,* Taitetsu Unno writes:

When we realise that we are all sustained by both visible and invisible forces in our world, we should be humble and grateful. But the reality of human nature is that our karmic impulse goes against both humility and gratitude. To acknowledge this truly is to experience the sadness and sorrow of what it means to be human. But deeper and profounder than our feelings is the heart of great compassion that takes us in (Unno 1998 p92)

Gratitude involves humility. Letting go pride, we allow in the feelings of appreciation. We allow ourselves to see the hidden workings of the universe, the compassion that surrounds and maintains our lives. This is both moving and difficult. There can be many tears.

Nei Quan

Nei Quan, or *Naikan* as it is known in Japan, is a form of life review that is personally challenging, profoundly moving and often extremely therapeutic. Naikan was developed by Yoshimoto Ishin, who lived 1916 to 1988. Ishin was a Pureland Buddhist from the Jodo Shinshu sect in Japan. Having experienced a tough form of spiritual practice within that tradition called *mishirabe*, Ishin wanted to create a therapy that could be used to bring its benefits to lay people. The original method of doing *mishirabe* used introspective methods similar to *naikan,* but also involved strict fasting and not sleeping.

Naikan is a well developed method in Japan. It is used therapeutically with clients from a variety of backgrounds and has also been widely used in the prison service, where it has proved very effective in lowering rates of recidivism. Being used in such mainstream settings, it has been well researched, although most material published on the subject is in Japanese. Different styles of presentation have also been developed, allowing it to be used in regular therapeutic settings as well as the traditional intensive immersion style retreat.

David Reynolds, who is probably the most well known Western proponent of *naikan* method, has developed its use as a Western therapy, combining it with the Zen inspired *Morita* method. Reynolds has written a number of books on these therapies, but his first book *The Quiet Therapies* (Reynolds 1980) offers a good introduction to the subject. More recently Greg Krech has also produced a good book on the subject (Krech 2001).

At our centre, we have developed a form of retreat which broadly follows the traditional *naikan* method, but uses a somewhat different group-centred format or retreat. We call these retreats *Nei Quan* retreats, using the Chinese form of the name to distinguish them from events using the traditional Japanese methods.

In both forms of retreat, the central element is the use of particular questions to facilitate an inward enquiry (the words naikan or Nei Quan mean inward enquiry). Usually this enquiry centres on a relationship that has been significant in a person's life, often starting with the primary care giver, the mother or person who stood in for mother. A period of time is taken for review. Often this begins with the first three years of life. When this period has been fully explored, a process which might take half a day or a day, the enquirer moves on to the next three years, and so on. This progression is made according to the instruction of the retreat leader.

The questions that are traditionally asked are:

What did this person do for you?

What did you do in return?

What trouble did you cause?

In the Nei Quan retreat, the retreatant is asked to focus on these questions and to look for concrete examples that illustrate their answers. For the early years, memory is substituted by deduction. Mother must have fed the baby, changed it, bathed it and so on. The retreatant can reflect on the times in which this was happening too. Maybe it was war time and the baby caused the mother anxiety. Maybe the parents living circumstances were difficult or there were family conflicts. Maybe she lived in a part of the country which she hated or had to give up a job that she loved because she had the baby.

During this reflection, the retreatant stays in an allocated area of the meditation room. Each retreatant has his or her own space, which is demarcated by plants or small pieces of furniture. Retreatants may sit, lie down or even stand if they wish. They may also use drawing or writing, and many do make extensive use of these methods of exploration. The whole retreat is conducted in silence, and retreatants do not communicate with each other directly except in the formal sharing circles held at the mid-way point of the retreat and at the end. Usually the retreat takes place over five days.

At intervals the retreat leader will give talks, which focus the retreatants' attention on the subject. He or she will also go to each retreatant in turn, probably daily, and invite the retreatant to give an account of their process. This account is received in an appreciative silence, but no response is made other than an appreciative acknowledgement and an invitation to either continue reviewing the same period, or to move on to another section of time.

Retreatants normally leave the retreat space only to sleep and use bathroom facilities. Food is brought to them. The food on a Nei Quan retreat is an important part of the experience as it is always very carefully prepared using a lot of raw and fresh food. Presentation is very important and the retreatants receive beautifully arranged trays, which have clearly taken much care to prepare. Being cook for a Nei Qan retreat is itself a beautiful meditative experience that takes the whole attention of the person in that role for the duration of the retreat.

The message behind the food is one of love, but it is also a love that, being human, can get it wrong. Although retreatants can tell the cook at the outset of the retreat if they have allergies to any foods, and occasionally send notes back to the cook on their trays, for the most part, they eat, or refuse, the food they are given. This produces a powerful replication of the life situation. We are given immense richness, but sometimes what life brings us may not be what we would choose for ourselves, given a free choice. Others try to help us, but sometimes they do not meet our expectations. We have habits of expectation which can make it difficult for others to give.

Sometimes the experience of being fed in this way can be quite transformative. I remember one retreatant who struggled a lot with the way that food was served. I could tell he was having difficulty because I was cooking and his tray kept coming back with the food half eaten. I felt sad at this because I was trying hard to find dishes that would please him. About half way through the retreat I found some beautiful green pears in our local shop. They were perfectly ripe and so attractive I decided not to cut them up, but to give each person one on their tray. When I took the trays into the retreat room, I saw the face of this particular retreatant fall again. He had returned all the pervious fruit I had offered, so I was not surprised, but I still felt a bit sad. However, when I returned later to collect the trays I found that the retreatant was busy drawing a picture of a big green pear. The pear had disappeared from the tray, and his face looked radiant as he turned to look at me.

Later that day we had the sharing round which customarily happens mid-retreat. The pear had been a turning point for him, he explained. When he saw the tray he had thought that it was a large green apple. Expecting it would be hard and sour, he had felt his heart sink again. When the tray was set down in front of him, he hardly looked at the pear, leaving it on the plate and toying with the other food. Suddenly, though, he looked again at the tray and realised that he had not even looked at the piece of fruit properly. He had just made the assumption that it would be unpleasant. In fact he loved pears, and when he picked it up and bit into it, his feelings suddenly welled up and tears began to flow. How often did he mistake something beautiful that was being offered for something he didn't want? How unappreciative! He spent so much time trying to control situations so that others could not mess things up for him, that he hadn't noticed the good things that were around too.

Nei Quan is a cathartic process. People often feel very moved when they reflect on the way that they have been supported and cared for by others. They may feel overwhelmed by sadness at how much they have not appreciated the love and attention that others have given. Against this background, even recognising the failings, the mistakes, which a parent has made, the retreatant's feeling for them softens. Such failings have so often been just part of an attempt to get things right which has backfired. Seeing the whole picture of another person's life, we appreciate more of the pressures that cause them to act as they do. We feel gratitude for their effort and concern, even if its effects were not as we would have wished, or we feel sorry that they were so bound up in their own bitterness that they could not love well and lived an isolated life.

These retreats frequently change people's lives. Even when a person has experienced a neglectful and abusive childhood, finding a different relationship with the parent through Nei Quan work allows a kind of respect for the parents' autonomy to emerge. Sometimes also it also brings memories of good moments and kindnesses to compliment the painful ones. But it is not intended to be a method to pour sweetness over bad circumstances. It is an investigation of the truth. We do not pretend people are never mean or abusive, but the truth is that no one is completely bad.

Finding respect for others as separate beings who are not part of our self-world, but have their own pain, conflicts and hopes, is the basis of our Buddhist approach to therapeutic work. Not just in Nei Quan, but in other methods such as journaling, psychodramatic exploration, biographical work and talking therapies, exploring the experience of others, and their histories, thoughts and relationships, provides a potent experience of releasing the world from our personal agendas and seeing others as people with their own value and beauty. Doing this, we often feel deep appreciation and gratitude.

Pureland practice, a path of gratitude

The experience of Pureland Buddhism is that we develop appreciation. This is not just for what others have given to us, or for the world we inhabit, though these are important. The central practices and teachings are grounded in an attitude of appreciation that goes beyond the worldly to the transcendent. The practice is deeply rooted in the sense of other-ness, an appreciation of the reality of a measureless beneficent presence beyond the limits of the self-world. This practice, as we will see, centres on devotion to Amida Buddha, the immeasurable expression of Buddha in the universe. It is a practice that expresses deep joy and gratitude, that reaches out in the wistful longing expressed by yugen, and that gratefully allows the practitioner to rest in the knowledge that despite their imperfection, they are blessed.

The emotional impact of these teachings can be seen in Honen's account of his conversion experience. On reading Shan Tao's commentary on the Contemplation Sutra, he was suddenly overcome with emotion. His gratitude to the Buddha and his sense of unworthiness came together in a great outpouring of joy. This was the teaching he had been seeking. This was the religious doctrine that he had intuitively sensed. This was a practice which could be available to everyone and bring salvation to ordinary people, not just to the religious elite. Despite his humanity which inevitably left him unable to practice perfectly, he was still loved. Amida Buddha had provided a way to practice that he and others could follow.

With such a realisation his heart opened up to the universal embodiment of love that Amida represents. He wept for joy.

> *In an excess of rejoicing, although there was none to hear, I cried in a loud voice: "In the past, when Amida Buddha was still engaged in practice as Dharmakara [Bodhisattva], he had already established this practice for persons of limited capacity like myself!" Joy pierced me to the marrow, and my tears fell in torrents. (Jurokumonki, JZ. 17:66 quoted on Jodo Shu Research Institute web site)*

Pureland practice is simple. The nembutsu, the act of calling on Amida Buddha, is an outpouring of the heart. This simple phrase forms a bridge between the practitioner, limited and flawed as he or she is, and the immensity of the universal love and immeasurable generosity that Amida embodies. It is an expression of gratitude, a deep cry of joy that erupts from the heart. Across the divide of separateness, it brings us into contact with the universal light.

CONCEPTS INTRODUCED IN THIS CHAPTER

- We are not separate in thought or action, but are dependent upon the process of others
- Gratitude and appreciation
- Nei Quan and other-centred approaches to transformation

CHAPTER FOUR

JIRIKI AND TARIKI

The boat of the eightfold path
He sails across this rough sea
Having traversed it himself
He now carries us across
(from Nagarjuna's hymn)

The teachings of Pureland Buddhism are rooted in the same understanding of the conditioned nature of the human mind as those of any other Buddhist school. They view the person as being deeply enmeshed in processes of attachment and self-aggrandisement and as infinitely capable of selfish, hostile and otherwise ill-motivated actions. For Buddhists of any school, this is nothing new.

The difference that Pureland offers is in its view of the solution to this situation. We cannot just walk away from our karmic patterns. The path of spiritual practice that attempts to wipe the slate clean is arduous and long. It is not necessarily impossible, and indeed, the sutras suggest that many have accomplished the task, but Pureland came to see this route of personal effort as being beyond the capabilities of most practitioners.

It was noted that in the time of the Buddha large numbers of people had become enlightened, whereas in later times the process seemed to have become much more elusive. This troubled Buddhists of later ages. A view grew up that as the world moved further from the age of a Buddha, it went through a series of stages, and that, in each of these, it became more and more difficult for people to achieve enlightenment. In medieval Japan, the view grew up that the world had reached the final stage, referred to as the age of *Mappo*, and that in this time reaching enlightenment through one's own efforts had become impossible.

In chapter one of the *Senchakushu*, Honen says

> *In these days it is difficult to attain enlightenment through the Holy Path. One reason for this is that the Great Holy One's time has now receded far into the distant past. Another is that the [ultimate] principle is profound, while [human] understanding is shallow…. We are now in the age of the final Dharma, that is, the evil world of the five defilements. The Gateway of the Pure Land is the only one through which we can pass [to enlightenment]. (Senchakushu chapter 1)*

Thus the Pureland approach offered an alternative. It was seen as an easier route to Buddhist practice, and ultimately enlightenment.

If people in the time of Honen believed that they were in the Dharma-ending age, how much more so are we, eight hundred years further on from the Buddha's time? If the age of *Mappo* was already upon them, what age are we facing now? The troubled world in which we now live indeed seems to be facing an ever more bleak future. The impending disasters of war, shortage and climate change compound the spiritual malaise of our age and renewed religious passions seem only to further entrench the human positions which exacerbate these problems. The necessary wisdom seems in short supply, and yet a spiritual transformation seems the only hope that humanity has of transcending the destructive forces which threaten us. What practice, what grace, is it possible to avail ourselves of in these dark times?

Escaping the avalanche

Japanese Pureland Buddhism uses the terms *Jiriki* and *Tariki*, often translated as *self-power* and *other-power*, to indicate the two modes of spiritual practice found in Buddhism, but indeed identifiable in other religions. *Jiriki* is self power. This is the approach that involves eliminating our attachments and delusions through our own efforts. *Tariki* is other-power. It is the approach that relies upon faith.

The idea of two paths, the path of effort, or *self-power*, and the path of faith, or *other-power* have been present in Buddhism since its earliest days. It is possible to trace their roots back into Indian Buddhism, and probably even to the time of the Buddha himself. Different people approach religion in different ways. When we look at how Buddhists practice across the world today we can see practitioners of both kinds represented in many Buddhist traditions. Western Buddhism, however, has become dominated by the self-power style of practice. This is probably because it compliments our Western views of independence and personal achievement. Perhaps also for some it is a reaction against their childhood encounters with other faith-based religions. Pureland Buddhism is an other-power school and, perhaps as a result of this, has made less headway in the West. It is time to redress the balance.

When I am talking about the Pureland approach with people who are new to these ideas, I often find it easiest to introduce the basic conceptualisation by inviting the listeners to reflect on the following scenario.

Let us imagine that a man is walking in the mountains. He is enjoying the fresh air and good views and the warm winter sun. He has no thought for danger or difficulty. He is on a good path and all seems well for the expedition ahead.

As he saunters along, appreciating the scenery, however, he hears a rumbling sound above him on the higher slopes. Looking up, he sees the snow further up the mountain is shifting. No doubt the sun has loosened it, and the flow of melt water has dislodged an area of snow from the rock face, creating a small avalanche.

The man is instantly overcome with fear. He suddenly becomes acutely aware of the dangers of such occurrences and that there may be little he can do to escape being buried alive in the snow. He fears he will be swept away entirely, and struggles desperately to move out of the course of the descending mass. But it is to no avail. With a great thunder of falling debris, he is engulfed by the icy cloud. He falls, curling his arms over his head, submitting to his situation.

Gradually the avalanche settles and the snow stops crashing down the mountain around him. There is silence. He is still alive.

At this point the man realises that he has been lucky. Cautiously he uncovers his head and looks up. The snow bank that has collapsed was not a large one, but its force has swept him off the path, into a crevasse just below, where he has become lodged, chest-deep in snow. Although he is not completely overwhelmed, he is stuck in the snow and unable to move or escape. He will soon be soaked. He becomes frightened, realising that somehow he needs to get himself out of this predicament or face hypothermia.

As it happens, before he left his lodgings, the walker's host lent him an ice axe. Being polite, he took it with him, despite doubting its usefulness. After all, he had no intention of straying from the well trodden routes. Now, however, he begins to realise its potential use as a small shovel. With difficulty he manages to extract from its pouch on his belt, and starts to dig the snow away from round his body.

It is not easy. Fast as he digs, new snow seems to slide in around him. He cannot get his arms properly clear of the surface in order to throw away the snow that he is digging out. It just seems to keep slipping back into the hole. The snow extends for some distance around him and the sides of the crevasse are slippery. Digging his way out is going to be a long process.

Nevertheless, in the absence of help there is nothing else to be done. At least the digging is giving him some hope of progress and keeping him warm. But as he continues, the man remains stuck in the snowdrift as before, and is becoming tired and disheartened.

Meanwhile, down in the valley, the mountain rescue team has set out. They have seen the avalanche from below and have come to the affected area, searching for survivors. The trapped man is still digging and trying to scramble out of the hole, albeit with diminishing enthusiasm, when the members of the mountain rescue team draw near. He pauses. Maybe he hears a voice or sees a movement. Looking up, he sees the figure of a man in bright orange overalls, standing on a large rock some distance off, and looking across the snow field in his direction. In relief, the man calls out.

Has he been spotted? Perhaps he will not be seen in all the vast expanse of snow. Safety is so near, yet he cannot reach it through his own effort. He can only rely on the other man's skill for his survival.

The rescuer is carrying a rope coiled over his shoulder. He knows the mountains well and is prepared to climb if necessary in his task of rescuing survivors of mountain accidents. Alerted by the cries, he looks round. He sees the man struggling in the snow, a small figure, some distance away.

With hardly a second thought, and with the ease of one whose daily work involves such tasks, the rescuer throws the rope across the space between them. It lands just beside the walker. The man sees the rope and gratefully drops the ice axe in order to reach up out of his snowy chasm and catch hold of it with both hands. He grasps the rope and loops it round his waist as the rescuer instructs him. Soon he is hauled to safety.

This scenario illustrates the human predicament. It also illustrates the two approaches to Buddhist practice. One approach can be equated to trying to dig ourselves out by our own efforts. This is known as the route of *self-power*. The other route involves allowing ourselves to be rescued. This is known as the route of *other-power*.

How, then, are we to understand the image? Our minds are engulfed in delusion. This is a common understanding in all Buddhist schools. We may imagine that we are in control of our lives. Just as when the man sets out from his lodgings, the sun is shining, and we feel well equipped for our journey. We are neither aware of our limitations or of the potential pitfalls that we may encounter. Only when things start to go wrong, do we recognise our predicament.

In fact we are already buried in an avalanche of delusion. We each carry with us a store house of conditioned patterns of thought and action. We cling to things that confirm our sense of self. We are locked into habitual tracks and limited vision. Unlike in the story, these heaps of delusion have been accumulating from time immemorial. It is in our nature as humans to accumulate complex layers of habitual responses, attachments and narrow-mindedness. We become rigid in our view of the world and of others and in our sense of who we are.

My previous book, *Buddhist Psychology*, explored the processes whereby patterns of thinking and acting are created and maintained. It described how our patterns of view and action reinforce one another, and how they become something that we cling to because they reassure us with their familiarity and because we have become identified with them. This identification creates our sense of self. The delusion is all we know, and we cling to it as if our existence depends upon it. Just as the young girl I observed with the beach ball, described in the previous chapter, was thrown into confusion and anxiety when her script ran out, so too we feel threatened and uncomfortable when we step out of our familiar territory. But our self becomes a trap, limiting our capacity to move "out of our box" into new thought or experience. It keeps us walled up, just as the sudden influx of snow prevented the walker from enjoying the afternoon stroll.

Jiriki and Tariki

Understanding the theory of conditioning is one thing, but to be able to recognise our own patterns of conditioned response is more difficult.

Firstly, our experience has always been acquired through our own perspective. We only ever see things our own way. Of course, we may have a variety of personal perspectives. When we think of things one way, we see them in a particular way, when we shift our position, we may see things differently. The young adult, for example may become used to seeing the world one way, and then, on becoming a parent, may suddenly see it very differently. People with prams are a nuisance in the supermarket check out until one is struggling with one's own offspring, and so on. Such a variety of experience can give us multiple perspectives which can help us empathise with others who are single, or who have children. At the same time, we never cease to view the world through our personal viewpoints. We never really know what it's like to be in another's shoes.

This may seem obvious, but the implications are substantial. The way that we see the world is shaped by our thought patterns and our past experiences. It is part of our way of being, and thus part of who we think we are. It is as much a part of us as our hands or face. We identify with our view-point, without even realising that we are doing so. Indeed, it is so much a part of us that we often assume that our personal perspective on the world is the objective truth. This is the nature of conditioning.

Secondly we have an investment in keeping our habitual patterns of perception constant because they are directed towards things that act as indicators of self (*lakshanas*). In other words, this personal view point implicitly gives us a feeling of identity. We know who we are because we inhabit a world that is viewed through a filter of our personal interests, assumptions and misconceptions. This perceived world is like a kind of mirror image of our sense of self. It supports that sense of identity and gives us evidence of our existence.

Escaping from the cycle of conditioning is therefore no simple task. We may achieve some limited progress through our efforts, but trying to get free of all conditioned behaviour is often a counter-productive route. The notion that we can eliminate conditioning through our own efforts is so often flawed. We are immersed in *fathomless blind passion*. We may understand and identify the behaviours, but as fast as we try to change them, further layers of habit energy inevitably seem to creep in, whether these take the form of smugness or irritability.

As it was for the man in the avalanche, so it is for us. As fast as the man dug, the snow fell back into the hole. As fast as we make progress, new manifestations of delusion appear in our behaviours. To imagine that we will be able to get ourselves out of this situation through our own efforts, from a Pureland perspective, is simply grandiosity. We cannot save ourselves through our own power. To get out of our psychological trap we must find something outside ourselves to rely upon.

Whether we try to dig ourselves out, or whether we reach for a rope, the ultimate concern is that we get out of the snow and onto the safe ground beyond. The path to enlightenment means getting out of our state of self-preoccupation. Different Buddhist approaches offer different ways to achieve this. Some focus on eliminating the delusion through the deconstruction of our conditioned processes (*samskaras*). This involves great mental effort, but since it is mental processes that are the source of the problem, concentration upon them can simply create more layers of mental structure and does not necessarily solve anything. The Pureland approach offers a different way to reach the solid ground.

From the Pureland perspective, we cannot rescue ourselves through our own effort. Even our effort is part of our mess. To get out of the avalanche, something else is needed. The man needed a rope to hold onto. Similarly, if we can grasp onto something that is beyond our personal world of delusion, we can be saved.

The other-power, *tariki*, approach is the approach that involves reaching for the rope that is thrown across the snow field. The, *jiriki*, self-power approach involves finding our salvation through diligence in practice. *Tariki*, or *other-power* approaches place reliance on what is beyond our self-world as the source of transformation.

But reaching out to catch the rope involves taking a risk. The man needs his hands free to catch it, so must release his hold on the axe. He must let go of his attempt to save himself through his own efforts before he can be helped by others. What if the rope does not reach him? Can he trust the rescuer not to let him down?

Reaching out is frightening. It often feels safer to stay within the limited orbit of our own strategies. For the man caught in the avalanche, it was easy to reach for the rope because he was already tired and willing to try another approach.

I remember as a child being instructed in basic lifesaving. We were told that if a person was in difficulties in the water, we should be wary of swimming out to them too soon. If the drowning person still had energy, they would cling to anyone who came near, in such a way that might make swimming impossible for either of us. It was likely in this instance that the struggling person would drag both of us, rescuer and rescued, under the surface. Instead, if we were attempting to save the person, we should circle them at a safe distance, reassuring them and waiting till they were ready to trust us completely. Only then was it safe to approach and pull them to the shore in the recommended way.

It is often only when we feel we have no choice that we are willing to take the risk of fully trusting another. So long as we feel we can do it ourselves, we continue to cling to the idea that we can indeed make things work through greater and greater effort. Some are more trusting and more willing to take a risk than others, but for many of us it is only when we recognise our complete incapacity to help ourselves that we allow others to take over and help us.

At a spiritual level, this willingness to allow *other-power* to take over from *self-power* is a moment of renunciation. It is the act of taking *refuge*. For Honen it was the confrontation with his spiritual failings, and the recognition that for most people salvation was impossible on the path of self-power, that brought him to seek another direction. Recognising our limits brings us to the point where we no longer struggle. We are willing to let go and allow ourselves to be rescued. It is often only when all else has failed that we go for refuge.

Taking the boat: Nagarjuna

Pureland Buddhism has roots that can be traced back to Buddhism's earliest days. In his commentary on the Three Pureland Sutras, Hisao Inagaki (Inagaki 1994) writes of his view that Pureland has its roots in the Samadhi experiences of Shakyamuni Buddha, the historic Buddha. In particular the Amitabha Samadhi which Shakyamuni seems to have transmitted to some of his disciples, forms the basis for early Pureland practices.

Shakyamuni Buddha recounted stories of a number of other Buddhas, either of the past, or of other worlds, and Amitabha Buddha was one of these. Amitabha literally means limitless light. Together with another Buddha, Amitayus, who is the Buddha of infinite life, these figures are seen as combining in the figure of Amida Buddha, the central figure of devotion in Japanese Pureland practice.

The tradition of devotional practice was thus well established from the earliest Buddhist times. Nagarjuna lived in the second century CE in

Northern India, a high caste Brahmin, he converted to Buddhism and studied with the different Buddhist traditions of his time, the predecessors of both the Theravada school and Mahayana schools. He is widely regarded as the greatest Buddhist teacher ever to have lived after the time of Shakyamuni himself. A great philosopher, who is particularly noted for having developed theory about the nature of *shunyata* or emptiness, his work is highly revered by Mahayana schools, all of which regard him as one of their founding teachers. His philosophical reasoning took Buddhist thought to new levels of sophistication and his verses on the middle way are widely studied.

Although he is generally thought of in the West as a great philosopher and proponent of the theory of Shunyata, Nagarjuna was also a devotee of Amitabha. Devotional practices centred on Amitabha were clearly a big element in Nagarjuna's religious experience. Nagarjuna saw these practices as the most effective way to achieve non-retrogression, a stage well on the route to enlightenment. Besides his philosophical treatises, Nargajuna left verses in praise of Amitabha which show a deeply devotional and quite ecstatic relationship with the Buddha of infinite light.

One of the images which Nagarjuna introduced was that of the two paths to practice. One he described as being the difficult path, and the other as the easy path. He likened these two paths to a choice of routes for the journey from India to China. On the one hand, one might cross the Himalayas on foot, and on the other, one might travel by boat. Both paths arrive at the destination, but the sea route is pleasant and easy, whereas the mountainous route is hazardous and difficult. The difficult path that is being alluded to here is the path of personal cultivation, which involves study and practice, whereas the easy path is that of devotion and faith.

The image of the boat which Nagarjuna uses is interesting, for it has some parallels with the image of the raft which the Buddha uses. In the

Snake Sutra (MN22) the simile of the raft is used to represent the Buddhist teachings. In that sutra the Buddha speaks of the teachings as being a raft to take one across the river to the other shore, but says of the raft that it is not something to be clung to. Similarly Nagarjuna sees the boat of the easy path as a method of transport to take us to our destination, and not an end in itself.

In his hymn to Amitabha, Nagarjuna talks of the Buddha, Amitabha, boarding the *boat of the eightfold path*. This represents the path of the religious life which the Buddha follows. Nagarjuna then talks of Amitabha, having himself already made the journey, carrying us across. In other words, because the Buddha has already set out the path to enlightenment, by allowing ourselves to be carried by him we can also reach the other shore. Devotion and faith are the requisites. It is not necessary for us to struggle along the eightfold path by our own effort.

Not only is it unnecessary, but one might argue, the extremes of self-power also constitute a negation of the work of the Buddhas. In trying to replicate their actions and resisting the path they have provided, we make their effort redundant. Self-power feeds an "each man for himself" philosophy and works against altruism.

The social context: problems of self-power

The two paths, *jiriki* and *tariki*, self-power and other-power, described in the previous section, represent two patterns of approach to spiritual practice. We should not, however, imagine that the principles behind them apply only in the sphere of formal religion. We can rely upon self-power or other-power in many aspects of our lives.

As we have seen, Western culture has placed great emphasis on individualistic values. Self-power styles of operating pervade many areas of modern life. This has brought with it various social effects that are not necessarily helpful to our society.

One aspect of this more individualistic approach is seen in the growing popularity of personal growth activities and of the psychological therapies which underpin them. Popular culture is everywhere offering invitations to build self-esteem and to engage in self-exploration and personal discovery. Business takes heed of psychological testing and assessment, just as former cultures consulted oracles and soothsayers for guidance (probably with equal levels of success). While this culture has brought undoubted benefits for some, it has contributed to a social ambiance that measures individual success in both material and psychological arenas and sets implicit standards against which many people measure their lives.

Concern for psychological well being is echoed by concern for material and lifestyle success, the latter often being taken as an indicator of the former. People are measured by their standard of living. Of course this has always been so, but in modern times, the emphasis on such indicators of individual achievement creates, among other things, an increase in use of material resources. This means an accompanying stress on the environment. As the numbers of single person households increases, each individual requires a range of material goods that previously a family might have shared; a car, a washing machine, furnishings, entertainment equipment and all the other paraphernalia of modern life. Even those who do not live alone tend to live in smaller units. Families are small and members of the households often pursue quite separate lives, with diverse interests. Much less time spent in collective activity. Many couples have a car each, and, since the pursuit of two careers may involve living some distance from work, increasing travel becomes the norm.

A big factor in the move towards increasing individualism and consumption is the general increase in personal expectations. Most people are not prepared to make do with the material limits that their parents and grandparents experienced at similar life points. When I was a child we always lovingly saved and ironed gift wrapping paper, to re-cycle it at the next Christmas or birthday. To rip the paper off a gift was frowned upon as greedy and wasteful. Later I recall my mother buying rolls of festive paper at Christmas, but these were always thin and tore easily. That was what was available at the time. Now one rarely receives a gift that is not wrapped in thick, good quality paper, often with ribbons and cards attached. A trivial example, but one that shows how, in so many ways, our expectations have crept up over the years. There is a feeling of entitlement, and almost of an obligation to live at a certain level. Personal fulfilment has become an expectation and Western lifestyle today is far more focused on consumption than it was fifty years ago. Twenty years ago, the "me generation" were exploring personal fulfilment through encounter groups and new age therapies. Now the pinnacle of personal achievement is more likely to be measured by a good salary and a fast car.

Besides the hunger for material goods, people now look for increasingly sophisticated methods of relaxation. They travel more, taking advantage of cut-price holidays, often able to consider more such breaks because they have delayed having families and so have greater spending power. To support such lifestyles, each person seeks their own career and salary, working longer hours. Working longer hours, people rely more on a variety of convenience products. Highly packaged foods replace home cooking.

Personal achievement of this kind is not good for our planet. The resources put into material goods that are scrapped after a few years use, and into production costs, are high; so too is the energy consumed in these processes, and in transportation of goods and people. Nor is the emphasis on achievement good for people's mental health. Far from getting happier with our material well being, levels of psychological distress are increasing.

Other effects of individualism are felt in the delivery of services. In particular, the helping professions have increasingly become focused on enabling people to become more self-determining and more personally successful. They train people in self-sufficiency. In good professional practice, the aim is to facilitate but not to impose; to follow, but not to set the lead. This has undoubted benefits, and where such moves have been properly supported with resources, rather than cynically used as a cheap option, we have seen many benefits from this kind of client-centred approach. But such benefits may come at a cost, and that cost is associated with the underlying philosophy of individualism in which such approaches are grounded. Short term benefits in autonomy may mask longer term problems as communal support networks are eroded.

Similar trends are found in many fields. We can see them in therapeutic work, medical and para-medical services and social care for example. Long gone are the extended hospital stays in which the bed-bound patient lay for days and weeks, waited on by armies of nurses, doctors and other hospital staff, their every movement, bowel or otherwise, monitored and recorded. Most of us prefer the shorter periods as in-patients that modern surgery and drugs offer. For the relatively able and wealthy, looking after our own interests is often pleasanter. On the other hand, for some people, such trends create situations of extreme isolation and hardship. Without resources, the most needy members of society are often left uncared for. Many of the homeless and rootless people who now hover at the edges of society would previously have been housed in long-stay wards. Bad as these were, the street does not seem an improvement. It is not impossible to provide good resources in such settings but in practice, care in the community has often become a few lessons in self-sufficiency and a door onto the street. Not everyone can cope alone.

At the same time, in many professions regulation is increasing. Registration of psychotherapists and counsellors hovers increasingly on the professional horizon. Alternative therapies are starting to set up systems for accreditation. In most professions, codes of ethics and professional practice create safety nets for those who fall into difficulties. The power of the professional to harm as well as heal is recognised. But these protective measures are mostly concerned with the framework in which the service is offered. They are seen as creating the boundaries within which the person receiving help is encouraged towards autonomy. The ideal of self-sufficiency is still paramount.

Such regulation seems part of a greater social movement towards individual autonomy and rights. Its ethos is often fostered within a framework that can be judgemental and legalistic. A culture of complaint and litigation is growing, although at the same time much commercial life has become impersonal and frustrating, the omnipresent call centres replacing personal service, and customer services often seem more concerned with protecting the interests of the company. The move towards individualism does not necessarily bring better services in the long run.

The details of different professional situations can be discussed elsewhere, but my concern here is with the underlying trend in modern society towards the individualist and materialistic value system that encourages people to look towards increasing levels of personal achievement and accumulation whilst discouraging dependency. This trend towards a society where personal autonomy is highly valued does not necessarily create a happy situation in the medium to long term. Although initially people relish the increased standard of living, the move towards longer working hours does not necessarily create the quality of life imagined. Creating more choice and flexibility in medical and social services brings great gains for the able and the informed, but may leave the more vulnerable members of society with inferior or limited facilities. Protecting service users and consumers from the unscrupulous has obvious benefits in gross cases of abuse, but often creates a culture in which organisations operate to protect their interests rather than to deliver the service users would really like. A more co-operative, mutually supportive approach, on the other hand, often produces benefits that are unintended. To some degree, society has been in rebellion against the worst excesses of paternalism, and from attitudes now seen as antiquated. On the other hand the move towards self-power attitudes also has its difficulties.

It is perhaps time to review this trend and to look at alternatives. Just as religious thinking has elements of self-power and other-power, so too, in helping situations we can encourage aspects of a person's behaviour that are autonomous or we can help them find refuge in relationships or places where they will be supported. We can encourage them to rely on self-power or we can move towards a more other-power approach, where values of mutual support, trust and collective effort are higher. All approaches offer some balance of these two elements, but the pendulum at present is somewhat weighted towards self-power. It may be time to redress the balance.

Trusting the other, finding refuge

When a person seeks help from a professional, it is usually because the approach to life that he or she has developed is not working. Things are not as they should be. Sometimes there is a practical problem. Often there are emotional dimensions too. The person's attitudes and thought processes are also wrapped up in the problem, and often at its root. We are all bombu, enmeshed in ordinary layers of delusion, pride, and despair. Sometimes, however, our mental processes threaten to overwhelm us. We no longer feel able to handle them on our own. At that point we may seek help. We feel adrift and look for someone to help us get out of the mess.

For most people, the decision to go for help to a professional arises out of a sense of having reached the end of the line. The lone struggle is not working and it is time to involve an outsider. The person's own efforts have failed.

We could say that at that point, the person makes an act of faith. Not knowing what to expect, he or she goes to a stranger, willing to take the risk of trusting another person with what are often their most intimate experiences. Behind this act is a level of confidence, maybe built on some real knowledge of the particular person's style and capabilities, maybe a more generalised confidence in professionals, or in people in general. Whatever its basis, however, in the initial encounter a lot is likely to be unknown. There is often some ambivalence around trust, and indeed the process of establishing trust is a big factor in the success of many long term helping relationships. Nevertheless, that first step of reaching out to another for help is an act of faith which takes considerable courage. As the recipient of such faith, we should feel great privilege and responsibility.

The act of seeking help involves a shift away from old coping strategies. The time of crisis is one in which old self-structures are often weakened. The support systems may have been eroded, and the sense of self challenged. It is therefore a time when a person may open up to new possibilities. It is also a time of fear and threat. At such a time, the person may also retreat into greater levels of defence. The experience of affliction can, after all, be the trigger both for the creation of self, and for the discovery of spiritual strength. Such spiritual strength is a gift. We cannot will it to be there, but sometimes, almost miraculously, it appears.

The experience of grief and sadness, pain and affliction that is *dukkha* opens the door of our self-prison. It breaks the cycle of self-building at least for a short moment and creates the opening for new patterns of response to develop. Thus it offers us the possibility of new ways of relating and behaving. When habitual coping strategies fail, this failure provides the impetus towards a new course of action. The new course may be healthier or less healthy. As we saw in the example of the young man who had experienced the car accident, described in chapter one, a crisis point may offer an opportunity for deep transformation. It may also be a point at which the client begins to trust others rather than trying to be self-sufficient. In a perverse way, the experience of losing faith in one's own endeavours may offer a dawning of a different kind of faith. The healing process requires a safe space and it is often through the experience of being in psychological contact with others, and feeling supported, and not through the injunction to be independent, that healing happens.

Self-power, other-power and the work of Carl Rogers

An important contributor to western psychological theory was Dr Carl Rogers. Rogers offered a model of therapeutic change that was extremely simple in its conception, which has been deeply influential in the development of counselling theory and practice. His central theory was that if the therapist provided certain conditions the client would inevitably move towards psychological health and would experience measurable change in positive directions. These necessary conditions have been presented in a number of formulations in his different works, but generally referred to as the *core conditions*. Rogers' approach has been called client-centred therapy, or person-centred approach.

Rogers lived and worked in North America. In the second half of the twentieth century, when he was practising and writing, the human potential movement was at its height there. Rogers writes in the language of that movement, and thus might be seen to promote a self-power route. On the other hand, the implication of his work seems to fall more comfortably within a set of ideas that are much closer to the *tariki* position. This positioning perhaps lies behind the fact that Rogers' ideas have been widely taken up by Pureland Buddhist groups in Japan. These groups may well feel an instinctive affinity for his views. For example, in chapter eleven of this book I will describe the work of Gisho Saiko in Japan, who was an enthusiastic participant in Rogers' person-centred movement and also a Jodoshinshu priest, psychologist and academic in Kyoto.

Rogers' theory asserts that it is the therapist's role to offer the right conditions for therapeutic encounter. This involves providing a psychological space in which the core conditions, which in their simplest, commonly used, formulation are empathy, congruence and unconditional positive regard, are available. The client, according to the theory, will naturally grow psychologically healthier as a result of these circumstances. The therapist should make no other attempt to affect the client. For this reason early Rogerian work was termed non-directive, though this term was dropped as it was too open to critique. Human interaction is a subtle and often slippery process and avoiding directiveness completely is almost impossible. Inevitably we influence others by our responses, verbal and otherwise, by the way that what we hear tends to focus on what interests us and by the way our attention is caught by certain words or images. Basically though, despite discussion of these finer points, the point of the method is simply to trust that, given the right conditions, the healing process will unfold.

In this way of thinking, trust plays a big part in the person-centred approach. Firstly the therapist must have trust in the theory that the core conditions will, themselves, be sufficient to allow the natural change to occur. Secondly the therapist must also trust that the client has the potential, known as the self-actualising tendency, to grow psychologically healthier without further interference. Having this trust, or we could say, these articles of faith, the therapist offers the core conditions to the best of his or her ability. Developing empathic presence involves being able to get psychologically alongside the client, and to see the world "as if" through his eyes. Here yet another act of trust takes place. The therapist trusts the client to allow him to walk alongside for a while. At the same time, the client learns to trust the therapist and to become more open and less rigid in his world-view.

Rogers' description of the *fully functioning person,* for example, in the chapter *A Process Conception of Psychotherapy* in *On Becoming a Person* (Rogers 1961) is of a person in the flow of their experience, a person who trusts others and embraces life. Although still framed in language that values the autonomy of the self, the attributes of that self include a shift from psychological rigidity to more fluid experiencing, with *situations experienced and interpreted in [their] newness, not as the past* and *the self [becoming] increasingly the subjective and reflexive awareness of experiencing. .. less frequently the perceived object* (ibid pp152-153). This view of the person emphasises engagement with the world. When we allow for the self-based language of this Western approach, it is not so different from the Buddhist view of the person who has made spiritual progress. Such progress is made in the context of relationship, and with the support of another's presence. The core conditions provide the container for trust.

It could be added at this point, that Heinz Kohut, (1913-1981) the originator of the theoretical approach known as Psychoanalytic Self Psychology, also placed a strong emphasis on empathy in his work. He, however, saw the lapses of empathy that naturally occur within the therapeutic process as highly significant to the therapeutic process, as these points forced the client to re-adjust his mental image of the therapist. This work is interesting in demonstrating a number of factors.

Firstly, the failures of empathy disrupt the client's world view. When our world view is kept in tact, we process around our habitual tracks. It is only when our perceptions are challenged that we change. Secondly, seeing others as functional parts of our world, we do not see them as individuals in their own right. The failure of the other to operate within our expectations forces a revision, and enables the possibility of a real meeting. In particular, the therapist, having in all probability been seen as an idealised other, is now seen as human. The client has to adjust to a world that is not just there to serve his needs, he has to grow up. Finally though, the therapist's lapse of empathy is an aspect of their *bombu* nature. Failing to be perfect is part of who we are as humans. If this is not hidden, but is allowed to be visible, we offer others an opportunity to really encounter us as fellow human beings, and that is therapeutic. We no longer have to be perfect ourselves and neither do they.

In Rogers' view, empathy is fundamental to the therapeutic process. Whilst the therapist develops skills in empathy, the client develops trust. Held in a situation where judgement is, as far as possible, suspended, he experiences the holding presence of another, maybe for the first time. This situation can be viewed as somewhat akin to the act of taking refuge, and the fundamental aspect of Pureland practice, the *nembutsu*.

The second element in Rogers' trio of conditions is congruence. This is the element of honesty. The therapist does not put on a pretence, and may in some cases voice feeling responses or thoughts which have arisen in her in response to the client's story. Kohut sees the failures of empathy as important because they break the illusion of perfection, and similarly these congruent interventions reveal the human presence of the therapist, offering the client the opportunity for real encounter.

Real encounter is the foundation for trust. Although we may dream of the perfect source of love and support, we actually trust humans who are prepared to be open about their flaws. We do not trust people who seem to be hiding behind an idealised façade. We do not trust people who are psychologically unavailable. When we cease to trust others we lose faith in a much broader way. Many psychological troubles arise from people's loss of faith. Life troubles and difficulties in relationships lead a person to feel they can no longer trust others. The person-centred movement, with its emphasis on relationship, creates an opportunity for trust to be rebuilt and faith in other human beings to grow once more.

Rogers put great emphasis on trust. Others within Rogers' circle, notably Eugene Gendlin, produced variations on his method that placed less importance on such relational qualities. Some of these methods drew on Rogers' belief in the capacity of each person to grow psychologically, the *self-actualising tendency*, but also emphasised empowering the client to develop healing strategies for himself. To some degree these methods were an attempt to extend the ideas of autonomy and personal control into the therapy room, and in this, to have political impact on the therapy profession. In this respect, Rogers himself had been part of a *third force*, a movement of innovative therapists who sought to move away from what they saw as the authoritarianism of, on the one hand the psychoanalytic traditions, and on the other the behaviouralists. The movement that gave therapeutic autonomy to those who sought their own solutions took this process one stage further. In addition to Gendlin's work, we can see a similar motivation behind such methods as co-counselling.

The move to give clients more sense of power in the therapeutic relationship was an important step in the development of the profession. It introduced the possibility of a much more genuine way of relating, in which the therapist could not hide behind the professional mask so easily. But it had its draw backs, in that it contributed to the kinds of trends toward individualism and the pursuit of personal rights that we have already discussed.

Gendlin's approach was inspired by research that had been done into the behaviour of clients who were successful in therapy. What Gendlin observed was that clients who did well were those who body referenced their experiences. These people tended to follow their *felt-sense* when exploring personal issues. Gendlin realised that this observation of the felt-sense was something that could be taught, and he developed a set of techniques which he called *focusing* (Gendlin 1951). The techniques of *focusing* could be taught to clients and used without the presence of the therapist. In many ways this was the ultimate act of empowerment. *Focusing* practitioners were called teachers, not counsellors or therapists. Their work was aimed at giving people responsibility for their own process.

Whilst in some ways *focusing* was similar in spirit to Rogers' person-centred method, in other ways it was very different. It moved the locus of responsibility away from the therapeutic environment, and created a technique based method that, once taught, could be used anywhere and effectively removed the need for a therapeutic relationship. The person-centred method, on the other hand, rested centrally upon the therapeutic relationship. The therapist created the therapeutic container within which the client was psychologically held, and this process of holding enabled change to occur.

For Rogers an essential precursor to therapeutic change was that therapist and client be in psychological contact. Not only this, but the therapist should also be congruent, being present and in contact with the client, and also genuine in the way she expresses herself. In other words, for therapy to take place, the therapist must, as far as possible, be experienced as a real person by the client. Her presence should not be a performance or pretence at caring, but should involve real human concern and warmth.

In these descriptions, we can see that Rogers own approach relied far more on the quality of presence, of otherness, in the healing process, and thus was advocating an approach much more in line with an *other-power* position than Gendlin's more self-directing approach, which is clearly *self-power* in style. Although the two were theoretically close in some respects, they differed greatly in whether their methods were basically *Jiriki* and *Tariki*.

In Rogers approach, the therapist is *other* for the client, offering a benevolent presence and place of refuge. At the same time the therapist also takes refuge in her own article of faith, the therapeutic process. This faith holds both counsellor and client and enables change to occur. For both counsellor and client, the therapeutic process remains a mystery. The therapist attempts to offer the basic conditions that she believes will be therapeutic, and these conditions offer universal qualities applied in a unique situation. How change actually happens, however, is not something for which we have an explanation. Offering the core conditions itself is an act of faith. Providing good enough empathy, genuine openness and warm regard to a stranger involves trust both in the client and in the activity which is taking place.

Faith in the self-actualising tendency allows the therapist to accompany the client in areas of psychological encounter that are confused or frightening, dark or unbounded. Although described in the language of individual assertion, the engagement of this healing process is not something that therapist or client can choose or deliberately engage in. All they can do is to be willing. It is a process that must be surrendered to. It is *other-power.*

A Safe Harbour

The notion of *other-power* is central to a Pureland approach. Although it seems to go against the tide of much of the theoretical and popular thinking of Western society, with its emphasis on self-determination and improvement, and of much of the Buddhism taught in the West, it is not in fact so far removed from most people's experience.

Although we like to imagine that we are the authors of our own experience, our lives are inextricably enmeshed in the ideas, behaviours and functions of the society to which we belong. We cannot conceive ourselves as separate, nor can we touch originality in our creativity.

Within our complex web of relationships, we are inevitably dependant. The West creates even greater dependency for its citizens than exist for those in poorer societies, as food production and fuel requirements are out of proportion to availability at local levels. We assert our independence but in reality live in a state of dependence.

We live with the myth of our own potential, but even at the heart of the human potential movement, find that psychological change depends upon powers that are greater than any of us can even conceptualise. This is the power of love, of unconditional acceptance and of the real other.

In Pureland the notion of refuge, common to all Buddhist schools, becomes the natural expression of our faith in *other-power*. The source of spiritual life is the focus of our practice. Although we may take refuge in other people, in physical objects and places, ultimately it is our relationship to the transcendent which sustains us. The following chapter will explore the way in which that relationship with the transcendent other creates our spiritual strength.

CONCEPTS INTRODUCED IN THIS CHAPTER
- Jiriki and tariki; self-power and other-power
- Nagarjuna and early Pureland ideas
- The Western theories of Carl Rogers, Heinz Kohut and Eugene Gendlin as examples of other-power and self-power approaches

CHAPTER FIVE

A RELATIONAL PSYCHOLOGY

> Dark volcanic crags
>
> Erupting from the bracken
>
> Break the winter sky
>
> In cold air rising, my heart,
>
> Embracing the sunlight, leaps
>
> (poem: *Bradgate Park*)

Today the snow has gone. I look out from my window. Dull clouds hang; heavy, grey. Toward the horizon, far out across misty layers of fields and trees, veiled by the poplars on the river plain, light hovers.

Landscapes touch us.

As humans we live in environments. We are always in relationship with our world. From the moment of our birth, we are surrounded, contained, expanded by what we see and hear and feel. Since this is true of all humans, and indeed all life, we cannot know what it would be not to be in relationship with a world. Our existence is thus conditioned. Our minds mirror the surroundings we inhabit. They are not, and cannot be, in isolation. The world creates us. The physicality of our environment imprints on our being. Dark hills create dark, reflective minds; the open grasslands give us space to dream. The sky dome lifts our hearts.

The physical environment is not all, though. We are also in relationship with other people. Most of us, day to day, surround ourselves with other humans. They may be family, friends, work colleagues, acquaintances, or simply the milling population of our city transport systems and commercial precincts. Even when we are alone, others are in our thoughts. Their words come to us in books, newspapers and radios and their images embrace us from the television screens and advertising hoardings.

Two of my children are twins. Now adult, I sometimes wonder how it was for them never to have been alone. Even in the pre-birth state, where most of us experience a kind of solitude, to share those watery lodging with another: how radically different. Yet even in the womb, we all relate. We hear body sounds, perhaps without recognising what they are. We feel warmth. Babies suck their thumbs and move their bodies before birth. They react to light and sound. Sensation grows into awareness of a world beyond self, even as we lie in the womb. At first the boundaries are blurred. The hands that wave before the face, fascinating objects in the visual field, seem to hang and move as independent entities. Everything is other.

Gradually we learn that we inhabit a body, discovering its capacity to move and feel. Gradually we learn to separate our experience, to find the edges of "me". Gradually out of the primordial soup of undifferentiated experience, objects emerge and we start to connect with special people. Gradually we connect the experiences of sight and touch and sound and taste and smell, and recognise that through these senses, we are connecting with a world of objects. Relating becomes conscious.

So we are enmeshed in a world of others. And yet, within our world, whilst always relating, in another way, we are still utterly alone. We see, we touch, we feel, but we cannot know the heart of another. We can only surmise. Our senses convey experiences, but they do not perfectly mirror what is there. Like narrow bridges, they connect us to the object world, but only allow limited perception of it across. They are, as we say, conditioned. Clouded by expectations and limited understanding.

And when we face death, we cannot take another by the hand and go together. We simply slip away alone.

This is the paradox of human existence: never alone, yet always solitary.

In this chapter, we will explore the way that our experience is created through our encounter with others. In particular we will look at the way that we are inspired and changed by such encounters. In daily contact with the ordinary world, the extraordinary manifests. If we are open to the *yugen* quality of daily experience, we can reach through it to something altogether more uplifting. The inexpressible universal truth, the Dharma, is touched through subtleties of imagery and atmosphere.

Spiritual depth becomes manifest through natural allusions. This is the intense beauty of Saigyo's poetic works. The mystic and poet's experience is embedded in an intimate relationship with his environment. Concrete, commonplace reality holds the religious experience. The universal is revealed in grains of sand and drops of water. In the brooding clouds we see the spiritual struggle. In the obscured sunlight, we glimpse the divine. Encountering the world, we open ourselves to grace.

Trying to look at or to describe the spiritual source directly is like looking at a faint star in the night sky. We see it from the corner of our eye, but each time we try to look at it directly, it disappears into the darkness. Or maybe it disappears into the light. Even the attempt to write is flawed. Words simply do not do justice to the theme. To describe the experience of such a moment requires vocabulary that has long since become hackneyed. But seeing the frost upon the rough boards of the garden fence catching the morning sunlight, my heart recognises something of that intangible quality. I am moved.

We have seen how modern trends push us towards individualism and self-sufficiency. Not only does this lead people to resist dependency, and to defend their autonomy, even in intimate relationships. It also creates a fragmented society. The self-perfection project is glorified, as the pursuit of personal optimisation becomes the philosophy that drives society. The project grows, taking many forms. Progress is measured in personal success. Each strives for their own material salvation. Yet such individual success does not breed contentment. Arid experiments in lifestyle change may be chic, but they create a deeply felt isolation for many.

Such isolation is not the solitary life of contemplation that nurtured the hermit-monks of medieval Japan. The latter created a way of being which, despite its separation from human company, was embedded in profound communion with other forms of life in all their myriad aspects. Modern isolation by contrast is lived amid the cacophony of city life, divorced from the natural world and from the silence in which the universal can speak.

Relationship is in our humanity. Without it, we wither into shades and spectres.

Awakening to the world

The Buddha, Shaykamuni, founder of the Buddhist religion, lived in the fifth century BCE. Shakyamuni is the honorific name given to the man who was born Siddhartha Gotama. The name means "sage of the Shakyas", the Shakyas being the tribe into which the Buddha was born. After his enlightenment, Shakyamuni Buddha taught for more than forty years. He was one of the greatest teachers of his age, and accumulated around himself a large group of followers. Some followers ordained as *bhikshus* and *bhikshunis* (monks and nuns), while others remained in lay life. His followers included members of his own family and others drawn to him by his wisdom and insight.

The Buddha's teachings, the *Dharma,* came from his experience of the universal truth. It derived from insight that came through his experience of *enlightenment*. It was insight into the nature of existence and human experience. The Buddha's Dharma was not invented but realised.

Shakyamuni's search had taken him through physical extremes and advanced practices. He had studied with many of the great teachers of his day. Yet still he felt dissatisfied. No teaching answered the questions with which he was wrestling. No teaching seemed to him to adequately address the existential realities of birth and death that he was struggling to understand. He drove himself to extremes of fasting and bodily penance in the attempt to overcome affliction, but these efforts failed to satisfy him. He was alone, near starved and unable to continue, lying by the roadside at the edge of a forest. A pitiful sight, he touched the heart of the young woman, Sujata, who was going to make offerings to the forest gods. She was so moved at this chance meeting with a wandering ascetic who had pushed his practice to such extremes, that she stopped in her tracks. Instead of making the offerings, she gave the food to the starving holy man. Her human kindness changed the course of Shakyamuni's spiritual life. Eating, he found the strength to continue. At the point of desperation, he accepted Sujata's gift and found the resolution to search further.

Now determined to find the answers to his question, he sat down to meditate, vowing that he would not rise till he discovered the meaning that he sought. He was alone once more in the forest, surrounded only by the trees and creatures of the night. He meditated. Beneath him he had made a mound of grass to keep him off the bare ground. Above him, was the tree, known after as the Bodhi tree. Before him, was the expanse of the sky. He was alone; alone with the darkness.

On the night of his enlightenment, a storm blew up. Tropical storms are powerful, with torrential rain and wild winds that whip the trees into a frenzied dance. Rain and wind raged about him. Legend tells that a large cobra spread its hood above him to shelter him from the downpour. Whatever, he sat on in meditation through the night, undistracted.

Whilst the storm raged around him, another storm was raging inside him. He struggled with his inner torments, his mind and the storm, battering his consciousness. Through the night, Shakyamuni was beset first by images of his own history and then by temptations and troubles. His mind was tossed on a sea of desire and aversion, but he sat steady. Neither storm swayed him in his resolve.

In the morning the storms had passed. He looked up toward a clear sky. Dawn was just breaking on the far horizon. The sky was still dark with just the tinge of light that heralds the new day, far out in the distance. The stars were fading with the early light, but still, bright and clear among them shone the bright pinpoint of light that we now know to be the planet Venus. Shakyamuni looked up from his meditation and saw the morning star. Its brilliance touched him. Seeing it, he was transformed. In that moment, he saw everything. He was enlightened. He became Buddha.

Through the ordinary we glimpse the universal. The infinite is available in the everyday reality of the world if we are willing to see it. The morning star rises every morning. How often do we see it? How often do we allow it to touch us? It is in encountering our world that we are changed. Sometimes in simple ways, other times profoundly, if we are willing.

The story of the Buddha's journey to enlightenment is one of encounters. His journey had begun with an encounter. According to the teachings, before the start of his journey he met with the four sights of a sick man, an old man, a corpse and a holy man. This first encounter inspired him to go forth into the spiritual life and to search for an understanding of the nature of suffering. On his journey he met many teachers. His encounter with Sujata was instrumental in his decision to resume the spiritual search, and it was through his encounters with Mara that the Buddha struggled to overcome his spiritual obstacles. His final experience of enlightenment came through seeing the morning star. Relationship changes us and moves us into new ways of thinking and seeing things. If a person is prepared to be open to change, the relationships that occur spontaneously in their life can be the catalysts for important insights.

Amida: the measureless

Shakyamuni Buddha taught for more than forty years. He left a vast wealth of teachings. These were collected in written form as the *sutras*, the religious texts of Buddhism. Because there are so many sutras, different Buddhist schools tend to revere particular sutras, and these vary from school to school. For the Pureland schools, the Pureland Sutras are key texts. One of these contains the story in which the Buddha taught about Amida Buddha. As we have seen, Pureland Buddhism places central importance on the practitioner's relationship with Amida Buddha.

The Pureland schools of Buddhism are *other-power* schools. They emphasise a spiritual path of connection. They see the ordinary person as enmeshed in their sea of karma that will not be exhausted through personal effort. They place importance on faith and on the relationship with a source beyond self as the source of salvation. They are *other-power* schools. The energy that is available to us when we engage with the world, and when we feel our heart longing answered, in Pureland thinking, is that of Amida.

The name of Amida means "without measure". Amida Buddha is the infinite Buddha; the archetypal Buddha, the experience of Buddha that is always available to us. The *-mida* part of Amida's name is related etymologically with the word metre, and the *a-* prefix denotes a negative. *Buddha* means awakened or enlightened, the state in which the clouding of perception that self-preoccupation creates has dropped away. In the ideal, the enlightened state is that of *nirodha,* where the pursuit of escape has ceased and the energy flows freely. Amida Buddha is thus an embodiment of the universal or the limitless.

The Larger Pureland Sutra tells the story that provides the mythic structure to our understanding of Amida Buddha. This important text describes a teaching given by Shakyamuni to his followers. It takes the form of a conversation between the Buddha and his disciple and cousin, Ananda. The scene in which the teaching takes place is at the Vulture Peak, where the Buddha has gathered with a vast crowd.

The circumstances of the teaching, described in the sutra, suggest that the teaching took place relatively late in the Buddha's career, and according to the account given in the text, 12,000 monks and innumerable bodhisattvas were present to hear the Buddha's words. We can probably assume that these numbers are exaggerated, since *Mahayana* sutras tend to be somewhat lavish in their descriptions. They are inspirational rather than historic documents. Nevertheless, many of the people present are listed by name and clearly a large crowd were present when the Buddha gave this significant teaching.

At the beginning of the sutra, Ananda notices that the Buddha is looking particularly radiant. He comments upon this:

"The Blessed One's sense powers appear serene, the colour of his skin is pure, his countenance is cleansed, radiating with a golden glow. As the jujube fruit turns bright yellow in autumn, pure, cleansed, radiating a golden colour, or as a skilfully made ornament of Jambu River gold displayed on a white cloth shows its purity, so the Blessed One appears radiant today.

Oh Blessed One, I do not ever recall seeing the Tathagata so serene, purified, cleansed, and radiant as I do today. This thought occurs to me "Today the Tathagata dwells in the sphere of most rare Dharma! the sphere of Buddhas! Today, the One who is the Eye of the World is centred upon what must be done by a guide of the world! Today, the One who is pre-eminent in the world dwells in supreme bodhi! Today, the Honoured of the Gods possesses all the virtues of a Tathagata! The Buddhas of the three times contemplate one another. Could it be that you are now bringing to mind all the other Buddhas? Are you gazing upon the tathagatas, arhats, samyak sam-Buddhas of the past, the future and the present? Is that why your august presence shines with such a radiance today?" (Larger Pureland Sutra 5-6. All quotes in this section come from the edition of the Pureland sutra used in the Amida School)

In response to this, Shakyamuni Buddha begins to give a teaching.

The Buddha tells how, long, long ago, there was a Buddha of an earlier age called Lokeshvararaja Buddha. At the time in which this Buddha was teaching, there also lived a king who, having heard of Lokeshvararaja Buddha's wisdom, renounced his kingship and became a monk. The monk took the name of Dharmakara. Dharmakara resolved to become a Buddha himself. So strong was his resolution that Lokeshvararaja Buddha, appeared before him.

On seeing Lokeshvararaja, Dharmakara pours out a hymn of praise to the Buddha, a beautiful piece of poetry, which expresses his own aspiration for Buddhahood. Dharmakara's aspiration, however, is not simply for his own spiritual fulfilment. His primary motivation is the salvation of others.

"Let me become a Buddha and the multitude of beings will all enjoy my primordial nirvana world. By indiscriminate compassion, I will enlighten all"

Hearing his resolve, Lokeshvararaja conjures before him innumerable Buddha-lands, of the kind that he might create and inhabit if he were to achieve enlightenment. Dharmakara wonders at these lands. The sight of them deepens his aspiration. Visions have that capacity. To see what is possible, is to engage with the possibility of its fruition. The vision inspires. It makes us bigger people. It draws out our capabilities.

Having thus been strengthened in his aspiration, Dharmakara asks Lokeshvararaja to teach him the way to achieve enlightenment. Lokeshvararaja replies that Dharmakara already knows the answer to this. So Dharmakara is returned to the vision. Setting the Buddha lands before him, he remains in contemplation. With serene mind, he then adopts the practices necessary for the creation of a pure Buddha-land. Seeing the infinite possibilities arrayed before him in these glorious lands, his heart knows its course. The resolution that arises culminates in his expression of forty-eight vows.

The Forty-eight vows of Dharmakara are central to the Pureland understanding of the Buddhist path. These vows express Dharmakara's resolve not to achieve enlightenment unless he can create a Buddha-land in which all beings can have the best possible conditions for attaining enlightenment. These vows represent a concrete expression of compassion.

As Dharmakara speaks his vows, the earth shakes, flowers rain from the sky, and spontaneous music is heard. A voice proclaims *"Surely you will attain the highest, perfect Enlightenment"*

Dharmakara continues to practice for many aeons, and eventually attains Buddhahood, becoming a Buddha known as Amitayus, which means infinite life, and creating a Western Buddha-land, the "land of peace and bliss". This land is that which is commonly referred to as Sukhavati or the Pure Land.

Amitayus, as we have seen is one of the names by which Amida Buddha is known. Amida is sometimes referred to as Amitabha and sometimes as Amitayus, but as we can see from the Larger Pureland Sutra both names refer to the same Buddha. In this sutra, the Buddha Amitayus is referred to repeatedly as the Buddha of infinite light, even though the name literally means infinite life; in Sanskrit, *ayus* means life span, whereas *abha* means light, thus Amitabha Buddha is more usually referred to as Buddha of infinite light. Such references underline the fact that Amitabha, Amitayus and Amida are all aspects of the same figure. Amida Buddha is measureless both in light and life, in space and time.

Dharmakara's vows are of central importance to Pureland Buddhists, and in particular, the eighteenth vow has become of great significance. It emphasises the recitation of the Buddha's name.

Oh Blessed One, may I not come to the complete awakening if, when I have done so, living beings inhabiting other worlds
  who conceive a longing for awakening,
  who listen to my Name,
  who set their heart upon being reborn in my Pure Land, and
  who keep me in mind with settled faith,
  are not assured of meeting me standing before them in full retinue and glory at the time of their death, such death thus being completely free of anxiety.

Through this vow, Pureland Buddhists came to understand that if the practitioner sincerely recited Amida's name ten times with deep faith, birth in the Pure Land would become a certainty. Thus recitation of Amida Buddha's name came to be seen as the sole requisite for salvation. On the basis of this understanding, the practice of calling the Buddha's name, which is called *Nien Fo* in Chinese or *nembutsu* in Japanese, became the primary practice of Pureland schools.

Doctrinal debates have developed over the centuries about the exact nature of the required practice. Some questioned whether the number of recitations of the Buddha's name were important, others asserted that the state of mind indicated by *settled faith* was essential. These debates, however, do not detract from the centrality with which the practice of calling the name of Amida is regarded in all schools of Pureland.

In our own tradition this practice of calling on Amida's name is expressed in the words *Namo Amida Bu,* which roughly mean "Homage to Amida Buddha", or "I call on Amida Buddha". The recitation of nembutsu, whether chanted or spoken, forms the central focus of Pureland practice. It is an expression of the heart's longing. *Namo* means "I call", *Amida Bu* is like the answering voice of Amida Buddha. This simple phrase holds within it the meeting of self and other, practitioner and Buddha. It is a practice of encountering the indefinable.

Face to face: encounter and change

Ananda saw the Buddha's radiance and was moved. The encounter was significant. Encounter changes us. It transforms us. It heals us. When we encounter someone of great spiritual presence we are touched. The meeting changes us profoundly. When a person is in a state of inspiration, that inspiration rubs off on us.

The Pureland Sutras are full of images of encounter. As we have seen, encounter is powerful because it takes us outside our self world and into relationship with that which is other. In this context, we can think of the other as *what is beyond self.* The other may be a person, a physical object, or even an idea. Meeting the other, transformation occurs. The other may be a Buddha, as in the sutra, but equally we may be deeply affected by an encounter with something that is quite ordinary. It is the act of really meeting with something that is beyond our constructed self-world which brings change.

Most of the time, we do not see things as they really are. We distort them to fit our expectations and personal agendas. We don't really engage. It is said that Buddhas are enlightened by everything. This is because in seeing everything without this self-focused agenda, they are in a constant state of full engagement with the world. For them, it can equally be said that the whole world is Buddha. It has the capacity to enlighten. In true encounter, all is awakened.

For most of us, though, our encounters, whether with other people or with the world of objects, are constantly being contaminated by our self-centred view. Our vision is only partial. The more compelling an encounter becomes, however, the more we are drawn towards seeing the other as they are, without our preconceptions shaping our view. Encounters can shock or surprise us, bringing us out of our self-preoccupation.

Some experiences catch our attention. They are more likely to break through our clouded mentality. Sometimes this is because they are grand or inspiring, but simple things can also break through to us if they catch us in the right frame of mind. Sometimes it is the simplicity of a situation that touches us. The morning star is always there if we are willing to see it.

At the beginning of the Larger Pureland Sutra, we are told of the meeting between the Buddha and Ananda. Ananda is inspired by the Buddha's appearance. He immediately expresses reverence. He honours his teacher, prostrating to him, and then he asks the Buddha his question. He suggests that Shakyamuni himself must have been contemplating other Buddhas. He sees the Buddha light reflected in his master's face, and as he does so, he feels the inspiration of all the Buddhas with whom Shakyamuni has been speaking. Encountering his teacher in this ecstatic state, Ananda himself feels inspired, a reflection of the Buddha's state, and is able to experience something of what his master is experiencing as he encounters the Buddha realm.

When we are with others who are inspired, it is like that. We feel the glow of their inspiration enveloping us. We walk with them in the light. Ananda's mental state was changed by seeing the Buddha. The Buddha's mental state had already been changed as he contemplated other Buddhas.

Both were inspired. Both changed.

Some encounters are important and life changing. Meeting an important teacher or listening to a rousing speaker can move us to do new things. When another person is inspired, it is infectious. We feel good. When we meet with someone who is happy and in love, we generally feel joyful. When we meet someone who is excited by a new insight, we catch their enthusiasm.

This morning my husband, David, was reading us some of the most recent material that he has been writing. It was about philosophy of religion. He is very excited by some second hand books on theology that we acquired last week. These have given him new directions in his writing. As we listened to him reading his most recent chapters and saw his animated expression, everyone in the community became very excited by the ideas. Conversation over the dining table got very lively.

People are excited by hearing other people's enthusiasms. The excitement that we felt participating in the lunchtime conversation certainly came in part from the actual ideas that David was sharing. We all like to discuss concepts, and it is not uncommon for people in The Buddhist House community to get very animated in doing so. On the other hand, the material under discussion was not the only factor present. David's passion for the subject was infectious. I am sure that much of our excitement this morning came from the animated way in which he read his work. This is part of the human process. Emotions and mental states pass between us on a visceral level. We catch each other's enthusiasms. David was excited by the books. His excitement was conveyed to us. He encountered the ideas through the books. We encountered him, and through him, the ideas.

As the Larger Pureland Sutra unfolds, the theme of encounter continues. Dharmakara goes to meet Lokeshvararaja. This encounter provides the opportunity for his transformation. The sight of Lokeshvararaja moves

Dharmakara to expound his great hymn of praise. Being in the presence of this all-powerful figure, he is immediately filled with spiritual aspiration. His heart calls out in joy.

The archetypal meeting between Dharmakara and Lokeshvararaja echoes the encounter between any spiritual seeker and the source of spiritual energy. Of course, it also mirrors the encounter that is actually occurring between Ananda and Shakyamuni. Dharmakara is on a spiritual path. He has heard the teachings and is seeking out their source. Lokeshvararaja is the Buddha of Dharmakara's time, the all-enlightened one, the most spiritually complete being who can be imagined. Dharmakara's out-pouring of joy is a song of spiritual transformation. Lokeshvararaja's influence has changed him and made his aspiration possible. Through encountering a figure of spiritual perfection, Dharmakara is enabled to achieve his aim. He is enabled to benefit all beings.

It is common for those who have most benefited others to themselves have had significant encounters which set them on their path. The Buddha encountered the holy man walking across the market place. Honen encountered Shan Tao through his writings.

Encountering mind objects

In the Larger Pureland Sutra it is interesting to notice that, at the point when Ananda encounters the Buddha, he says "this thought has occurred to me…" He might equally have said, "I am wondering if…" The difference is probably not coincidental.

In using the former phraseology, Ananda refers to the thought as if it were something that has a momentum that is separate from his will. In the phrase as it stands, the thought is represented as having arrived unbidden. This mode of expression suggests that thoughts come into the mind as spontaneous appearances. They are beyond our control. In other words, our thoughts are subjects that we encounter. They are not part of our selves. Wisdom is something that comes from outside the self. Knowledge is acquired or given and not innate.

At the time of the Buddha, people thought of the mind as having six sense doors. These were identified as six organs of perception, each of which was constantly grasping after objects. The six sense organs in this Buddhist model were the five sense faculties that we think of today: sight, hearing, smell, taste and touch. The sixth sense faculty is called *mano-vijnana*. This is the faculty of mental perception, or, in popular parlance, the mind's eye. Mano-vijnana perceives all the "objects" which we think of as passing through the mind. These include thoughts, dreams, visions and other mental phenomena. They are perceived by mano-vijnana in just the same way as visual objects are perceived by the eye. A thought arrives and becomes the object of mano-vijnana's perception. Grounded in this understanding, Ananda perceives his arising thought as something that arrives in the perceptual field of his mind, and not as something of his own creation. One might call it a visitation.

Our thoughts are not original. They are an assemblage of second hand pieces. Nothing originates within. In many ways, the early model of the mind sense spoke more closely of the true situation than our modern way of viewing mental process. Of course, we often imagine that we are authors of our own ideas. We congratulate ourselves on our clear thinking and our wise insights. But what would exist in our minds if we took away all that we have received from elsewhere? Our knowledge, concepts and even our patterns of thought and expression are all borrowed. We are the custodians of wisdom, transmitting it from past generations to future ones, however imperfectly. Maybe a little is lost along the way. No matter. The Dharma is always there to be found. Thoughts come and go of their own accord.

Encounter as an unequal process

Although in modern society it is popular to think of encounters as being the meeting of equals, it is worth noting that the significant encounters of the Larger Pureland Sutra are not between people of equal status. Indeed, it is the inequality of these meetings that is efficacious. Most meetings, in fact, involve an encounter between an ordinary person and a figure of spiritual perfection. Ananda is affected by his sight of the Buddha. Dharmakara is inspired by Lokeshvararaja Buddha. Ordinary people are saved by Amitayus. Even where the meeting seems more a meeting of equals, as when Shakyamuni Buddha encounters the host of previous Buddhas, there is still an implication of a hierarchical relationship. Shakyamuni consults with his spiritual ancestors. He seeks out wisdom from those who have gone before.

Of course it is not always necessary for an inspirational meeting to involve such inequalities. There are examples of people who have been inspired through meeting people of equal or lower spiritual or social status. But the type of meeting with great figures described in the sutra is not an uncommon source of inspiration, or starting point for setting a person on the spiritual quest.

We have already explored some aspects of the inbuilt inequalities in many helping relationships in a previous chapter. The therapeutic relationship involves an intense meeting between two people. It is also, in a sense, a one way relationship. One person seeks help, or, to use a term borrowed from the religious setting, seeks refuge. We are therefore talking about an encounter that is also founded on inequality. The power dynamics of a helping relationship are complex, but certain features of the relationship make inequality inevitable. The helper offers psychological containment to the helped. The client looks to the therapist to support change. The client shares personal, and often embarrassing, material. The therapist discloses only limited personal data. The disclosure of irrelevant details about the therapist's life is generally considered counterproductive to the therapy process. In the present climate which values equality, the value of inequality is often overlooked. Yet, it is the willingness of the therapist to take on the role of carer and to provide a set of therapeutic conditions that creates the possibility of change.

We can see how this inequality occurs if we consider the role of congruence in therapeutic encounters. In the last chapter we explored the work of Dr Carl Rogers, who placed considerable emphasis on the importance of congruence as a condition for psychological change. This condition is provided by the therapist's commitment to deep honesty in her mode of interaction. This congruence has two aspects to it. Firstly, it creates the conditions for a meeting that is genuine and honest. In this frame it is possible for the client to experience the real otherness of the therapist and thus move beyond his own self-projections. The latter will not inevitably happen, for some clients are very locked up in their self-worlds, but it makes the possibility of something approaching genuine encounter more likely to occur.

Secondly, in order for this direct encounter to take place, the therapist has to set limits on her own openness. In this, the distinction between congruence and self-disclosure becomes apparent. Although the therapist's presence needs to be genuine, *in as much as she relates to the client*, she must be circumspect in references to her own personal views and experiences. The therapeutic space needs to be safe and clear of the therapist's own agendas. If it is not, the client is unlikely to be able to use the situation and may feel imposed on, or even harmed. A therapist should be able to put her own agendas aside to a sufficient extent that she can offer the core conditions. This does not require the therapist to achieve a state of perfection. Indeed, as Kohut's theory suggests, it is her human mistakes that are often the therapeutic factor in the encounter. Broadly, however, it is the therapist's ability to hold a clean space for the client which offers conditions for change.

Therapeutic encounter, then, relies upon the inequality of the meeting. It relies upon the complex nature of relationship in which some aspects can be highly transparent, whilst other aspects remain hidden. It relies upon a balance of inter-personal power that creates asymmetric conditions for the two participants. Accepting such factors, the nature of the power dynamics in a given therapeutic relationship can be explored.

So, encounter is important in that, when we meet one another, we step out of our habitual patterns and open ourselves to relationship. But it is not important for us to know the other person that well. Encounters can be intense but of limited scope. The most significant encounters we experience are often with others who are quite unknown to us, except in some specific. The effective therapist is not known by their clients as a rounded person. They do not know, for the most part, details of her personal life. But in other ways, she completely meets them. In some ways, the power of the meeting actually arises out of the kind of relationship that is not contaminated by the kind of assumptions that arise from knowing details of another's life.

This is how it is in Pureland practice. Amida is measureless, unknown and unknowable. All we see when looking toward Amida's realm is light. Yet the encounter which follows from nembutsu practice is deeply transformative. We call out to Amida and sometimes we experience a deep sense of Amida's presence, but we do not need to know Amida.

Vision and encounter

Reading the Larger Pureland Sutra, one is struck immediately by the visual quality of the text. In particular, light is an important aspect of Pureland imagery. In the sutra, Dharmakara sees Lokeshvararaja, and his spontaneous hymn describes the radiance of Lokeshararaja's face. Ananda sees the radiance in the Buddha's countenance when they meet. Towards the end of the first section of the sutra, the Buddha Amitayus is described in terms of light, offering a further visual image:

"44. The majestic light of Amitayus is the most perfect and extensive of all. There is nothing like it. The light of all other Buddhas does not surpass this light. The light of Buddhas first extends a fathom, then a league, then two, three, four or five leagues, then a whole Buddha land. Some Buddhas illumine a hundred Buddha lands, some a thousand, but the light of Amitayus illumines myriads of world systems, numerous as the sands of the Ganges, to the east, to the south, west, north, above and below.

...[the list continues with a series of epithets, all describing aspects of Amitayus' light] .

Amitayus is thus associated with light. Amitayus is another name associated with Amida. Amida is also represented as light. The practitioner hopes to see the light of Amida, and it is towards Amida's clear light that they go at death. Amida is associated with the setting sun, and in the *Contemplation Sutra,* another of the key Pureland texts, the visualisation of the Pure Land begins with the visualisation of a sun set.

The visual aspects of the sutra are not limited to images of light, however. Scenes as well as people are described as visual sources of inspiration. There are many examples. Dharmakara is shown many Buddha lands by Lokeshvararaja. Following this sight, he is inspired to make his forty-eight vows

"23. Then, immediately, Lokeshvararaja described in detail the good

and bad reserved for humans and devas in the vast number of Buddhakshetras, and explained how some are gross and some subtle, and, as he did so, Dharmakara, because of the strength of his longing, was able to see them all appear before him. He saw the whole matter with unprecedented clarity and there arose in him a great singularity of purpose: a supreme vow.

Later in the sutra, the Pure Land itself is described. The imagery here is lavish. Clearly these images are inspirational to Ananda and the rest of the audience present, and they remain a source of inspiration for Pureland practitioners. The visual quality of the account is so vivid, it must be intended to engage the senses. Reading it or hearing it, we enter into a kaleidoscope of colour that is quite hypnotic in its repetition and poetic language. For example, we read:

54. Furthermore, throughout that land are trees made of the seven gems. There are trees of gold; trees of silver; trees of coral; trees of amber; trees of agate; trees of ruby; and trees of lapis lazuli. Then there are trees of two precious substances, trees of three, four, up to all seven. Some gold trees have silver leaves, flowers and fruits. Some silver trees have gold leaves, flowers and fruits. Some coral trees have leaves flowers and fruit of amber. Some amber trees have leaves flowers and fruit of coral. Some agate trees have leaves, flowers and fruit of ruby. Some ruby trees have leaves, flowers and fruits of agate. Some lapis lazuli trees have leaves, flowers and fruit of all sorts of jewels.

The description continues. There are pools of many colours and precious stones, magnificent buildings and the gardens are filled with beautiful creatures and people. Colours glisten. Senses are soothed and excited by not only the spectacle but also sounds, smell and taste. The air is fragrant, the water warm or cool as desired, and the inhabitants of the Pureland taste and smell the wonderful food that arrives spontaneously at meal times without the needing to actually eat it.

The emphasis on such visual aspects of the Pure Land probably reflects the origins of Pureland practice in the experiences of *Samadhi*. There is a strand of thought that suggests that Pureland Buddhism has its origins in the *Samadhi* or higher meditation states that Shakyamuni Buddha himself experienced. This idea is put forward by Inagaki among others and can be found in his extensive introduction to the Pureland Sutras. Whether or not the experiences went back to the historic Buddha, it does seem likely that the visions described are of this nature.

Many of the *Mahayana* sutras contain similar descriptions of Buddha realms and of magnificent figures of Buddhas and Bodhisattvas and other celestial beings. These also seem to draw their inspiration from the actual experiences of the ecstatic spiritual states of early spiritual adepts. Studying such descriptions, practitioners of later times would gain visions of the Pure Land and other transcendental realms for themselves. Often such practice was accompanied by other attempts to gain visionary experiences. People undertook intensive retreats, such as the ninety day nembutsu retreats, first developed in China, and later brought to Japan. In such intensive retreats, where walking and chanting continues uninterrupted throughout the three month period, the practitioner seeks a spontaneous vision of Amida Buddha. On Mount Hiei near Kyoto, it is still possible to take such a retreat in the "yolked" temple where they have been held for centuries.

Visionary experiences can be an important form of encounter in the spiritual life. Although modern attitudes place little importance on such experiences, many of the great teachers of the past experienced spiritual transformation through undertaking visionary practices or spontaneous experiences of this kind. Honen's dream encounter with Shan Tao was a turning point in his life. Shinran, founder of the Jodoshinshu tradition experienced a dream vision of Prince Shotoku, which led him to become a follower of Honen. Eshin-ni, Shinran's wife dreamed of her husband as the bodhisattva Quannon.

Encounter as a gift

Spiritual resolution and transformation is not usually a one-sided process, brought about by the will. More often it is a process of encounter. It involves meeting a contrasting element which shakes us out of our complacency and rigidity of view. Attaining a vision, whether of Amida, the Pure Land or some other spiritual sign is not something that is under our control. We may create the conditions in which a *samadhi* is likely to arise through effort, but we cannot control whether the vision appears. The encounter is not something that can be engineered. It arrives of its own accord. It is a gift. Sometimes such experiences come in a quite different context, with no expectation at all from our side. For some people the religious experience comes out of the blue, challenging all their previously held assumptions.

In these kinds of experience, we are not changed through our own effort. The world changes us. We need to be willing to open up to the process but we cannot will it to happen. Change remains a mysterious process. All we can do is to have faith.

In a place of uncertainty, though, there is still a kind of faith that makes a difference. We can have faith that that change is possible. We can have faith that a benevolent process underlies human experience, as Rogers did himself in postulating the self-actualizing tendency. We can have faith in power beyond any of us that underlies the process of transformation and healing.

We do not need to be reliant on our own resources. We do not need to be perfect. It is surprising how many modern people think we do. Rather, perfection is outside us. It is the experience of otherness that makes life feel real. When we experience ourselves to be in relationship to something greater than ourselves, we let go of some of the struggle to independence and autonomy. We no longer have to have all the answers within us. We do not have to be perfect any longer.

In this chapter, we have explored the importance that the Pureland understanding places on relationship and encounter in the process of change. In particular we have seen how the relationship to an inspirational figure provides the source of religious transformation. Meeting such a person changes the way we see the world and the way we react to it.

We all seek inspiration. Even in recognising our own foolishness we may still long to meet others who are perfect. My own defensiveness of Honen (described in an earlier chapter) was symptomatic of that desire to conceive of a teacher who embodied the ideal. In one sense this is all illusion, but in another way, there is a deep truth in our perception of perfection in others. The other person whom we meet may be a foolish being too, but in them we can see reflected the perfection of something greater. In ordinariness, we see Amida's reflection. Just as the snipe and the marsh, the moon, the sun, the ancient rocks of Bradgate Park, ordinary phenomena, reflect the unseen dimension if we can but look in the right way, so too, the person we meet in the street or in our workplace can be Amida for us if we look with the right eyes.

Amida is the measureless; by definition, unknowable, or at least on the very edge of our knowing. Amida is the multi-faceted richness of the universe. Yet, in meeting the personified figure of Amida we can reach out towards that perfection. When we have a sense of that relationship to the immeasurable, we shine with reflected radiance.

When we truly encounter, we let go of the cloud of self-delusion for a moment. We are infected and our imperfection is no longer relevant. The dull grey pebble on the beach sparkles in the moonlight when the tide wets it. The tarmac road sparkles on a frosty night. Buddhism teaches non-self. The self is a trap we create through our fear and our clinging. Self is delusion. Beyond self is a world vibrant in the light of eternity. That world is measurelessly wonderful. Amida is the measureless.

CONCEPTS INTRODUCED IN THIS CHAPTER

- Amida, the measureless
- Encounter as a theme in the lives of Shakyamuni Buddha and other leading figures in Buddhist sutras
- Styles of relationship that offer the possibility of transformation
- The Larger Pureland Sutra

CHAPTER SIX

LACK AND LONGING

Grey tones; lake and sky
Two oarsmen navigating
An edgeless expanse
Engulf me, water spirits
Take me into your silence.
(Lake Geneva in mist)

Spring comes. The garden dances with daffodils and iridescent green euphorbia. The plum tree is misted with red-bronze leaves. The grass is growing.

As the sun streams through my window, my heart warms with joy.

The return of spring has always been important in restoring confidence in the processes of the natural world. This experience is deeply etched in the human psyche. The time when shoots reappear from the frozen ground is a time when nature manifests both in the beauty of the new freshness, and also in the confirmation of the continuing capacity of life to repeatedly resurrect itself. With each cycle of the seasons, the life process is re-born, grows, withers and dies. Impermanence manifests in the fluctuations of seasonal change. Yet behind this ever-changing pattern of growth and decay, something reliable continues. We can trust the seasons to return: never the same, yet always moving to the order of their own rhythms.

Those who live close to nature are particularly affected by the changing seasons. It is not surprising that most of our modern festivals, though wrapped in imagery and stories of our modern religions, owe their timing and their origins to the ancient seasonal markers of the year. The harvest was a time of plenty and feasting, but was also a time when the feeling of melancholy arose at the prospect of coming winter. The mid-winter festivals, set in the darkest time at the turn of the year, were a time for communities to come together for protection and comfort; a time for great fires and the retelling of stories. The arrival of spring brought with it the festivals of fertility and celebration of the survival of life through the long winter months. It brought hopes for the coming summer, a time for relaxation and plenty. It was the time for planting of crops for the year ahead.

In our centre in France, we feel the seasons much more acutely than we do in England. The natural world comes to our doorstep, and even, often, into the house. In winter we struggle to stay warm, lugging wood in from the hedgerows to feed the wood burning stoves. The crisp frost assaults our feet and our lungs as we do outdoor walking meditation. Mice and other small creatures creep into the crevices of the buildings for warmth and become bold in our absences. This winter we found a small dormouse curled up between two mattresses in the stack of stored beds, his tail wrapped around his slumbering body, and his breathing slowed so as to be almost undetectable. How I hope he will survive the winter hibernation and that on our next visit we will find his cosy nest vacated. The seasons are harsh as well as beautiful.

Spring comes with bridal veils of blackthorn blossom along the hedgerows and cowslips gleaming yellow in the lush new growth of grass across the field. Arriving birds twitter on the roof ridges and telephone wires, and soon the eaves and beams and crannies of the barn will support the summer lodgings of martins and redstarts. We will feel the warm sun on our backs as we work in the garden or sit to meditate mid-day.

Nature and the sustenance of faith:

Saigyo, the Japanese poet lived in intimacy with nature. In his mountain hut the seasons became the inspiration and the ground of his faith. His poetry reflects this experience of the changing processes of the year. Through the window of these descriptions of his daily experience we glimpse the rich colours of his spiritual life. Through the imagery of the seasons' beauty he portrayed the measureless wonder of his religious encounters. The yugen quality of his relationship with nature offers to draw us into our own experience of religiosity with all its indefinable complexity. In the glimpsing of the changing seasons Amida is with us.

In one poem, Saigyo wrote about the coming of spring.

While the old year lasted
Kasuga Field
was buried in snow.
Now it's spring
and new shoots are poking up.
(Watson 1991)

This poem counter-poses the images of the cold times of winter and the coming of spring shoots. Representing the old year, Saigyo describes the frozen scene of a snow-covered field. The new year, on the other hand, is portrayed as the time of growth. These images are presented through two contrasting scenes, which in the classic Japanese style, as with so many of Saigyo's poems, fall into the two halves of the piece: snow and winter, shoots and spring. The reader is invited to feel the physical qualities of the two images and to recognise them as representing a transitional process. We feel the transformation from winter to spring. We recognise the joy in the poet's heart as he sees the plants emerging from the soil.

But Saigyo is also taking us beyond the physical world. His allusions carry reflections of his spiritual experience and speak to our spiritual capacities. His poem expresses faith. The returning spring renews our faith in the cycling processes of birth. New shoots and new growth emerge from frozen land. The spring follows the winter. There is reliability, even when weather patterns seem to go awry.

The images of the poem also contain metaphoric allusions. Within the image, not only is our faith in the processes of nature invoked, but also the nature of faith itself is explored. Although the field is heaped with snow, beneath the snow, new shoots are preparing to grow. The bare earth is not lifeless. It already contains the seeds of next year's plants. In the same way, although we are caught in delusion, our faith is still growing and as soon as the opportunity presents it will be reaching out towards the light.

Faith is an elusive commodity. Many people will say they have no faith. They are fearful of the expectations that faith raises. If I say I have faith, they think, perhaps I need to feel certain about the future. Perhaps I need to know what will follow death. Perhaps I need to move mountains.

I was sitting on a rather bumpy flight recently, and the man next to me noticed that I was reading a Buddhist book. "Oh, you won't be worried by this" he quipped, "I'm sure you stay nice and calm whatever happens" As someone who has a clear religious affiliation, I often find myself being expected to live up to other people's expectations. People want to believe that someone else knows.

But faith is not thus. Faith is found in the repeated movement of our lives out into the unknown. It is the willingness to live without certainty and sometimes despite fears. We all trust the chair on which we sit and the air that fills our lungs to be there moment by moment, despite the possibility that in the extreme chairs may collapse or air be polluted. This is a kind of faith. Faith is the power that transports us through life despite the doubts that assail us, which prevents us falling into a paralysis of anxiety.

At a simple level, we all demonstrate our faith with every step we take.

We may feel that we have no faith to rely upon, but yet we are prepared to walk on the ground. We have confidence in the earth beneath our feet. Each step we take is an act of trust. Our past experience has led us to believe in the solidity of ground. Time and again our faith has been confirmed. If by some accident of geology or engineering the ground gives way, we feel our faith shaken. To be caught in an earth quake brings particular horror. To see the ground sway and shake is deeply disturbing, evoking very primitive responses in us. That is what happens when that which we trusted as solid collapses beneath us.

We all have faith. Often, however, it is locked up in the struggle to create security. We place our faith, perhaps unwisely, in the immediate, the comforting and the self-created. We use our faith to endorse our delusion, placing our faith in the mundane and the insubstantial. Our attempts to shore ourselves up against the ravages of *dukkha* are, however, flawed. Thus our investment of faith may be placed in quicksand and not on solid rock. But under the snow, the shoots are growing. Though it may be locked in improbable diversions, our ability to trust even the most transient security may become the seedbed for a healthier expression of faith, which is always ready to emerge.

Our inherent healthy faith is often experienced as a feeling of yearning. We are locked into our everyday lives, but, from time to time, something happens which catches our energy and pulls at us to give attention to things that lie beyond the mundane. Our energies are caught by something beyond the horizon of our attention. We long for something more spiritually engaging, but often do not know what the object of our longing is.

Longing:

The quality of *Yugen* draws us into relationship with that which is situated in the far distance. As we read a poem or look at an image that has this *yugen* quality, our attention is pulled towards the horizons of our world. Everything is swathed in mist and fades to a subtle greyness. We feel yearning and wistfulness.

Yugen catches a feeling that is both primitive and familiar. Although impossible to express directly, and therefore masked in the language of poetry, the feeling that is expressed through this quality is something we recognise. We sense that the poem written with *yugen* holds a profound truth. The imagery goes beyond our everyday worlds and brings us into that same space and time that poets of the twelfth century or tribal peoples of prehistory inhabited. It places us in a timeless, cultureless space.

Yugen expresses the primal searching of the heart. It is the feeling that we experience when we allow ourselves to open to the layers of life which are ordinarily obscured from view. It is the experience of reaching out into the darkness without knowing what we will encounter. It is the experience of dancing with the mystery of life.

Although some people struggle with the idea of faith, most people recognise the feeling of longing. When I talk with people about this quality of longing, I find most people know what I mean. They recognise the feeling that arises in the heart when they look into that far distance. They know the way the body inclines towards the sunset and the sea, and the mellow comfort that wraps like a blanket around the soul. They feel the bristling of the spine as wild geese fly noiselessly across the grey sky at dawn.

Longing is a thin line thrown out across the heap of delusion in which we are caught. It is our attempt to create a lifeline to what is beyond our mundane perceptions and experiences. It is the attempt to escape from our self-world. Longing is the dawning of the spiritual. It is the reaching out towards the unknown. It is the seeking of the immeasurable. In our longing we stretch out fingers of hope towards Amida. Our hearts cry towards the infinite Other.

Craving and longing

In his books, *Lack and Transcendence* (Loy 1996) and *A Buddhist History of the West: studies in lack* (Loy 2002), David Loy explores the thesis that a "sense-of-lack" is the driving force behind human societies. People sense the insubstantiality of their nature. They struggle with what Loy describes as *the groundlessness of their being* and they seek solutions that give meaning and solidity to their lives. In other words, they have a sense that their identity or sense of self is not as solid as it seems. This fragility creates anxiety which drives a feeling of craving.

> *"..Groundlessness usually manifests in our consciousness as a gnawing feeling of lack, the conscious or repressed sense each of us has that "something is wrong with me." On this account, even fear of death and desire for immortality symbolize something else. They become symptomatic of our vague intuition that the ego-self is not a hard core or consciousness, but a mental construction, the axis of a web spun to hide the void."* (Loy 1996 p51)

The insubstantiality of the self-world is a fundamental Buddhist tenet. We are all in a state of *avidya,* literally not seeing, or as it is commonly framed, ignorance. We do not see what is true and cling to what is illusory. We do not want to believe that our constructed worlds are impermanent, and instead build our sense of permanence by shaping our experience into an identity that, we tell ourselves, will remain solid.

Loy also equates his concept of *lack* with the Buddhist concept of *dukkha* (affliction). In making this analysis, he is referring to the fact that in the sutras, *dukkha* is described by a list of experiences which contains both unavoidable life experiences, and phenomena that might be seen as resulting from our experience of these existential afflictions, notably the *skandhas*. We can find an example of this mix of elements in a number of sutras, for example in the *Sammaditthi Sutta*.

> *Birth is Dukkha, ageing is dukkha, sickness is dukkha, death is dukkha; sorrow, lamentation, pain, grief and despair are dukkha; not to obtain what one wants is dukkha; in short the five skandhas are dukkha. This is dukkha.* (MN9.15)

This listing leads some traditional commentaries to offer a complex understanding of *dukkha,* the first Noble Truth. *Dukkha* is not only identified in terms of the primary events that give rise to affliction, such as sickness, old age and death, but also in terms of a second category of *dukkha*, namely those phenomena that arise as a result of our reactions to primary *dukkha*. In our experience of affliction we compound it by chasing delusory distractions which, one way or another, then let us down.

In the sutra description of dukkha, the list of elements includes primary sources of *dukkha*; the events of birth, ageing, sickness and so on. These are indisputable, and for the most part inescapable, facts of life. The list also includes emotions: sorrow, lamentation, pain and so on. These could be thought of as responses arising from the primary sources of *dukkha*. Some of these could be thought of as primary reactions, the energy that arises with *samudaya*, the second Noble Truth, and others might be part of a secondary reaction to *dukkha,* part of the habit energy that we generate as we try to escape from that reaction. The final element in the list of forms of *dukkha* is the *skandhas*. These could be seen as a secondary form of *dukkha.* They are a product of, and dependent on, the *samudaya* described in the second Noble Truth. Sometimes referred to as the five aggregates of clinging, as we saw in *Buddhist Psychology*, they describe the process which creates the self structure.

When we experience affliction, we tend to react initially at a visceral level (*vedana*). We grasp at things which might act as distractions, or we reject things in order to keep ourselves feeling safe. These responses form the basis for habit patterns which in turn create the structures of the self. Once in process, the *skandha* cycle becomes self-maintaining. We repeat reactions, and through this create a conditioned world view. This maintains the patterns. Although initially we create self to avoid experiencing *dukkha*, the habitual responses become a more generalised avoidance or distortion of experience and themselves cause further *dukkha*.

The teaching of the *Four Noble Truths* suggests that the spiritual task is to unhook from the object of clinging (*trishna*). Instead of becoming caught in patterns of avoidance, it would be healthier to face painful experiences. The *skandhas* however represent the usual human response to *dukkha*. They create compounded misery as they lock us into unhelpful and often painful patterns of behaviour.

In this way, the description of *dukkha* quoted above can be seen as suggesting a self-compounding model of affliction. Things happen that are afflictive. We have feelings that arise from the afflictive events, and as a result of these we escape into habits of distraction, craving and attachment, which are the basis of the *skandha* process. Life events can be afflictive. Our responses to them create further affliction.

The *skandha* process itself could be described as growing from a *sense of lack*. It is built upon craving (*trishna*). Thus, any feeling of lack may arise from our feeling of insubstantiality and from our feeling of craving. An intuition of the insubstantiality of the feelings of permanence we have created through the self echoes all our existential fears. This compounds *dukkha,* leading to more craving. The problem of craving is central in the Buddhist interpretation of the human situation. Craving, sometimes translated as attachment, is at the root of the self-project.

Craving (*trishna*) arises in reaction to the insecurity of our existence. Our sense of self is based upon such delusion and, as Loy suggests, we suspect its' groundless nature. This suspicion creates fear of our own insubstantiality, which in turn is *dukkha* and so gives rise to further craving. The cycle is self-perpetuating. We fear our vulnerability and create a sense of permanency by clinging to delusions. These attempts then compound our feeling of vulnerability as we sense that not only are we physically subject to decay and death, but also that our sense of who we are is founded on false premises.

Social applications of Loy's model of lack

Loy discusses the social as well as personal implications of his interpretation. The processes described operate not only at the individual level, but also at a social level. This is a view I would agree with. Craving for sensory distraction, identity and finally destruction, the three *samudaya* processes, unfold in the histories of nations just as readily as in our personal lives, with terrible consequences.

Loys sees history as driven by a sense of lack. This operates also in modern times. In this time of countless global dangers and conflicts, the route to sanity requires a reappraisal of our situation. Not only is it spiritually healthy for individuals to recognise bombu nature. It is essential to the survival of our planet that nations too see their fallibility.

Just as the individual clings to sensory distractions in the face of daily stresses, so too nations develop cultures based on accumulation. Consumerism has become an industry in much of the world, driving huge machineries of corporate finance. The search for resources fuels conflicts. As conflicts deepen, national identities become more entrenched, amplifying the cycle. The ground of this pursuit of comfort and identity is *dukkha*.

Dukkha arises when we do not get what we want, and as a society we become ever more greedy. *Dukkha* arises when we engage in processes of self-building, the *skandhas*. Nationalism and power-struggles based on identification with nations or movements are increasing. *Dukkha* arises when we face death and destruction. At a planetary level we are faced with serious threats to our environment that could wipe out human cultures and many other species.

We live in a time where global catastrophes are being announced with alarming frequency. The last sixty years has seen a shift in human consciousness, brought about initially through the recognition that nuclear warfare had the potential to create destruction at a level hitherto unknown. In the past wars have been terrible in their brutality, and people have feared an ending of civilisation at many points in history. Never before, however, has the potential existed to wipe out human life on the scale that nuclear war would. People of my generation grew up with the knowledge of the fragility of the human position. A bleak back drop to ordinary life, the four minute warning that might herald all-out nuclear attack haunted our awareness. Images of fractured landscapes and lifeless ruins became part of modern mythology, not so different from the ancient shades. We speculated idly on how we would use those last four minutes, knowing in our hearts we would probably be too paralysed by fear to do anything.

With time, other threats have encroached. Environmental challenges, for example, sometimes seem to overshadow earlier fears of war, though in the event it is unlikely the two will be separately realised, but rather that a crisis of resources arising from climate change will initiate ever more bloody conflicts, and perhaps precipitate the eventual Armageddon.

Dukkha precipitates craving and clinging. Craving and clinging create the sense of lack that is *dukkha*. The sense of lack drives us to grasp and cling in ways that are destructive and bring greater *dukkha*. The problem is self-perpetuating. Some countries' attempts to create safety through gathering resources and building national strength, create added stress for others. These others respond aggressively. Conditions become more stressed internationally and everyone becomes more fearful. Just as we respond to personal threat by building personal defences, so too, national identities rigidify in the face of international fear.

In observing this, we should also be mindful that in the ultimate extreme, the response to *dukkha* becomes destruction. When the defensive strategy of self-building fails to quell the discomfort of *dukkha,* the next stage is *abhava* (destruction). When nationalism fails, warfare may degenerate into purposeless destruction.

Although we have not yet reached such depths at a global level, in recent years we have seen many insidious moves in this direction. Recent wars have been widely perceived as dishonest. Presented as for the benefit of ordinary people and righting injustices, they have seemed to many to be fuelled by national interests and the drive to secure oil reserves. The accompanying tightening of national boundaries and immigration laws build hatred, creating an outcaste group of peoples upon whom negative emotions can be vested and amongst whom resentment and strategies for revenge understandably grow. Beyond resentment lies despair which creates a will for total destruction. Though glorification may be a motive, some suicide bombers may not be concerned with building self.

Fear increases and government policies and some media sources build the sense of impending threat. Tighter and tighter controls invade many areas of life that were previously seen as sacrosanct. The libertarian tradition that opposed identity cards in the 1950s and welcomed refugees of numerous world conflicts from the Eastern block to Vietnam is viewed with the same suspicion and amusement as a maiden aunt speaking of sexual morality.

Living with perceived threat creates waves of greed, manifesting in the proliferation of consumerism, and in the appropriation of resources from poorer countries. Hate increases in society, both for the enemy abroad, and for groups within our own countries – the refugee, the condemned person or the social misfit. Driven by fear, the strategies of escapism and isolationism, and the increasing emphasis on national and group identities, are all attempts at finding permanency. Despite the upsurge of religious alignment in the world, it is an age of little faith.

Trishna and *Yugen*, craving and longing

The teachings on craving (*trishna*) describe the process of delusion, the foundation of our *bombu* nature. These are cycles of compulsive and self-building behaviour that keep us trapped in our ordinary nature. This craving contrasts with the feelings of longing expressed in the word *yugen*. *Trishna* is the compulsive, escapist craving that leads toward self-building. It is inwardly directed, and has the effect of distancing us from others. *Yugen* expresses the kind of longing that seeks what is other. It looks beyond self towards the universal and the transcendental.

Sometimes people make the mistake of thinking that Buddhism proscribes loving relationships. This is not so. Indeed, the opposite is actually the case. The craving and attachment that is to be avoided is *trishna,* the compulsive craving for things that will distract us from our real situation. *Trishna* is driven by our attempt to escape reality, specifically *dukkha*, and tends to cut us off from others. It leaves us isolated in our deluded self-world. Love for other humans or the natural world is not problematic in as much as we respect their independent existence. It is the way we subvert our relationships and surroundings to build our personal worlds that is problematic. We create the illusion that we can control our environment, but if we really love others as they are, we do not cling to them or demand particular responses. We want the best for them. We do not seek their affection for us as part of the bargain. Of course, in practice, most of us love imperfectly. But in as much as we are able to really love others, we do not indulge in self-building *trishna*.

The qualities of *trishna* and *yugen* may sometimes be difficult to distinguish. Spiritual longing seeks its object beyond the self-world, but in practice it can sometimes be hard to tell the line between the kind of religiosity which is grounded in escapism and a real sense of the transcendent. We are *bombu* practitioners and the two are often confused and coexistent.

This coexistence of self-building with the heart-longing that instinctively looks beyond personal agendas is particularly difficult to disentangle, given our facility for building a sense of self through the way we see the world. The perception of others, whether human or divine, is filtered through our self-building perspective. We almost inevitably distort the world we see to fit our egocentric needs. This is a process so habitual that it is quite automatic and unconscious. Whether by selection or distortion, we look for signs (*lakshana*) that indicate our personhood.

Thus, the spiritual figures to whom we relate take on our hopes and projections. Just as the psychotherapist becomes the container into which transferential longing is poured, so too our gods and angels become the receptors of our self-building process. We are always in danger of making God in our own image and then longing for that God, fuelling our narcissistic dreams. This is a facet of our innate grandiosity.

Recognising this tendency to glorify our spiritual desires and through them to support our craving for security and permanence has brought many to question the basis of religious experience. Is the search for transcendent religious experiences, and particularly the search for authoritarian deities and theistic religion, a part of the pathology of *trishna*? We crave escape.

In our craving we create imagined authorities who can provide the permanence and stability we long for. Thus religious experience, according to this way of thinking, may simply be more craving and delusion.

Loy is rather of this view, and proposes that the attempt to reach beyond self in seeking a religious focus outside ourselves is founded on delusion. Instincts of self-creation and spiritual searching seem, in his understanding, to simply express the same existential fears. Despairing of our own permanence, we seek permanence in some external force. We create the illusion of an eternal Other to replace our fallen Self. Both are rooted in delusion and grandiosity.

These ideas pose questions about the nature and foundation of the longing which is so much a part of human experience. Do these ideas threaten the foundations of an outwardly orientated spirituality such as Pureland Buddhism? Is the longing that so many people feel for a spiritual dimension simply a pathological response to the existential reality of our impermanence? Is longing for Amida or some other manifestation of transcendence a facet of a deluded nature? Sometimes such dynamics may indeed be at work. People seek solace in systems of belief and do project their desires for love, immortality and omniscience onto the figures of worship. This is part of human nature.

The element of projection, however, is only part of the story. In our desire for solace, it is common to seek external sources of power, greater than ourselves. We look for strong, often parental figures. We attribute to them, or project onto them, such qualities as we feel that we ourselves lack. We make them all powerful – the rescuer, the comforter, the saviour. This process of *projection* happens in human relationships all the time. Anyone in a caring role, a therapist, a Buddhist teacher, or in other similar situations, is frequently a recipient of other people's longing. One learns to be aware of the power of such unrealistic forces in helping relationships, and also to recognise ourselves putting false expectations on others. It is a common occurrence.

As humans, we feel our insignificance and fragility acutely. Consequently we are drawn into searching for others as sources of help. The fact we search does not, however, diminish the fact that external sources of help actually exist. Our hopes and expectations may be unrealistic and driven by our sense of neediness, but this does not mean that help is unavailable. Indeed, external contact is generally the only source of help that can pull us out of self-perpetuating cycles of delusion.

Transference phenomena are the product of being deeply embedded in a delusory world. We seek to perpetuate our self-world through deluded relationships. Perception is distorted by self phenomena. This does not mean, though, that there is no reality outside the self-world. Once caught in distorted patterns of relationship, we may gradually find our way through the projections to a real relationship. We do this through the continuing presence and support of others around us. The reality of the other creates the possibility of eventual encounter. Creating meaningful relationship breaks us out of the cycles of self-entrapment. Meeting, person to person, creates the bridge to psychological and spiritual transformation.

Longing for a rescuer often originates from a feeling or experience of insufficient quality of relationship in the past. It is a grasping response built out of the reaction to the *dukkha* of that situation. Rebuilding trust in the other provides a way out of that pattern. Thus, the longing for another can be both an expression of the deluded desire for an all-powerful rescuer and an intuition of the power of contact with the other to heal. Within the deluded striving, the seeds of faith are fostered. Shoots grow beneath the snow. It may be that we project our neediness and our sense of omnipotence onto powerful others in the human sphere, but this does not diminish the fact that there is a person, existing in their own right, who is the recipient of the projection. This person may actually become the source of our healing. We sense this deep in our being.

When it comes to our religious life, the fact that we project our longings onto a spiritual figure does not negate the possibility that there is a spiritual source to whom we can relate. Equally, just as in our imperfect meeting with other humans we experience moments of real encounter, and through these, gradually heal our psychic exile, so too, within our spiritual devotions, it remains possible that we may glimpse the Other despite our imperfect beliefs and practices. The fact that we long imperfectly does not negate the presence of Amida.

Nembutsu, the heart's call:

Nembutsu is the expression of spiritual longing. Practices of calling the Buddha's name are found in all branches of Buddhism. They may express praise or reverence, affection or identification. The form of nembutsu is itself not very different from other forms of calling. For example, the Pali phrase *namo tassa bhagavato arahato sammasambuddhassa*, which roughly translates as *homage to the blessed one, the worthy one, the completely perfected Buddha*, is widely chanted in Theravada and Mahayana contexts. Bodhisattvas and Buddhas are acknowledged in similar forms of words. We may call on the Buddha, *Namo Buddhaya*, on Quan Shi Yin, *Namo Quan Shi Yin Bosat,* on bodhisattvas such as the bodhisattva of wisdom, Manjushri, *Namo Manjushraya* and so on. Such practices are devotional. They are intimate expressions of religious feeling.

When I was visiting Thailand a few years ago, I was staying with my husband in a large training temple on the outskirts of Bangkok. It was a temple where a lot of Westerners stayed for meditation retreats, and when we had met with senior monks to discuss our respective views of Buddhism, they had been keen to explain that their practice was about developing the mind and was not religious, something we found a little strange. While we were looking round the temple, which was in the Theravadin tradition, however, I got into conversation with one of the monks about his practice. I discovered that the practice had other dimensions. The temple specialised in teaching walking meditation, and we noticed that on the marble tiles of the floor there were many lines that had been marked out in plastic tape. What were these for? we asked.

The monk explained that this was where you practiced walking meditation. How did you do this? we asked.

The monk's face lit up. He stood at the end of one of the lines and made *gassho*, the gesture of placing the hands palm to palm at mid-chest level, right in front of the heart. First, he explained, you said a prayer to the Buddha, and then you started to walk. As you walked you said in your head "Buddho, Buddho, Buddho". We asked what the purpose of this practice was, and were told that this was something one did in order to invite the Buddha into your heart.

We smiled in recognition. As so often in the East, the practice was deeply devotional and indeed deeply religious. It hardly differed at all from what we did in our nembutsu practice, except in small details of language and form. It was essentially the same practice of calling the Buddha's name. We showed the monk how we did walking nembutsu practice and he smiled and nodded warmly. It was a wonderful moment of mutual recognition. We came from different continents and from traditions that apparently lay opposite ends of the Buddhist spectrum, and yet our practice and our religious experience seemed very close.

That temple also had several small shrines on its roof, including one devoted to Quan Shi Yin, a figure not generally associated with Theravada. These were clearly well used by the Thai devotees who left many offerings. In most Eastern Buddhist countries it is similar. Regardless of tradition, temples, roadside shrines and household altars are the focus of a Buddhism which is primarily devotional, heartfelt, personal and which often involves some form of calling out to the Buddha. Devout Buddhists in the East practice in many ways, but these devotional expressions are an important element in all the traditions I have encountered.

Devotion to Amitabha or Amitiyus is widespread. Tibetan, Chinese and most East Asian countries have practices which centre on Amitabha, Amitiyus or Amida. Practices of calling Amida's name in the form of Nien Fo are found particularly in Chinese Buddhism and those countries influenced by China. It was from China that the practice spread to Japan.

Nien Fo or nembutsu practices are often the practices of ordinary people although they are widely practiced in monasteries as well. Travelling in Vietnam we soon discovered that the way to delight the elderly Vietnamese women who pulled at our Buddhist clothes and asked "Catholic?" "Buddhist?" was to reply Namo Adida Phat, which is the Vietnamese form of nembutsu. This would be greeted by great explosions of glee and profuse bowing. Once more, our devotion to Buddha was shared across barriers of language and culture.

Nembutsu practice speaks the language of the heart. It expresses feelings that are hard to put into words. We sense the transcendental, the presence of mystery in the universe. Our heart strives to reach dimensions that are hidden from ordinary sight. We call out of our longing without really knowing what it is that we long for. Namo Amida Bu. The phrase is like a cord thrown out into the darkness.

Sometimes on a foggy day you can stand on the side of a ship as it comes into dock. You can watch as ropes are thrown out, but if the fog is thick, you cannot see the quayside where they must be anchored. The great hawsers must be guided by smaller lead ropes and these are passed across through a combination of shouting, and experience so that they can be flung

over the anchorage points to secure the vessel. Seeing these ropes extending into the murky gloom can be quite eerie. Sound is muffled, though
maybe a distant fog horn booms out. Sometimes nembutsu can feel this
way. We call out into the unknown space of the spiritual realm, only to
watch our cry disappearing into the darkness. Our sense that it is received
and held is a matter of faith. We trust Amida is present.

From this perspective, nembutsu becomes a bridge between us and
Amida. Sometimes like the great bridge at Millau it skims through the
clouds so that its end is shrouded from sight. Other times the air is clear and
we sense Amida's presence more strongly. Our view is always misted
though.

In its two halves, the practice embodies the tension of the cord that
passes between ourselves and the unseen focus of our calling, Amida.
Namo expresses our deep longing. It is the call we make across the well of
delusion. We seek Buddha. We cry out. We long to encounter Amida, the
great Other. In our smallness, we reach for the immeasurable. In the second
part of the phrase we are answered. *Amida Bu* comes the echoing response,
and the immeasurable, unknowable Other meets us.

In our daily practice at The Buddhist House we recite our *Summary of
Faith and Practice* the doctrinal statement of our Order. This summary is
based on Honen's last one page testament, the *Ishimai Kishomon*, which
itself is a central text to the Japanese Pureland tradition. In this text there is
a reference to reciting the Nembutsu in faith that we will be reborn in the
Pure Land *without even knowing what rebirth in the Pure Land truly is.* We
call and we have faith that our cry receives an answer, but we do not have
the capacity to perceive Amida directly. We cannot really know what
Amida's vow truly is. This is the limitation of our *bombu* capabilities. We
have faith that there is a world beyond self. We have a faith that beyond our
measuring there is something that is measureless. Beyond conditioned

existence, there is the unborn. We have confidence that we can trust things which are real and not of our own making. Despite our troubles, our insubstantial delusions, the sun rises each day. We have houses in which to live and food on the shelves in the shops. Somehow we are cared for. Life carries on despite our doubts.

Most of us recognise the feeling of diffuse longing that is expressed in the quality of *yugen*. We know the pulling at the heart, the yearning that seizes us as the great red ball of the sun sinks from view behind the distant lines of cloud on a summer evening. We know the sigh of the soul that greets the departing swallows gathering on the telegraph wires in the chill of early morning as autumn approaches. We feel the misty greyness of the marshes at dawn drawing us into a melancholy quietude. We long to reach out beyond the mundane. This longing is the seedbed of our faith. It is the intuition of the transcendental.

CONCEPTS INTRODUED IN THIS CHAPTER
- Concepts of Faith
- Longing (yugen) and Craving (trishna)
- Nembutsu as an expression of longing

CHAPTER SEVEN

FAITH AND THE ENGAGEMENT WITH THE OTHER

> Traveller pushing his way
> Through a summer meadow
> Grasses so thick
> His sedge hat seems
> To float over their tips
> Saigyo (Watson 1991)

Our religious sense is like the air we breathe. It is in us, around us. It holds us in life. Mostly we don't think about it, but sometimes we are aware of its force. To try to pin down the nature of this experience is like trying to catch the wind. When the wind blows, we know it is there. We see its effect. Yet, if we try to get hold of it, it runs through our fingers. Wind is moving space. Empty. We reach out to touch it, and the wisps of air simply disappear into nothingness around us.

We can stand in the wind's path. We can try to defy its presence and feel its pressure on our bodies. Other times, we can feel it play gently on our hair and skin and clothing, enjoying the subtle nuances of sensation. Our experience of faith is like this. Sometimes it is so strong we can lean against its force as if held by a wall of stone. Then it drops and our spirit plummets like a kite from the blue expansive sky.

When my children were small we lived in Tynemouth on the North East coast of England. Our road ran down to the sea front, and when the wind blew from the north it seemed to come straight from the arctic wastes and into our front hall. One particular afternoon I set out for a walk with my twins, who were maybe two or three years old at the time, heading down the road towards the sea. They were well wrapped up in snow suits, for it was winter. I held one on each side of me, a small woollen mitten in each hand.

We had intended to walk down to the harbour, which lies in the lea of the ruins of the medieval priory there on the promontory. We wanted to see the waves. This was an exciting prospect, as the sea would be whipped up by the on-shore wind, and pounding the long stone built breakwater that shielded the mouth of the river. You could not walk on the breakwater in such weather. It was shut to pedestrians lest someone were swept out to sea. But you could stand on the hill top above it and watch the spray breaking in great rushes of water that rose high into the sky before crashing down onto the walkway.

That day, however, the wind was so strong that, as we left our house, I and my two small companions could make no headway against it at all. Each step we took returned us to the same spot from which we attempted to move forward. Though we leant into the force of the gale, we could not make any progress. After a few minutes of trying we gave up. We simply had to turn around and walk in the opposite direction; such was the strength of the wind. Its' power was both terrifying and exhilarating.

A World of Dharma

Today I am writing out of doors. It is summer and the days are hot and skies blue. We are in France at our community's summer retreat. This is a good space in which to explore the qualities of religious faith. Close to nature, I feel surrounded by so many small wonders, and great ones. It is an ideal space in which to practice a religious life. It feels impossible not to be touched by the proximity of the myriad forms of life and non-life that abound here. I am reminded of Saigyo's poem *Even a person free of passion would be moved.* Everywhere, nature encroaches and shakes us out of our self-preoccupation.

Here we watch a fascinating parade of insects of different shapes and colours; beetles, green, black, iridescent, are everywhere, flocks of many varieties of butterflies rise from the flowers in the garden. Last night two huge dragon flies circled the yard at dusk among the usual bevy of bats. Congregations of birds inhabit the old buildings and the woods around the house, interrupting us with their twittering and sometimes enthralling us with deep melodious calls. On the ceiling of the outside toilet a mother spider cares for her hundreds of babies with such dedicated attention, delicately lifting stragglers back into the family web. Above us, the sky constantly changes with the progress of the day and movements of weather systems. Clear blue in the early morning, it deepens to vivid cobalt towards mid-day. In the afternoon a scatter of small clouds form on the horizon, which build to become almost threatening as the evening moves on, before clearing to give us a spectacular sunset. At night when the last vestiges of sunlight have finally faded, a thousand bright points of stars break into the pitch darkness, taking us out from this small planet into the vast expanses of space.

We have come for our summer teachings, the study of *Dharma*, the Buddhist doctrines. Around us a different kind of *Dharma* unfolds. *Dharma* is the deep truth of life. It is the eternal, universal nature of things that was always there to be discovered. It is that which holds us. It is that which challenges us. Here amid the teeming life of a small piece of forgotten countryside, *Dharma* breaks through everywhere in the daily encounters with the natural world. We meet otherness moment by moment. Amida is omnipresent in myriad forms. Our religious sense is awakened.

Here, under the shade of the walnut, I notice the light breeze that rises and falls, rustling the leaves and sending the shadows dancing across the screen of my lap top. This wind feels gentle and understated. And when it drops, I miss its presence and wait its return. It softens the heat.

The religious sense arises thus. It breaks upon us without our bidding.

Our encounter with the spiritual is not really under our control. We can bring ourselves into spaces where it becomes more likely, just as, in bringing ourselves here, we are inevitably more aware of the seasons than we are back in England. It cannot, however be forced. If negativity prevails or worries encroach, I may be too wrapped up in my own concerns to notice the life around me.

Our religious experience, and with it our faith, ebbs and flows like the moving air. It is invisible, yet effecting. Of the material world and creating a bridge between the creatures that inhabit it, it hovers in the mid-ground between the visible and the unseen. It is substance and space at the same time.

Sometimes it seeps away into a breathless calm, a fragile hiatus in which only stillness remains. We are left, just the sound of our own breath in an echoing space. Breathe in. Breathe out. Heart beating against the silence. Other times it is solid and challenging as that wall of air my children and I encountered on our walk. We are stopped in our tracks. We are changed in our direction.

Like the wind, our spiritual nature is infinitely varied. Sometimes it is the delicate ripple of grasses in the field as we do walking meditation, other times it is powerful, the wind that moves ships at sea or turns the sails of the windmill, generating electricity. Sometimes it buffets us like the gale that rattles the windows and throws tiles and chimney pots scuttering along the pavements, other times it is the dancing surface of a lake, whipped into a myriad sparkling lights.

Life events contribute. The brushes we have with *dukkha,* pleasures and disappointments, all create whirlpools in our spiritual life. Like summer storms that blow up from nowhere out of a clear blue sky, a sudden bereavement or new relationship can turn our personal world upside down. With this turmoil, our religiosity is affronted or enhanced. But then, life and the spiritual are inseparable, although some may think it otherwise. We are beings of faith.

Shinran and Shinjin

Shinran was a disciple of Honen. His life spanned the late twelfth century and much of the thirteenth, for he lived to be 90. Having been orphaned at an early age, he entered monastic life at the age of eighteen. He spent the first twenty years of his religious career on Mount Hiei, studying the teachings of the Tendai school, which were the prominent form of Japanese Buddhism at that time, and well established with the ruling classes.

Not much is known about Shinran's time on Mount Hiei, though scholarship does suggest that he spent some time as a *doso*, a priest associated with the ninety day nembutsu retreats which were held there. In this, he would have received a significant exposure to Pureland practice. He also seems, like Honen, to have reached a point of some disillusionment both with himself and his capacity to train, and with the lifestyle of the temple, where many monks were engaged in rather unmonk-like lifestyles, competing for power and honour, either fighting each other or acting in rowdy, undignified ways.

Despairing of this life, he left Hiei and, returning to Kyoto, undertook a hundred day intensive retreat. On the ninety fifth day of this retreat, Prince Shotoku, an early ruler of Japan who introduced Buddhism to the country and who had since taken on semi-legendary qualities, appeared to him. As a result of this vision, Shinran was inspired to take a new direction. He immediately left his retreat and went to visit Honen, who was teaching at the time from his small hermitage.

Studying with Honen, Shinran came to believe that faith, not practice, was the essential to salvation. He understood that human effort was flawed, but Amida's vow was the source of salvation.

Professor Albert Bloom comments: *His religious experience gave him a penetrating insight into the defiled nature of human existence which became the foundation for his understanding that salvation is through faith alone. (Bloom 1968 p7)*

Shinran studied with Honen for six years. He was a devoted disciple, as evidenced by his well known statement that he would not regret his devotion if he followed his teacher, Honen, even to hell. This, he added with typical forthrightness and humility, would not be a great sacrifice for him as he was destined there anyway. Nevertheless, Shinran's devotion illustrates the power of the relationship between disciple and teacher. His devotion to Honen was a great source of inspiration, mirroring his devotion to Amida. During this time, Honen also demonstrated his faith in Shinran, allowing him to copy his work, the Senchakushu, and to draw his portrait. Both these acts were signs of particular closeness between the two men. Honen also validated some of Shinran's ideas, notably that both good and bad people could be given faith, and thereby salvation, by Amida, and that salvation in this life was possible.

In 1207, the authorities on Hiei having become increasingly hostile towards Honen and his followers, a crisis occurred in Honen's movement. Following an incident in which two court ladies ordained in Honen's group, the two monks who had introduced them to Honen's circle were executed and both Honen and Shinran along with others of Honen's followers went separately into exile. Shinran was sent to Echigo in the North of Japan. Honen was sent to Shinkoku in the South of Japan.

At some point around this time, Shinran married. The historic details are unclear and some versions of Shinran's life record him making a first marriage, and even having a child, before he left Kyoto. What is clear is that he married Eshin-ni after having gone to Echigo. He took up a life style that was, as he put it, *neither monk nor layman*, continuing to preach the message of Amida's vow, whilst developing family life. This new lifestyle was something that Shinran relished, for his passion was to find ways of teaching that broke out of the traditional social limits and doctrinal rigidities that had prevented the Buddha's message being taught to the common people. Shinran and Eshin-ni had a number of children, probably six. They were living in a remote rural area, learning to survive by simplifying their lives. In exile, Shinran had to face difficulties which as a priest he had not encountered. He had to learn the practicalities of living. As Bloom says, *He was a priest without privilege, he was a layman without experience.*

We can read more of Eshin-ni's life in her surviving letters. These were written after Shinran's death, and show the circumstances of his later life. In his book *Letters Of The Nun Eshin-ni: Images Of Pure Land Buddhism In Medieval Japan* (Dobbins 2004), James Dobbins also offers good commentary on her earlier life and on the times of Shinran.

Shinran's new situation gave him a sense of mission. Living in close proximity to farmers and other working people, Shinran's desire to teach nembutsu to ordinary people rather than to the elite, always an aspect of his ministry, was strengthened. He also came to understand more profoundly the nature of the precarious life situations of most people living in the ordinary world, as opposed to the monks who lived lives that were much more rarefied. According to Bloom, *He was led through his difficulties and hardships to look deeply into the nature of human existence, and he became acutely aware of the strength and indispensability of the passions and instincts in the struggle for existence. He saw that people were inextricably bound by their passions, which were necessary to maintain life.*

(Bloom 1968 p20)

Honen returned to Kyoto in 1211, shortly before his death, but Shinran remained in exile, moving to Kanto in 1212 where he stayed till around 1235, continuing his mission to bring the Dharma to the common people. When he was about sixty, Shinran returned to Kyoto. The reason for his return to Kyoto is uncertain, but once in Kyoto, Shinran settled down to write a number of books. Here he produced a large collection of commentaries, letters, hymns of praise to Amida and other writings.

Shinran is known for the singularity of his emphasis on faith. He saw faith in Amida as the essential element that brings about rebirth in the Pure Land. In particular he saw the conversion-like experience, the moment of being embraced by faith and opening up to Amida, as the essential basis of that salvation. This experience was called *shinjin*. The experience of *shinjin* he grounded firmly in Amida's vow, the vow of Dharmakara to rescue all who called upon his name. Amida's grace was without discrimination and was given without measure. Shinjin was a gift from Amida and an experience of grace.

Even faith was not something to be cultivated through effort in Shinran's view. It was a gift, bestowed through Amida's infinite love. The experience of *shinjin* was instantly transforming but could not be engineered or attained through effort. It came, and one could only prepare for it by being willing to receive it. Later it might transmute into *anjin*, or settled faith, but in its initial flowering it was something that swept a person's life onto a different course.

Shinjin, thus, is not mere faith or entrusting; it is fundamental religious experience in the here and now of Amida's compassion, the realm of infinite wisdom transcending samsaric life. The Pureland path as seen by Shinran not only leads to non-retrogression in this life, but to the

realisation of supreme enlightenment at the very moment of death.
(Commentary on Shinran's collected works P110)

The experience of *shinjin* is something on which Shinran laid great emphasis. Although Honen used other words to express the relationship with Amida, Shinran always used the word *shinjin*. This word expresses an experience that is total. It is a moment of completeness, an experience in which there is a sense of overwhelming presence. The practitioner feels completely filled by Amida. The moment of *shinjin* is, in Shinran's view, a moment that it is all consuming. The Other comes completely into our minds and hearts. Of this experience, Professor Takamaro Shigaraki, retired President of Ryukoku University writes

Shinjin is totally different from [other words for faith] in that it has no intimation whatsoever of "looking up to" but expresses a condition of trust in Amida Buddha and his Vow to save all beings everywhere at all times. In this entrusting there is no subject, no object, no "I believe in something." It is an entrusting relating to the Sanskrit word prasada, which describes a condition that is very calm, still, pure. (Shigaraki writing on the web site, "What is Shin Buddhism")

Here Shigaraki likens shinjin to the clarity of mind that opens up when personal struggle subsides. Such moments of clarity are rare, even in the spiritual life. Mostly, our minds struggle and race, filled with doubt and resistances. Our bombu nature grasps after certainty on our own terms. Sometimes, though, clarity breaks through. The mental chatter ceases. At such points we might experience the Other overwhelming us, filling us. Such an experience does not demand belief in anything, for there is no need. Everything has come to us with enormous clarity. In this we can see how the experience of *shinjin* and the Zen experience of *satori* can be descriptions of similar experiences. In the opening of the heart, self drops away if only for that time.

Losing faith

In the modern world many people feel that they have lost faith. The gods of our ancestors are to no avail and the forces of nature are unleashed to the hands of science. There is no predestination and often no destination either.

Yet the capacity for faith does not die. Its objects may become small and insubstantial – the pension, the holiday, the relationship – but humans continue to live by faith. This human function is as basic as breathing. It is the complement to our conscious nature. As long and as far as we have awareness, we also have faith. Without it we could not live. We would drown in fear at the dangers and sadnesses we perceive around us. We would fall into despair when life's realities became apparent. If animals have no awareness or knowledge of matters such as future and death (though it may well be human conceit that leads us to imagine that this is so) they have no need of faith. Having eaten the fruit of the tree, however, we know our nakedness and, without faith, live in fear.

Thus the daily continuation of ordinary things requires a kind of faith. This is so even in mundane matters. We need faith to labour all week for a pay packet. It is faith in the system that pays us, faith in our colleagues and in the technologies on which we rely. We have faith in transport systems and postal services; in medical and social support. We have faith in the norms and systems of our society. Such faith upholds the structures of our lives. It is faith of small scope.

These structures create the defences against our existential fears. They support our identities and our material comfort. For this reason we cling to them. But such clinging is symptomatic of a lack of deeper faith. It dulls our capacity to trust and makes us mechanical. We trust procedures and systems rather than trusting life. Mundane faith is often grounded in the psychological manoeuvres which we saw in the last chapter which construct a sense of permanence and stability out of the realities of impermanence and change that buffet our lives. Through our mundane faith we build a false world. Mundane faith roots us in a system of thinking and living that creates order in the chaos of life and death. It is interwoven with delusion, but it gives structure to our lives.

Not all mundane structures are bad or unhelpful. The structures give context and form to society and create possibilities for enlightened action as well as deluded. The day to day details of financial systems, employment, communications, and so on all hold great possibilities for good. It is their subversion into the building blocks of attachment and self-building that may limit us and tie our faith to the transient and the material.

Other levels of faith extend beyond the day to day. These are concerned with our individual and shared continuance as humans. They underpin our basic ability to live. Such faith may, again, be deluded. For example, we may have a kind of faith that things will go on in the same way for ever, leading us to live as if we were immortal, for ever young. Even though they know intellectually that things will be otherwise, it is common for humans to act as if their days were limitless. Thus beliefs often co-exist with an opposite sense of impending loss and disaster. Acting as if life will continue for ever, we may be haunted by fears of impending doom. We are not consistent. We often run several scripts simultaneously.

Nevertheless, despite our fears and premonitions, we still act on the basis of a kind of deep confidence in life. Most of us continue to plan futures, often years ahead. Our assumptions about the future happen on both conscious and unconscious levels. The implicit faith involved is only revealed if circumstances change. A sudden diagnosis of terminal illness shocks us to the core, not only because the imminence of death is brought home, but also because we have previously presumed on three score years and ten, or longer. We trust life and have faith in its continuity.

Beyond our personal survival, we have faith in future generations. We start a relationship and have children, presuming they will continue in the years ahead. We plant forests that will mature beyond our lifetimes, and write books that will pass knowledge on to those who are to come. It is perhaps, part of the malaise of our generation, though, that our trust in the future has been shaken. Human capacity for destruction has grown to a point where the certainty of human life continuing on this planet is no longer assured. Such dark thoughts torment modern people and pull at our capacity for faith. And yet, faith continues. Like grass that springs up in the broken concrete of a bomb site, faith grows back. It is a human quality.

Faith of this kind is second nature. It pervades our mentality. It is part of the human bargain. Life could not continue without being grounded in faith. To enter into dialogue with other people, we need at least a modicum of mutual trust. To function in everyday life, we need faith in the continuing provision of ordinary necessities; water, air, food and warmth. This is mundane faith. It is the ordinary, the substance of mind.

Lack of mundane faith means to fall into paranoid psychosis. The person who trusts nothing inhabits a lonely world, framed by fear and cut off from contact with others. Disabled as completely as someone whose limbs do not function, he is utterly alone, fighting unseen enemies that invade even his mind. There is no rest, no relief. Relentlessly he retreats from the haunting presences. This psychotic state is, however, simply an extreme version of the ordinary deluded state. We all withdraw, we all struggle to trust life. In this case, though, even the mundane level of faith is compromised. So sanity depends upon faith. A person without basic faith becomes unable to function or communicate.

Diminishing faith is driven by fear. Shrinking from life, we satisfy our needs for faith at the mundane level. The ordinary person relies upon their own resources and those of their functional world. But deeper faith sometimes surprises us. As we recognise our place in the order of things, deeper faith that is not dependent on our own efforts may arise. In seeing beyond our individual position, we glimpse the measureless. Deep faith goes beyond the mundane level. It is grounded in trust that goes beyond the limitations of self-reliance.

Mundane faith and materialism

For many people, the objects of their faith are secular. They are often concrete and substantive, and belong to the mundane world. At the same time they are insubstantial and transitory in the spiritual realm. Such objects of faith bring transitory comfort, but they do not satisfy the real longing of the heart. They are more of the nature of objects to which our senses and ego-driven cravings attach; the objects of *trishna,* the escapist craving that leads us away from reality into a constructed and limited world.

There is a spiritual malaise in lives that have become too caught up in such attachments. The modern trend towards materialism has not brought happiness in its wake, and though each year brings new brands that are ever more exciting in their possibilities, we never seem to quite achieve the peace of mind or even the leisure time, promised by these new technologies.

Perhaps I am getting old. It is hard to believe now that in my childhood a refrigerator was considered the height of modernity and objects like a car, a television and a record player only made late appearances in our household. Yet life was not so different. The material horizons have changed somewhat, but people lived within the scope of the commodities they had available, as they always have.

In fact the material object alone is rarely the whole component of mundane faith. It is the symbolic value of the objects, rather than their intrinsic worth, that is most significant. We may be attached to having the latest or the fastest or the most attractive or the most expensive, rather than to having the thing for its own usefulness. We may be grasping at a dream of convenience or comfort or perfect happiness and hooking it onto the object we purchase. We may be more concerned with future improvements than appreciating what we have.

I was talking recently with someone who had returned from a remote area of Nepal. She had adopted a village there in the hopes of improving the conditions of its inhabitants. In the village, many basic facilities were lacking. They had only very simple huts, and used well water and outdoor earth latrines. Back in Europe she had been working to raise funds to help the people. To her surprise, instead of wanting improvements to their physical environment, the people asked her to buy paint for their temple.

At first, this seemed a profligate way to spend the money she had raised which had been intended to improve their impoverished conditions. As we discussed the matter, however, we began to question how much our responses reflected our own priorities. It is easy as Westerners to assume that flush toilets and modern, hygienic kitchens are essential to good living, but humans have lived without these accoutrements for thousands of years and built great civilisations without them. Our priorities may be too biased by our attachment to our particular materialistic lifestyle.

Abraham Maslow, in his theory of the *hierarchy of needs*, placed basic material well-being at the base of a pyramidal model of human requirements. He suggested that material well-being is a fundamental need which must be satisfied before the higher levels of need could be addressed. Only when physical needs are satisfied can emotional, social and spiritual needs be addressed. Maslow's theory has been widely, and often unquestioningly, accepted in the West, where the material condition of our lives has taken on such high priority, but it raises many questions for the spiritual practitioner. It flies in the face of the experience of many devotees who deliberately court physical hardship and deprivation as a route to a spiritual life. What are the basic needs of human beings? Modern society with its surfeit of material comfort does not appear to have it right, but such is the faith of the modern person.

Cultivating Faith

Under the snow, shoots are growing. Within mundane faith, we find seeds which could grow to lift us out of the morass of ordinary delusion into what is called *deep faith*, the state of spiritual entrustment.

The mundane objects of our faith are not simply objects of mind. They are existent in their physical or abstract materiality. We should not forget that many mundane objects of faith are indeed abstract. A pension scheme has no more material substance than a demon or a unicorn. Although deeply invested with our personal needs and perceptions, such objects are potentially in the realm of that which is beyond self. They are other.

This other-nature aspect of our objects of mundane faith has the capacity to draw us back into connection with the real world. The person we fall in love with has views that do not coincide with our own. The train is running late and we miss our appointment. Our employer relocates to a new area, forcing a choice between a house move and a change of job. Such events keep us on our toes and engaging with life. They keep us in relationship with others. Sometimes they are small manifestations of warmth and love, which soften our hearts. Other times they are small afflictions which help us develop a more robust relationship with our surroundings. These daily challenges are essential to psychological and spiritual health. Spiritual maturity relies on an other-focused outlook.

Mundane objects also have the capacity to bring us into contact with the other in more profound ways. An ordinary object may take on unexpected luminosity. Flowers on the window sill suddenly shine with the radiance of life. The garden path, glinting in early light, becomes a path to heaven. A religious practitioner might choose to cultivate such perceptions deliberately, making ordinary experience symbolic of the transcendent. He might meditate that the person he is helping takes on the person of Christ or Buddha. She might receive food and clothing as gifts from God. He might imagine Quan Yin in every face on the bus or halos on every child in the school. Such exercises can help us bring the spiritual into the mundane and breathe life into our faith.

Many dare not intentionally venture beyond the ordinary. Even here, though, implicit spiritual truths may be manifest. Embedded in ordinary events, trust in universal energies may emerge. Such trust creates a rudder in a person's life, holding it on a steady course. A person may trust the provision of services and resources in his community, and behind this may have a deeper faith in the human capacity to give and provide. In the West, we all trust that shops will stock the necessities of life, and this may reflect a sense of a benevolent universe. The fact that people have children, creating a new generation, may be grounded in faith in the continuance of the life process and in a sense of connection with the eternal. Such manifestations of faith need respect. They may sometimes be just as deeply felt as faith expressed in more religious language. Different people have different styles.

Times of crisis can bring us into a more direct encounter with our faith. The spiritual metal of a person's life becomes apparent when they are caught by a sudden trauma. At such times, a person cannot avoid facing questions of life and death.

In the wake of the bomb attacks in London in July 2005, I saw a young man interviewed on a television news broadcast. He was an ordinary sort of guy, the sort of person you might expect to meet on a bus or in a pub. Not someone whom you would expect would choose to discuss spiritual matters in public.

As it happened, this young man had just narrowly escaped one of the bomb blasts, walking out of the station moments before the explosion had occurred. Not only this, but he had also happened to be in Sri Lanka a few months ago at the time when it was hit by the Tsunami wave of Boxing Day, 2004, and, a few years earlier, had been staying in Bali when bomb attacks on night clubs killed and maimed many tourists. Three narrow escapes. It was a good story for the television company.

It was clear that the experience of these three events had affected the young man deeply. Although he was somewhat shy to talk about the subject, when pressed by the interviewer, he said that he now had a feeling that his life was planned and that his purpose was to be present as a survivor at such events so that he could be of help to others who had been less fortunate. He intended to continue this vocation and to find ways in which he could do more to help others in the future.

The young man had also been struck by the way that different people had reacted to the disasters. Some were severely injured and could do little, but of those who were not so seriously hurt, some responded with panic, whilst others threw themselves into doing what was needed rescue survivors. These two patterns of response seemed quite instinctive. Some people respond one way, some the other. It did not seem to be a choice, but simply in the nature of human reactions. Terrible circumstances bring out the best in some people, while others are paralysed.

Extreme events can break through our habitual patterns of ordinary life and confront us with our nature. Such experiences can bring us to a point of deeper faith, or they can lead us to retreat into deeper levels of withdrawal from the world. Which way we go seems almost arbitrary. We are ordinary beings. We cannot determine in advance which path each of us will take in a crisis. Despite our best intentions, our responses to disaster often seem to lie in the lap of the gods. Cowards or heroes, the differences emerge through grace, not planning.

Faith without beliefs

The other day, a friend said to me "I am coming to think that Pureland Buddhism is about trying to discover what Amida is."

This echoed my own feeling. It is what makes writing about Pureland Buddhism difficult. We live in a world in which people want straight answers and there are so many questions for which I do not have any answers to give.

People ask: But who is Amida? What is Amida? Where is Amida? Is Amida a god? What do you believe? Some of these questions can be answered in terms of doctrinal statements and the descriptions found in the sutras. Amida is a Buddha. He lives in the Pure Land which he created far, far away to the West. He is not a god, but there are ways in which you might compare him to a god. He is not an all-powerful creator or a punisher. He will not intervene in daily life in response to prayers. He is however, a spiritual source outside myself, to whom I can relate, and is ultimately a source of salvation.

These answers, though, go no further in conveying the relationship a Pureland practitioner has with Amida than a Sunday school hymnal conveys the complexities of Christian theology.

Pureland is a path of faith. It is easy to confuse faith with belief. Actually the two are quite different and often opposite. It has been said that beliefs are what you have when you don't have faith. We cling to beliefs to protect ourselves from things we find frightening or threatening. We seek certainty to cross the abyss of our human isolation and to confirm our sense of security. Beliefs are often rooted in the kind of thinking that creates the god in the image of self.

Faith is willing to doubt. Indeed, it is only through our doubting that we discover real faith. It has been said that one who never doubts cannot have faith because they live in certainty. Certainty leaves no room for faith. Faith is the moment of reaching out without knowing for certain if we will be met. It is trusting.

Faith in Amida is faith of this kind. It is not limited or defined. As Amida is unmeasured light and life, space and time, so faith in Amida is grounded in all that is and might be. How better to express that experience than by following the heart intuition.

Discovering faith is for many people a homecoming. It is the recognition that, as we have always known, beyond all the iniquities of life, and there are many, there is something to meet our deep longing to trust. Reaching this point is not easy though. Many of us have spiritual baggage. It can be hard to hear that uncertainty is an aspect of faith, or that in expressing faith we do not open ourselves to divine judgement.

It can be the simplest steps that bring most healing in this respect. Returning to the basic processes of human life can bring a person back into contact with the trustworthy and thus restore faith. Gardening, talking with others, cleaning a room; all these ground a person in the ordinary world whilst at the same time, as in the imagery of Saigyo's poetry, pointing towards spiritual truths. Echoes of growth, of contact and of transformation are touched but never spoken. The universal is conveyed. Gradually faith returns, perhaps. Healing is invited.

Affliction as opportunity

Dukkha is everywhere. The events that have the potential to disturb our world of expectations and disrupt our habits of view happen all around us, all of the time. Often, though, we are too caught in our own concerns to notice the afflictions of others. It is only when our own life is threatened or we face a significant loss that we break out of the mundane trance and experience something that might connect us with our religious nature.

At such a point we become all too aware that we are vulnerable to the realities of life. Our attempts at creating a sense of permanence are shattered and we recognise our small nature as dependant beings. This crisis point is extremely painful. It is the point where the world we have created around us, that gives us our sense of security, is shattered. It is the point where we may become the hero, or may run away. This is the *Samudaya* crisis. It is the point when by grace we may grow, if we are lucky.

This point is an opportunity. In breaking open the shell of complacency of our ordinary lives, new, often greater possibilities emerge. Our sense of personal autonomy may be broken, or at least diminished, but such situations offer an opportunity for us to do things we would not otherwise do. Our world becomes bigger. We may experience a new sense of connection. We are part of a bigger system. We may discover a new sense of trust in something that is beyond our usual sphere. Or we may not.

New faith may arise from a situation of crisis but it is not inevitable that faith will come at such times. A traumatic event of the scale we have been discussing can lead to a loss of confidence. Previous strategies of self-protection don't work. Also, the event itself may have removed the sources of support on which the sense of self was created. Losing a husband, a woman loses the role of wife. Losing a parent, one can no longer be a child. Even adults in middle age, when a parent dies, often feel strongly this loss of role. No one exists any longer for whom they are the child. They grieve the loss of this vestige of the past. With unwelcome force, the self-structure is sundered. We experience this as an opportunity for spiritual insight or we may become even more strongly defended by building firmer defences.

Painful as times of disaster are, an opening is created. Faith is tested and shaken and can emerge stronger, but not always. The Tsunami has brought much soul searching. If there is an omnipotent God, how can such things happen? In the wake of hurricane Katrina, people joked that God must love the gays a great deal, for the gay quarter of New Orleans was left untouched whilst surrounding areas languished under flood waters. But such amusing reflections mask a deep disquiet. People lose faith when terrible things happen. This is not surprising.

Seeking reality

Our sense of longing is embedded in our intuition that there is something that is unknowable to us, but that is nevertheless deeply meaningful to us. Maybe there is something even more real than our mundane perception of the object world we inhabit. Although our perceptions are constantly coloured and distorted, beyond these distortions, there is something real. The world is not a projection of our minds. We project onto it, certainly, but it has its' own existence without our presence. To think otherwise would be extreme grandiosity.

What is other, by its nature, cannot be truly known. We can posit knowledge. We live in the world on the basis of perceiving good enough approximations of the physical objects that surround us. If we did not, we would starve and fall prey to all manner of accidents. Yet we never perceive our surroundings fully as other. There is mystery that always persists.

Go out into your garden and choose a small area of ground. If you do not have a garden, choose a park, or place in the countryside or even a spot by the bus stop. Take some time to be there so that you can do justice to these surroundings.

Look at the ground. What do you see? Notice how you look. What process does your attention take?

Probably at first you scatter your gaze over quite a large area. There are so many things to be seen that it is impossible for your mind to describe them all. It skips about and chooses details. Things catch your interest and others are not noticed. Or maybe your mind quickly becomes bored and dismissive. It's a grassy lawn – so what? Thoughts arise about the nature of the exercise. What am I supposed to see? Is there some deeper meaning about to be revealed in the process of observing the ordinary? We crave excitement. We look for specialness. The mind wanders and loses interest.

This is how the mind works. Like a monkey swinging from tree to tree, it nibbles here and there at fruit on the branches, discarding it half eaten on the ground. It finds bits and pieces of experience and uses them to build a patchwork image that satisfies its view of the world. This selective viewing is part of the self-project. The mind creates its own selections and uses them to reinforce its world view.

Having seen how the mind behaves given a free choice, confine your attention to a small section of the ground, perhaps as big as a dinner plate. This will bring focus and limit the selectivity.

First of all, notice all the growing things in your piece of ground. How many plants, mosses, fungi and so on can you see? Look closely. Probably if you had a magnifying glass or microscope you would see more. Keep searching. Keep investigating.

Now look at the ground itself? How is it made up? Probably you can see specks of different materials. There may be earth, stones, pieces of organic matter, and perhaps small man-made objects – fragments of plastic or glass or pottery. Whether your piece of ground is soil or some other substance such as tarmac or stone, you will still find it has many other materials on its surface and maybe embedded in it. Some may be organic, others non-living. Keep searching. Keep investigating.

Look at the colours in your piece of ground. Notice how even objects of the same colour are not uniform. Notice the interplay of light and texture. Notice the patterning of objects. When you have looked at the ground from one direction, move your head and notice how the change of light changes colours and shadows. Keep searching. Keep investigating.

Is there animal life in your piece of ground? Perhaps, as you are watching the space, an insect or other small creature surprises you with a visitation. If this happens, seize the opportunity. Look carefully. Notice the creature's complex body. Notice how it moves legs, wings, antennae and eyes. Notice its behaviour. Where does it go? What does it eat? How does it live? What is the meaning of its existence? How does it relate to you? Even if you do not see obvious signs of life in your area of ground, you can be sure that microscopic creatures are living in this space. What life do you imagine they have? How do you imagine they might perceive you? Keep searching. Keep investigating.

Spending time on this investigation, you will no doubt see a great deal that you would otherwise have missed. After all, we step over many such areas of ground in a day. This piece of ground is about the size of an area that you regularly cover with your two standing feet. However closely you look, however, there will undoubtedly be much that you do not see. Some non-seeing is due to lack of sensory capacity, some to lack of investigative interest. Our limits come in many forms. Perception is grounded in the questions we ask ourselves. All such questions are culturally determined, growing out of our previous experience, education and influences. The questions we ask shape what we see. They only partially help us to perceive reality.

We are limited in physical ways by our organs of perception. The senses are not only conditioned by our experience, but also by nature. We are limited by the size and qualities of our visual field and by the angle of vision. We do not see the play of infra red or ultra violet light or hear the ultra sonic cries of insects. We do not consciously sense magnetic and electrical fields.

Despite lengthy investigation, something as simple and mundane as a piece of ground remains a mystery. Even if we were to set all the scientists on the planet to investigate it, this mystery would remain irreducible. Beyond the known are always more unknowable layers.

It is a simple exercise. It nevertheless demonstrates the complexity of the world and the limitations of our view. As we walk along a street or look out of a window, how little we see. We cover so many footsteps in a day, yet our path is just one small part of the mosaic of human movement. Our view is one very limited perspective of the world. This world is inhabited by nearly 6,500,000,000 people, and each has their own view. Humans are only a small part of the animal kingdom, and have particular ways of viewing. Our world is just a very small planet in a vast universe.

Thus, even at the material level, the other is a great mystery. When we struggle to relate to it, we fall back into personalised approximations. Keeping our sense of wonder and our willingness to encounter the other requires a special kind of reaching out. Even the mundane world is Amida.

Metaphor and religious experience

In her book, *The Barn at the End of the World,* Mary Rose O'Reilly comments on the importance of metaphor in religious life. She points out that working with metaphor is not something that readily equates with scientific enquiry. It is a process that operates through the heart rather than the intellect. The intellect has its place, but it is our feeling sense for the imagery of poetry and art that helps us to draw on its wisdom. It is the same, O'Reilly suggests, with religious metaphors.

Religious ideas – and every idea apprehended by the heart – are metaphoric. But human beings want to turn soft metaphors into hard facts, and better control them. (O'Reilly 2000)

O'Reilly's view is that in trying to achieve philosophical tightness, the rich but fluid meaning of the metaphor is reified and thus made into something that is far clumsier and more rigid than was intended. This view, of course, is not the whole picture. Religious writing has benefited greatly from philosophical rigour, and popular writing may use imagery as an excuse for sloppy thinking which hides inconsistencies and partial views. But intellectual clarity is only one aspect of religious thought.

The felt experience of faith is central to the religious life. This often remains in the world of mystery which can only be touched by the soft descriptive power of imagery and metaphor. The experiences of the religious sense are of a nature that one struggles to put into words. Attempting to find words that are definitive and incorporating, can be a reductive, rigidifying and diminishing experience. As we grasp at the intangible it slips way into further distance. Grasping is an act of ego. It is the attempt to harness what cannot be contained.

As we have seen in the poetry of the Pureland hermits, metaphor is often a more potent mode of expression in the arena of religious experience than attempts to describe the experience directly. *Yugen* is metaphoric. It allows many levels of meaning to coexist, that do not require interpretation. A good metaphor not only tells us intellectually about an object, and indeed, this is probably the smallest part of what it conveys, but also gives us a feel for the object, its context and its impact and something universal that lies beyond it. We do not even need to consciously recognise these meanings to be affected by them. The image speaks from unconscious to unconscious.

Why do we see our soul reflected in the sea? Why do we see our sadness in the moon? In metaphoric imagery we can build associations and multiply secondary images. We feel the lapping waves, the churning depths, the unseen sharks, but even as we do so, we do not exhaust the layers of meaning. Each new nuance unfolds a new set of associations. Each helps us deepen our understanding in new ways. We flow through images as through a hall of mirrors. Life is infinite, complex and beautifully rich. The secrecy of its unrelenting depths adds to their power and the light we draw from them.

Dreams, like metaphors, are often best left uninterpreted. The attempt to contain with meaning cuts off the unconscious process that the images work on us. Better to dwell peaceably in their corridors and meander through their eerie glades than try to see pathways of the mind and find dark memories in their stories. They will make known to us those things we need to know in their own time. Yet appreciating their rich presence and inviting their nightly unfolding we embrace their healing quality. So too, religious experience, fragile as a dog rose on the hedge briar, appears, a gift to be appreciated in the moment, but not cemented into concrete analysis.

Amida, the Buddha of infinite life and infinite light, beyond time and space, remains a mystery. Amida cannot be contained in words. Inevitably, our description is metaphoric. But our experience of Amida lies in the experience of otherness. Amida is the infinite space beyond self. Stuck in our *bombu* nature we can only glimpse these expanses. Only occasionally does Amida break in on us. Sometimes in the spectacular, more often in the mundane, in our everyday experience, we glimpse the distance and look toward Amida's light. By its nature, the other cannot ever be truly known, and Amida, as the measureless, must remain mysterious. Yet we can sense the presence of Amida, as we feel the strength of the wind and see its force impacting on the landscape. Trees bend and birds are tossed high. Lives are thrown onto new courses by the spiritual tide. In our ordinary struggles with life and our interminable retreat into the compulsiveness of ordinary being, if we can look honestly, we may experience our religious sense as fully as in many high-flown writings. Looking deeply at our foolishness, we discover truth.

CONCEPTS INTRODUCED IN THIS CHAPTER

- Mundane faith and religious faith
- Shinran and the life of faith
- Metaphor, Mystery and the undefinable nature of all things

CHAPTER EIGHT

THE GATE OF CONTRITION

All the harm committed by me
Is caused by beginningless greed, hate and delusion
All this is the work of my body, speech and mind
I now confess everything whole heartedly
And resolve to begin anew

(contrition verse, traditional)

Many people complain that they feel guilty all the time. It has become quite epidemic. Women feel guilty because they do not give their children enough attention, or use convenience meals, or don't achieve promotion at work. Men feel guilty because they forget to buy flowers or don't remember to phone home at the right time. Adult children feel guilty for not spending enough time with parents, while younger ones feel bad when they fail their exams or when they do things of which their parents would disapprove if they knew.

Feeling guilty gnaws at us and keeps us awake at night. It makes us timid and apologetic. It leaves us depressed or resentful. It is the millstone we carry around with us, the shadow which haunts us. We may feel angry about feeling guilty, but then it is quite likely that we will feel guilty about our anger. Guilt is a slippery, uncomfortable emotion, which easily becomes self-preoccupying. Feeling guilty is very disabling.

Feeling guilty is not the same thing as being guilty. We often feel guilty even when we know we have done nothing wrong. Sometimes the feeling is not even attached to any action, but lingers like a kind of doubt at the back of the mind.

This kind of ill defined guilty feeling, even when it can be linked to a mistake or deliberately wrong act, is really the other side of the self-perfection project. It is the price we pay for trying to be perfect. Such a feeling may be the result of us believing that we should be able to foresee every potential pitfall in a relationship, or every need of a loved one. It may result from us believing we should always be tactful and loving and never tired or lazy. It may be the result of us feeling that we have let others down or that we have let ourselves down. It is the uncomfortable realisation of all those times when we are less than perfect.

Against this background, recognising our ordinary fallible nature is a great relief. It stops us from having to be perfect and from feeling unnecessary guilt. As long as we expect to get it right every time, we will keep disappointing ourselves. As long as we expect others to get it right for us, they will let us down. This will be doubly hurtful as we feel hurt or angry and then guilty for having such feelings. Others are also in the grip of the idea of perfection and may be conditional in their views of us, adding to our sense of guilt.

Foolishness is in our nature. We are ordinary people, living ordinary lives in ordinary ways and in doing so, we mess things up continually. We are not omniscient and we make mistakes. Recognising this we can be more relaxed in our approach to life. In turn, this probably makes us easier to live with.

Feeling that we are failing in the self-perfection project can make us defensive. We often feel frightened and vulnerable. We feel vulnerable to all the uncertainties of life, and death. We feel vulnerable to others and fear their criticism. In our fear we retreat into defensiveness.

Humans have few predators in the animal world. Our major threat is from one another. Whether physical or psychological, other humans inflict the wounds that cause us most grief. We are wary of the potential they have to hurt and maim us. Feeling this way, we fall into patterns of behaviour that create psychological barriers to protect ourselves from one another. We cling to our attachments and compulsions, building around us the armoury of self structures with which we are so identified. This adds to our burden of guilt as we sense our inauthenticity.

Besides such human threats, we are vulnerable to the forces of nature. Such is the perilous quality of our existence. We inhabit bodies that are skin bags full of fluids, surrounded by the jagged rocks of life. "Brutish and short", our existence is framed by the pain of birth and death and peppered with spells of sickness, discomfort and disappointment. We feel our vulnerability sorely, and shrink into psychological manoeuvres to diffuse it.

Our human tendency to defend ourselves by slipping into compulsive patterns of avoidance and attachment lies at the heart of the Buddhist teachings. We get irritable or proud, greedy or negative. We are gloomy about our own lives and those of others, or aggressive to friends and strangers. We want things for ourselves and take secret interest in others' misfortunes. In an average day, we act primarily out of motives that are riddled with self-interest and fail to notice the needs of others, or noticing them, ignore their implications. This is because we feel we have to defend against knowing their otherness. We have to maintain our sense of self and thus try to ward off the pain of our feelings of guilt. It is a viscous circle. Even when we care for others, we are frugal in our offerings, feel pride in our meagre generosity, confining our concern to those with whom we feel personal connection.

We are defensive, and our defence is twofold; against others and against ourselves. We defend ourselves against others, by rejecting or dismissing them as different or by hiding our own failings from them, a strategy driven by fear of retribution. We defend ourselves against ourselves, not allowing knowledge of our shortcomings to penetrate the illusion of

OK-ness that our minds create. We censor experiences or responses that contradict our self-image. This adds to our feelings of insecurity as we sense we are frauds.

Sometimes we glimpse our nature, but, as raw reality confronts us, we back off, shrinking into habitual comforts. We avoid and embroider, creating our personal strategies for warding off knowledge of our frailty and fallibility, and then out of these strategies we build our sense of identity. We reassure ourselves of our worthwhile nature, clinging to the positive aspects of this identity, or, conversely, by clinging to a negative self-image, we console ourselves, believing that we can fall no further and that no effort will improve matters (the corollary being that no effort is to be made).

Whether self-congratulatory or self-deprecating, we feed our complacency and reinforce our tendency not to see the reality of our nature. We cling to a consistent sense of self, whether positive or negative, because this supports our sense of personal permanence and keeps us at a degree removed from our vulnerability. This position is untenable. It is also hard work.

So it is that not only are we caught in all manner of negative patterns of behaviour, but also we are involved in complex processes of self-deception. Whatever the roots of our self-image, its construction out of filtered perceptions and a selective self-story creates a doubly deluded position. Firstly we act in harmful or deluded ways and then compound the delusion by denying it to ourselves.

Facing the reality of our nature is fundamental to any Buddhist approach to life and to mental health. It removes one layer of delusion. Honest recognition of our situation creates the basis upon which this approach rests. It means releasing energy and letting go some layers of pretence.

Most Buddhist traditions therefore include reflections on personal shortcomings as an important preliminary practise. In such practices a review of one's actions is undertaken before other practices, such as meditation or devotional acts, are commenced. The act of confession, and its accompanying feelings of contrition, creates the ground from which these other activities can arise. It makes a space. It helps us to let go of emotional baggage and mental games. It brings clarity. Contrition is thus seen as being of great importance in shaping our ability to change. Sometimes referred to as the Dharma gateway, it opens the possibility for new ways of being.

The Wheel of Life

Our *bombu*, fallible, nature is summarised in the teaching of *The Three Poisons*. This teaching, which is one of the foundational teachings of all Buddhism, describes the root processes of delusion. *The Three Poisons* are the three basic manifestations of clinging (*trishna*). In short they are the three logical possibilities; the three directions that our attachment or clinging may take. When we relate to things compulsively we do so by either grasping at them or pushing them away, or else we respond to them in some ambiguous or neutral way. The three poisonous roots manifest in many forms, but they can be summarised as compulsive grasping, *greed*; compulsive rejection, *hate*, and compulsive ambivalence, *confusion*. These three possibilities underlie all our compulsive clinging responses in some combination. In short, our lives are driven by greed, hate and confusion (in Sanskrit *lobha, dvesha* and *moha*).

Tibetan Buddhism uses a pictorial representation of the deluded nature of the unenlightened life, the cycle of *samsara*. This picture is called the *Wheel of Life* and it provides a diagram of all the different worlds that beings inhabit. The diagram depicts a series of concentric circles, each being divided into sections with pictograms, the whole circular world being held in the jaws of a ferocious beast. The image is a teaching aid. It is a reminder to all, and particularly the young *tulkus* for whom it was probably originally intended, of the pitfalls of the deluded life.

The beast who is devouring the wheel of life is Yama. He is red in colour and has great bared teeth that clench around the outer circle of the wheel. His clawed hands also grasp the rim, and he stares out over the top of the disc at the viewer, with large, piercing eyes. Yama is the lord of time. A frightening, yet rather flamboyant image, he serves as a reminder that our time in this life is limited. If we want to do something about the state of our lives, we should act quickly. Each day we accumulate more negative karma and lose more opportunities for change. Time is gobbling up everything around us. Practice is urgent. Time should not be wasted. In the words of the Zen verse *"Do not squander your life"*.

The wheel which Yama holds contains a series of concentric circles. These represent different Buddhist teachings about the nature of deluded life. Here is presented a depiction of *samsara,* the cycle of ordinary life. The teachings depicted offer different perspectives on the process of delusion. This is the *bombu* world, the world we build through our defensive responses to life.

Commonly, the outer circle of the wheel represents the cycle of *Dependent Origination*. In keeping with the traditional form, this teaching is set out as twelve pictograms. The cycle shows how each aspect of life is conditioned by the previous one, each mental state arises in dependency upon the last. This teaching can be interpreted in many ways, but taking a psychological viewpoint, it shows the intransigent nature of our foolishness. In parallel with the teaching of the *skandhas*, it illustrates the process by which the self-structure is created and maintained. For a fuller account of this process, you may refer to chapter 10 of *Buddhist*

Psychology. Here we may simply note that *samsara* is maintained through the cycling of our conditioned nature. Our minds are interminably circling the same mistaken tracks.

The next circle on the wheel of life represents the *six realms of existence*. It is divided into six segments, each of them illustrating one of the realms. In the uppermost segment are the *heavenly realms*. Here pleasure and diversion are boundless. Fountains play and palaces of jewelled splendour wait for the gods' delight. This is the realm of ease and relaxation, where pleasant abiding rewards the fortunate inhabitants. An enjoyable interlude in the cycle, but one in which spiritual progress is postponed. Below this, to the right, we see the realm of the *warring gods*. This is the space where power and pride predominate. Angry and jealous, its inhabitants fight for power, defeating one another and in turn falling prey to the weaponry of battle. On the left of the wheel, below the heavens, we see the *human realm*. This is the place where ordinary life struggles occur. Without the distractions of the heavenly space, here at least there is a possibility for Buddhism to be studied. Nevertheless, this human realm rests within the cycle of delusion. The realm of the *heavens, warring gods*, and *humans* make up the upper half of the wheel.

The lower half contains three further realms, seen as the less desirable births. Below the human realm we find that of the *hungry ghost realm*. This is the space occupied by *pretas* or *hungry ghosts*. These creatures, whose swollen bellies and thin necks grotesquely illustrate the extremity of greed, find even the most nutritious food to be as poison. On the other side of the circle, below the jealous gods, we find the *animal realm*, where life is dominated by instinctive drives from survival and reproduction. At the bottom of the wheel we find the *hell realms* where all manner of misery unfolds.

For the young Tulku, the wheel of life, with its colourful images of hells, served as a warning to encourage diligence. It showed how bad behaviour might result in terrible consequences, and should therefore be avoided. Karma and Yama were implacable. Despite the effort many Western Buddhists make to distance Buddhism from any suggestion of divine retribution, Eastern Buddhism has its own rich heritage of hellfire and karmic consequence. It is true that these are conceived of as being consequences of our own making, since there is no external source of judgement involved in the unfolding of karma, but the image of the hell realm is prominent, and has frequently been used in encouraging the practitioner to reformation.

Just as with the teaching of Dependant Origination, the teaching of the six realms can be understood in different ways. Traditionally taken as a description of the progress made through different life incarnations, it has also been taken in some contexts as a description of different human mind states. In his book, *Thoughts Without a Thinker* (Epstein 1996), for example, Mark Epstein explores the teaching of the Six Realms as tools for understanding the different psychological states through which we cycle.

An inner circle, within that of the six realms, shows a line of beings, who ascend and descend in an inevitable process of alternating self-improvement and decay. Although the conditions of our lives seem to improve, whilst caught in the processes of grasping, we inevitably return to the hell realms. Our bompu nature is such that even if we seem to make spiritual progress, we discover our fallibility with monotonous regularity.

At the centre of the wheel is a circle in which three creatures are depicted. These animals chase each other in a circle, each biting the next one's tail. They are a cockerel, a snake and a pig, and represent the three poisons, greed, hate and delusion. The cockerel represents greed, the snake represents hate, and the pig represents ignorance or delusion. It is no accident that these three root delusions are at the centre of the wheel. The whole cycle of unenlightened existence is driven by these fundamental processes of grasping. Our deluded experience is driven by greed, hate and delusion, the processes of attachment. Humans compulsively grasp at some aspects of experience and reject others and through this move inevitably into the lower realms, visiting the hells or battle fields, craving impossible comforts like hungry ghosts, or gorging insatiably as they express their animal nature.

Contrition and Pureland Buddhism

Recognising one's deluded state is a first step in the spiritual path. It can be a spur to practice, motivating us to continue. Understanding our nature is an act of deep honesty. It challenges us to engage with the real experience of our failings rather than simply arriving at a theoretical acceptance of them. Any spiritual practice can quickly deteriorate into a pious gloss on life. Deep truths convert into easy statements that have lost substance and impact. Facing the reality of our situation needs to happen in the muck and clutter of real daily situations rather than remaining tied to remote doctrines and images.

Basic human nature is confronted in the religious life through practices that involve making acts of contrition. These involve looking at our actual behaviour and seeing our shortcomings and mistakes. They introduce bite into our religious life. They provide a foundation for serious reflection. Acts of contrition are fundamental in many religious traditions, not just in Buddhist contexts. In most Buddhist schools, acts of contrition are considered an important aspect of practice, and this is particularly the case in Pureland.

Modern people may be less inclined to accept notions of hell realms as actual destinations for their future lives than people in the past, but the act of contrition still motivates us to change our ways. Seeing the negative consequences of our actions, and the frequency with which they are committed, is humbling and builds motivation to continue spiritual practice.

In addition to providing simple motivation, however, acts of contrition may help us to get beyond emotions which stifle us. In particular it addresses feelings of guilt and of pride. Often these are two sides of the same coin. Both arise from our desire for perfection.

Pride is a primary obstacle in our lives. It stops us trying new things for fear of failing. It makes us hard and unwilling to bend to others views or to co-operate. It stops us from admitting we are wrong and changing direction. It is a barrier to religious practice. Pride is one of the main symptoms of our struggle to build and maintain our view of ourselves as special cases. It encourages a false sense of entitlement, and makes us unwilling to change or to open up to others' guidance. Guilty feelings can sometimes result from our regret that we have let ourselves down in others' eyes, they can be injured pride. For this reason, contrition, which reduces pride, is an opportunity, a gate to the spiritual path, and the facilitator of spiritual growth. Recognising mistakes that have been made, the practitioner becomes more sober in his self-assessment and, with luck, abandons grandiosity, becoming more open to grace.

Thus contrition is commonly seen to reduce pride and to cultivate diligence, and is practiced in most schools of Buddhism.

In Pureland Buddhism, contrition has a special place. It takes on a particular importance in practice because it brings us to a deeper knowledge of our *bombu* nature. Knowing our *bombu* nature is a precursor to faith. An act of personal honesty brings us into direct knowledge of our real condition. We are far from extinguishing our past karma and are constantly generating new negative karma. The deliberate practices of reflection and review such as Nei Quan that address contrition remind the practitioner of how many daily acts cause hurt to others or damage to the environment.

They bring into focus the continual failings, large and small, that are part of human life. It gives real examples which become the subject of reflection.

Such insights can be confronting if we are still caught in trying to see ourselves as perfect. They demonstrate the meagre success of any attempt that we have made to change ourselves through our own efforts. They provide an opportunity for stock-taking. Sometimes it is apparent that we have made some progress in changing a particular behaviour, and this can be encouraging, but, when we are really honest with ourselves, our ability to transform ourselves is limited. There is always something else getting in the way of enlightenment. Maybe I have managed to control my temper better, or to become more aware of others' needs in particular situations, but I then discover plenty of other aspects of my life that are still grounded in selfish attitudes or thoughtless exploitation of personal advantage. For every small step forwards, I discover plenty of other areas of behaviour that are thoughtless or driven by dubious motivations. So it continues. As we grow in honesty, we begin to identify more and more layers of self-serving interests. We uncover an ever growing catalogue of greed, hate and delusion.

The most important learning that comes from this process is, however, not about how we can become better people, but rather, about how little control we actually have over our own behaviour. The *skandhas* are not easily abandoned and *dependently originated* behaviour is deeply rooted. Even when we are determined to master a particular habit of speech or action, we frequently find ourselves slipping up and falling back into just the behaviour we are trying to eliminate. Sharp words have left our mouths before we have had time to notice their arising At the end of the day, we realise that we have once more failed to telephone the sick friend. New Year's resolutions are broken within the week. The smoker knows how easily resolve is forgotten when cigarettes are being passed around.

Despite all our good intentions, we do not seem able to control our actions. Problematic behaviours do not cease simply at our bidding. The attachments and habit patterns which dog our lives are not easily defeated. We are not in control. We cannot find our own salvation. This is not an easy message for Western audiences, used to self-help books that offer step by step routes to self-improvement. It can be a relief though.

On the other hand we should not use this knowledge as an excuse to avoid effort to change specifics. It is just there will always be more to do. Devoting time to an examination of our lives in the light of practises of contrition, it is possible to respond at two levels. At one level, we see the implications of our actions and this may lead us to decide to act differently in the future. We sort out the real guilt from that which is compulsive and arrive at a truer assessment of ourselves. This is because we are evaluating our behaviour but we are not condemning ourselves. We are looking honestly, but not expecting to see perfection. We develop resolution. Such resolution has some, albeit limited, success. Sometimes, although it is hard to make changes through will alone, we do manage to effect change on particular behaviours. Such change often comes through the shock of really realising the effects of our actions on others and on ourselves.

At deeper level, however, when we see our actions and honestly appraise our behaviours, we arrive at a more sober view of our nature. We understand at a heart level the *bombu* quality of our lives. We recognise our endless capacity to generate karmic obstacles; our capacity to mess up and the frequency with which our minds are filled with greedy, harmful or emotionally confused impulses. We also see how ineffective our attempts to reform are. We become less convinced of our personal omnipotence and more open to the support of others.

This realisation of our *bombu* nature is the basis for spiritual transformation. We can see that in the lives of many great sages, particularly in the Pureland tradition, contrition has been the precursor to insight. King Asoka is said to have converted to Buddhism on seeing the dead lying across the battle field after his invasion of the country of the Kalinga people. Nagarjuna entered the spiritual life after an escapade with his friends went badly wrong and the rest of the party was killed. Shan Tao's teacher, Tao Cho reached his spiritual breakthrough after making an act of contrition. Honen awakened after he had despaired of ever mastering a single precept. Shinran saw the experience of *Shinjin* itself was intimately linked to recognition of our failings. The list is impressive.

According to the commentary on Shinran's collected writings, recognition of our deepest failings is the very root of *shijin*, the experience of complete faith. Honest insight into our true nature as *bombu* opens our hearts to Amida's transforming presence.

> *Shinjin is not a matter of believing in scripture, or placing faith in the Buddha, or anticipating a future life in the Pureland; it is not a matter of blind trust, vulnerable to uncertainties and anxieties. Rather shinjin is born from awakening to the fathomless evil of oneself made possible through the working of Amida; at its core is a kind of wisdom that comes with the realisation of things, including the self, as they truly are. Shinjin, however is more than wisdom; there is a radical transformation in which evil (good and evil of a foolish being) becomes good (the good of the Buddha) occurring at the depths of one's being. (Commentary on Shinran's collected works P107)*

The process of looking deeply into our behaviour brings to our awareness the great imbalance that exists between those actions we have committed and those things we have received. We recognise how little we have actually achieved through our own efforts, and yet how, in spite of this, our lives have been fully supported. The wonder of life and the manner in which its necessities arrive for us almost miraculously create an awkward adjunct to our recognition of our own ineffective attempts to reform. Of low personal capacity, we are nevertheless held by a process greater than ourselves. We live through Amida's grace.

Such thoughts transform the act of contrition from a cataloguing of our own failings into a deep appreciation of our position. We feel great joy and release. Far from generating despair and frustration, a feeling often arises, which embraces both the regret for what has occurred and gratitude for what has been received. These two feelings balance each other. In them, the bitter-sweet *yugen* quality, so characteristic of Pureland Buddhism arises. We are deeply flawed and yet deeply accepted. Beyond our perversity, there is much to be celebrated.

Confession, release and freedom

A protestant upbringing can leave a certain fascination with the whole art of confession. Visiting Catholic churches in France, those little wooden cubicles with their fretwork screens and ecclesiastical carving, which nestle in the side aisles of austere Romanesque churches or line up in regimental fashion behind the neat rows of chairs in the great cathedrals, evoke a strange mixture of attraction and horror. Their little curtains suggest a place of privacy and intimacy. It is tempting to imagine whispering to the unseen listener the dark secrets of the heart. No need to behold the flicker of eyebrows or the furrowing of the brow. Such thoughts become almost as seductive as that of taking a tall white taper from the box before the statue of the virgin and offering it to the willowy figure with her heavenward gaze. Anathema to the frugal protestant spirit, such spiritual indulgence seems an almost instinctive response, an act of universal religiosity.

The imagination flows on.

"Bless you my child. Go and sin no more"

Caught in perpetual guilt, a protestant child may from time to time find herself surprised by jealousy, yearning for the freedom of the Catholic skipping home, only a few Hail Mary's away from absolution.

To confess, to seek forgiveness, absolution, to offer devotion; these acts tug at our hearts and draw us. They touch a primitive part of our nature. The thought of finding opportunity to divulge the gnawing guilt or heartfelt regret inspires a craving for release and a longing to entrust the burden of our sins to the holy space. We long to walk away cleansed.

Of course, many Catholics will assure you that they have been left their share of guilt. That's not the point.

The point is that confession is the precursor to transformation and freedom. When truly made, and placed in a context in which it is heard by one who has a loving concern for the spiritual wholeness of the one making confession, it brings a space for change and letting go. Telling the secret breaks the hold of the transgression and releases the sinner from pride and the endless machinations of mind that try to adjust and reform the deed. Telling the secret draws a line.

Confession without forgiveness

The act of confession in the Christian context is, among other things, an act of seeking forgiveness and restored purity. The words of the confessor bring relief precisely because they mediate the divine forgiveness. The God of Catholicism is a God who can be loving and can take away the sins of the sinner. Through this God's grace, the follower is released.

The Pureland view is somewhat different. Pureland has no notion of judgement. It is precisely by knowing our *bombu* nature that we become aware of Amida's unfailing love. Confession is not followed by forgiveness. Forgiveness would suggest that we had behaved outside our nature and could return to a different way of being. It also suggests a return to the fold, a repair of the relationship. In the Pureland view, we are not forgiven because we were never judged in the first place. Universal love is unconditional. It holds us, whatever we do. Confession takes place in this context. It does not heal a breach, for Amida has never been absent, but it may lift a veil we have created. It brings us back into knowledge of Amida. We have done wrong yet we have not been punished. Love is unfaltering, whatever we do. We can stop trying to be god and to be perfect. We can relax and open to the greater process that supports us.

As a practice, we look honestly at the detail of our behaviour. What did we think of when the phone rang this morning? Did we notice who had done the washing up or put away the dry clothes? We realise that we are not as good as we would like to be. We also realise that this is how things are. It is still OK even when we are not OK.

In our daily practice at The Buddhist House we use *Quan* meditation as a means of personal reflection. *Quan* means enquiry. It is the Chinese term for the form of meditation known in Sanskrit as *Vipasshyana*. Insight meditation can be practised in many ways, and the form of *Quan* that we use focuses on personal reflection with the intention of gaining insight into the nature of our lives through concrete focus on behaviour and circumstances. It involves working with questions and identifying specific incidents and interactions.

Our period of *Quan* meditation frequently begins with an invitation to think back over the past twenty four hours and consider our interactions with others. This may be with people in the community, visitors, people we have met outside the house, strangers we encountered, or people we didn't even meet, such as those who provide services or resources for our consumption. How have we caused others harm during the past twenty four hours, and how have we helped them? What is honestly true? What have we received and what have we given?

Usually as we reflect it is all too apparent that we have received more than we have given. We have caused others hurt and trouble and have often overlooked it. We have built an inflated view of our achievements and our capabilities and under-rated those of others. Such reflections are sobering. Sobering too is the recognition that, as we become aware of our mistakes or of some uncaring behaviour, there is often a tendency to immediately slip into self-justification or to feel recrimination toward ourselves for letting slip our idealised self-image. We are tenaciously attached to seeing ourselves in a good light.

As we have seen, guilt and pride are often closely linked. Our self-reproach hides dissatisfaction with ourselves for failing to live up to our own standards. We are frustrated by our own imperfection and give ourselves a hard time in consequence, not because we are really contrite but because the facts do not support our image of ourselves as the perfect person. The recognition that it is our human lot to be imperfect is both a release and a challenge to our egotism. Yet this is just another aspect of *bombu* nature. The fact that I can write about such processes, confident that the reader will recognise them, demonstrates their pervasiveness. As *bombu* we are proud, grandiose and mistaken. We are also frightened.

Strange as it may seem, it is actually hard for most of us to realise that we do not have to earn favours from an external authority. We do not have to fear judgement. The expectation of judgement is deeply engrained in the Western patterns of thought. It is part of the theistic heritage that seems very hard to shift (even though it is an aspect that many theists today tend to play down). Even avowed atheists are theistic in their thinking in this respect. Pureland Buddhists have tended to regard such reliance on external sources of evaluation as superstitious, however.

Often we find ourselves playing mental games and trying to bargain where no bargaining is possible. We cannot believe in unconditionality. Imagining that we are acceptable despite all the mistakes we make runs against the grain. Surely there must be a reward for doing good. Anything else would be unfair. If this is so, it follows that bad behaviour will be punished. This has been our experience of interactions in the past. We do, after all, live with other *bombu* humans who judge and criticise us, and we learn to do likewise. We anticipate that conditionality pervades the universe.

Even in the teachings on the workings of *karma*, the unfolding of cause and effect, we see that negative actions are understood to bring negative consequences. These teachings are often taught in a Buddhist context. But as we reflect, the gifts that we receive to live each day and take for granted, go far beyond what we have earned. The sun, the air, the growing plants, the wealth of human compassion; these are not balanced by our meagre contributions to the planet's welfare. Though *karma* is relentless, we are blessed.

There is a further problem with accepting that we are not judged. Besides our sense of our own unworthiness, we often harbour an even greater sense of the unworthiness of others. Our deluded grandiosity creates a sibling rivalry par excellence. As we struggle with our own habitual guilt, we are unaware that we also resent the idea that there might be a universal acceptance that embraces all. In truth most of us want the possibility of achievement; to be able to demonstrate ourselves to be better than others and getting close to perfection. Even though the price is high, with its ticket of guilt and judgementalism, we would rather opt for a deity who measures our worth against others than for one who offers true acceptance and really does leave the responsibility with us.

There is a poem by the Japanese poet, Zuiken Inagaki (1885-1981)

Just as you are
Really
Just as you are

I often share this poem when I am talking about Pureland Buddhism because it seems to go to the heart of the matter so simply and so perfectly. At first its message is deceptively inviting. Most people are delighted by the idea of being fully accepted. But as the real intent of the poem becomes clear, its challenge emerges. To surrender to unconditional acceptance requires humility. It means being *just as we are*. It means letting go the pretence of being something else. We can only know that we are accepted just as we are when we recognise how we really are, when we accept our *bombu* nature.

When we reflect on our transgressions, we start to see the real nature of our condition. If we can see it, and in doing so stop trying to maintain the eternal cover-up, we free ourselves from the burden of trying to be what we are not and let go some of the delusion of grandiosity that all of us carry. Clouds drop away, a little, and our sense of being held by something greater emerges. Reflecting on our behaviour and sharing our reflections with others, we gradually start to trust that we can indeed be *just as we are.*

The confessional in the therapy room

Confession supports us in recognising our nature. It may bring with it feelings of regret. It supports our willingness to be honest with ourselves and others. It also allows us to experience that parts of our lives that we feel to be unacceptable can be told to another without dire consequences. Sharing our secret guilt with someone else, whose specific role is not to judge us, allows us to be guilty but not condemned.

The therapeutic encounter can offer a person something of the same function as the confessional. The therapist's consulting room is the place where, in modern society, the person can unburden himself of feelings of failure and shortcoming without, for the most part, fearing that it will be used against him. The therapist becomes the recipient of the client's secret guilt. Sometimes this is confided in veiled allusions and other times more candidly. Often the degree of honesty is directly proportional to the client's perception of the therapist's real capacity to withhold judgement.

Therapists are supposed to be non-judgemental. This is a basic tenet of most therapeutic training and, as with many dogmas, can be easily promoted without a deep examination of its implications. At a superficial level, many therapists implicitly take the idea of non-judgementalism to imply that they should always think well of their clients. But it is not a big step to move from this view to a position that makes it very difficult for the client to express guilt and feel properly heard. The interpretation of unconditionality that avoids seeing the negative aspects of people's behaviour unwittingly creates taboo areas, which clients often sense and instinctively steer away from. When therapists shy away from fully accepting the client's guilt, the client is denied the possibility of real unburdening.

The problem is that therapists are in general nice people. They want to encourage their clients and to see the best in them. They do not want to think of their clients as guilty. They are schooled in notions that guilt is unhealthy and to be avoided. More than this, though, they are embedded in a culture that is highly value ridden. It is a culture of villains and victims, perpetrators and the abused. It is a culture of health and illness, problem and solution. It is a culture where some things are seen as desirable and others not, where progress is sought and change anticipated. It is a culture deeply invested in judgement. For this reason therapists are reluctant to give ear to the client's guilt.

When clients talk of things they have done wrong, therapists tend to listen with a sceptical ear. They tend to try to take away the client's guilt, implicitly or explicitly reframing what is said. They tend to justify and reattribute blame.

"But what else could you have done? The way they had treated you, how else could you have responded? You meant well..."

Where knowledge of guilt is unavoidable, the therapist may embrace other philosophies. *Love the sinner, hate the sin* can serve to distance the deed and preserve unconditionality of a sort. But this is not a true acceptance. The slight of hand involved is sensed as deception or rejection. The *bombu* nature of the person is divided.

Emma tells her therapist about how she cheated on her long term boyfriend, Phil. The relationship wasn't going well, and one night at a friend's house she met Tony, whom she had known a few years earlier. She had always been attracted to him, but he had married someone else. That night she discovered that his marriage had ended. At the end of the evening, managing to get some time alone with Tony, she swapped mobile phone numbers. The next day she texted him, and so arranged a meeting. Within a few weeks she was having an affair.

When Emma talked the situation through with her therapist, it was all too easy to understand the conflicted emotions involved. It was easy to see that things were not going well with Phil. If Emma had been happy in the relationship, would she have been tempted by the chance meeting with Tony? Surely, the relationship with Phil must be coming to an end anyway. After all, the couple were not married, and there was no contract to stay together.

Such a line of thinking can lead us to see breaches of trust in relationships as inevitable. Being true to the heart becomes the criterion for authenticity and hurt that arises becomes the necessary cost of living in such freedom. Yet, such a philosophy makes us victims of our passions, living our lives at the mercy of unconscious forces. As feeling beings, it implies, we have only to determine the true nature of our feelings to know which course is right.

Another line of thought might lead the therapist to view the situation as representing a tangle of possibilities which Emma was bringing to be unravelled. Did she want to rebuild the fraught relationship with Phil, or disentangle from it and explore the, as yet unexplored, possibilities of a relationship with Tony? What would the two relationships look like in five years time? Which might fulfil her ambitions for a home and family, expressed in earlier sessions? Which would make her happier? This latter response is more mechanistic. It does not assume an underlying preference or decision to already exist, but weighs the options and trusts that optimal outcomes will become evident.

Both these responses can be perceived as non-judgemental. One values feelings as the source of direction, the other measures outcomes. Neither judges the morality of staying in the relationship with Phil or starting one with Tony. Neither comments on the manner of her meeting with Tony. Each invited Emma to reach her own conclusion or uncover her motivation.

At the same time, neither response allows for Emma's knowledge of her own guilt in the matter. Although Emma refers to having cheated, a phrase that suggests her own feelings of having behaved wrongly, neither approach allows for exploration of this. The implication in each style of exploration is that guilt is not appropriate. The first suggests an amoral situation in which the heart must be obeyed, the second, equally amoral, gives the mind predominance. Incidentally, the former places the human as hapless victim of their emotions, the second as master of their world. Each implies Emma's innocence, or at least avoids the notion of guilt. Yet Emma's need may well be for confession. It may be that she needs to acknowledge her guilt publicly. She may need to explore her feelings of contrition. In practice too, the avoidance of the subject seems to make the guilt too awful to be acknowledged.

Though well intentioned, such responses detract from the person's act of confession. They build the web of self-justification. They cut the person off from the truth of his human nature. In this they collude with the deep dishonesty which keeps us all out of the light.

Paradoxically too, they leave an unease. In his heart the person knows the truth of his position. When the fault is not heard but diminished, a subtle message is transmitted. This fault is too awful to be admitted. The person is not acceptable *just as he is*. Only by slight of hand, by deceit, can he be fully appreciated and held.

Giving space for the person to tell the truth and recognise the reality of his human state, the therapist gives the gift of true unconditionality. This is the real manifestation of unconditional positive regard, the core condition Rogers posits. To offer something less denies the *bombu* nature of the person and so restricts their being to a charade of pleasantries. *Just as you are, really, just as you are.*

Contrition and love

For Westerners, the idea of contrition is often coloured by negative associations. Coming from a framework of ideas in which judgement and damnation have been given a central role, contrition is perceived as something that is enforced and linked to external coercion. In Buddhism, however, the frame of thought differs, and contrition is seen as a personal act of relinquishment. It is an unburdening of the heart. It takes us into a place of deeper personal honesty and integrity from which we can recognise the reality of our nature. It is the act of recognising responsibility and letting go of the pride and self-building that stops us from compounding the state of delusion.

The role of contrition in Pureland Buddhism is particularly poignant to Westerners. Not only do we discover that in this tradition we are not judged for our mistakes and wrong deeds, but also, the Pureland doctrine asserts that it is our *bombu* nature itself which brings us to Amida's grace. Despite our bottomless capacity to create trouble, we are still inhabitants of a benevolent universe. Life continues. The sun shines. We receive more or less those basic requirements of life and we are surrounded by beauty and love.

CONCEPTS INTRODUCED IN THIS CHAPTER
- Contrition as a gate to change
- The Tibetan Wheel of Life as a model of bombu nature
- Confession, contrition and freedom
- Quan meditation and contemplation as a prelude to contrition
- Unconditionality and contrition in therapy

CHAPTER NINE

PATACARA AND KISAGOTAMI: GRIEF, LOSS AND THE DISCOVERY OF FAITH

I have seen the jackals
Eating the flesh of my sons
In the cemetery.
My family destroyed
My husband dead
Despised by everyone,
I found what does not die.
(Patacara in Murcott 1991)

The loss of a child seems an almost unimaginable tragedy for modern women in the West.

The first few weeks of life we may creep to the side of our child's crib at night, listening to the miracle of breath, almost inaudible. We stand, holding our own breath as the infant seems to hover for a moment in silence between the worlds of life and death, then, we breathe again, relieved, as, with a little sigh, he resumes his dreams. We touch the tiny fingers and find them warm as they curl slightly at the contact. We put our cheek to the tiny face. We stroke the fine, soft hair. We fear, as we love with a pain that aches in our chests, that this infinitely fragile preciousness may slip away from us, back to whence it came.

But with the weeks our confidence grows.

Of course it happens. Babies do die. Most of us know people who have experienced such a loss. Sometimes the child becomes sick, or dies of an accident. Sometimes it dies unanticipated and unannounced, slipping away in the night. But somehow it seems, until it does happen, that it will not. In our modern world, it is an outrage to our technological complexity. Child mortality is low in our society.

India of the Buddha's day was different. Just as in India today.

In the Buddhist sutras there are two accounts of mothers who became overwhelmed by grief when they lost their children. These are not the only stories of mothers who lost children. It was, after all, not uncommon in those times. But these two particular stories tell us something about the way the Buddha approached the subject of bereavement and grieving. They tell of how he helped the two women to face their situations and to turn around the depths of their grief so that they lived spiritually fulfilled lives.

In this chapter and the following one we will explore the subject of a Buddhist response to grief and loss in some detail. We will take the two stories as examples and we will look both at the general understanding of the subject that can be drawn from them, and the particular aspects of Pureland that they illustrate. This chapter will focus on the experience of grief and loss itself, putting the stories in the context of the teaching of the Four Noble Truths. The following chapter will look at the Buddha's response and the way that a relational approach creates a bridge for the grieving person.

The Story of Patacara

Patacara was the daughter of a rich house in Savatthi. One day, she was due to be married to a young man of her own rank. She had, however, already fallen in love with a serving man of her parents' household.

On hearing that her marriage was arranged, Patacara decided to run away with her lover. One can imagine she was a strong and somewhat reckless character to behave in such a way at that time. Certainly she was greatly in love.

Patacara and her lover went some distance away and set up home together. After a while, Patacara became pregnant. Now, it was the custom in those days that when a woman was ready to give birth, she return to her parents' house for the confinement. Patacara asked her husband to accompany her on this journey, but he procrastinated, understandably unwilling to face his in-laws. Eventually Patacara set out alone.

When her husband found out what had happened, he set out to catch her up. Half way to her parents' house, however, he found her already in labour. The child was born by the road side, and, having no reason to continue the journey, the new family returned to their home without visiting Savatthi.

A second pregnancy followed a couple of years later. Once more Patacara's husband delayed. By the time they set out, this time together and accompanied by their first born son, Patacara was again nearing the time for the birth.

It was a long way to Savatthi, and night was coming upon them. As they were about to settle by the roadside a terrible storm blew up. Patacara was already in the early stages of labour and her husband set off into the woods to cut banana leaves to make a shelter for his wife and child. He was gone a long time. Patacara waited and called but to no avail. In labour and in the dark she dared not try to find him.

Patacara was desperately worried, wondering why he took so long, but it was impossible to follow him. It is terrible to imagine the isolation of the young woman at this point; her older son, merely a toddler, huddling by her side, confused and frightened by what was going on, and the new baby coming closer with each contraction of her labour. The rain and wind lashed at them, trying to shelter as best they could, as the birth grew imminent. Then the birth itself, the child slithering onto grass of the roadside, to be bundled to her breast under the travelling rugs, still wet from the womb. And still Patacara's husband did not return.

By morning she was distraught with worry and, with first light, was just able to venture into the woods to search for him. But here the horror of what had happened became clear to her. Patacara discovered her husband lying, dead on the pathway. He had been bitten by a poisonous snake and had died instantly.

There was nothing else for Patacara to do but continue on her way. She followed the road toward Savatthi, carrying the new-born baby in her arms, while her older child walked by her side. Before they came to the town, the little party reached a large river. Normally this would have been easy to cross, but with the recent rains, the waters were swollen and fast running. Fearing to set out with both children lest she lose her footing, Patacara, told her older child to wait on the bank while she carried the baby across. The little boy stood watching as his mother set out into the surging waters.

The middle of the river was deep and Patacara had to lift the new baby on to her head to avoid it getting wet. As she held the child aloft, suddenly a large bird of prey swooped from the sky and took it in its claws. Patacara screamed, but it was too late. Her baby was gone.

At this same point, Patacara's older son, hearing his mother's shouts, rushed towards her into the stream. Perhaps he thought he was being called. Perhaps he ran forward in a childish desire to protect his mother. Whatever, the current was too fast for him to stand and he was swept away before she could reach him.

Patacara again had no choice but to continue her journey to Savatthi. Now she was alone. It was of no avail to seek for her children. Both were lost. She could only return to her parents' home and hope that she would be welcomed back. Once there she might find the support and love to recover from her terrible ordeal.

But a further twist to the tragedy was still to unfold. As she approached Savatthi, Patacara saw a very large funeral procession that was taking place on the edge of the town. Several bodies were being taken to the charnel ground together. Patacara asked a passer by who was being cremated that day. It was a sad story, she was told. During the storm, a mud brick house had collapsed killing the entire family. Patacara asked the identity of the family, only to discover that those who had died were none other than her parents and brother.

At this point, it seems hardly surprising that Patacara went mad.

For a long time she wandered the country, her eyes wild and her clothes falling in dishevelment from her body as she wept and wailed. She was no longer aware of anyone around her. People would taunt her and throw clods of earth at her, but she just carried on unaware of their presence.

Then, one day Patacara happened to wander into the Jeta grove where the Buddha was teaching a large group of people. When the crowd saw the mad woman, Patacara, coming, they immediately tried to drive her away, but the Buddha called to her.

"Come to your senses" The Buddha said.

Hearing his voice, Patacara immediately became sane. Seeing her unclothed state, she sank to the ground. A man nearby lent her a robe to cover herself and she knelt before the Buddha, telling him her story.

The Buddha said "I cannot take your losses away".

And so, Patacara came to her senses. She understood that no matter what unfolded, her loved ones could not be returned. She saw that her distress and madness could not bring them back. She felt confidence in the Buddha and took ordination there and then.

Over the following years, Patacara no doubt continued to feel her acute grief, but as she practised in the Buddhist community, she became increasingly peaceful in her heart. One day she was washing herself using a bowl of water. She noticed the little rivulets of water that were falling on the dusty ground around her bowl. Some ran a little way along the earth before they disappeared. Others ran for longer. Some ran for a long way on the ground before they were soaked into the soil. In that moment she saw that this was just how it was with life and death. Some lives were short, others long. Others were a middle length. This was just the way things were. It was not predictable or changeable. She could not control the process that determined life and death. With this thought she became enlightened.

Patacara became a great teacher in the women's sangha, deeply respected for her inspirational presence. In this way, her grief became the source of her strength.

The Story of Kisagotami

The second story that I would like to share here is the story of Kisagotami. Like Patacara's story, this involves the loss of a child.

Kisagotami was also the daughter of a rich man from Savatthi. Unlike Patacara, however, Kisagotami married a rich young suitor, chosen by her parents. Everything seemed perfect and Kisagotami enjoyed her status as the wife of an influential young man. Her happiness and pride became even greater when very soon she gave birth to a son. The couple were full of joy at the birth. It seemed that life held everything for them. However their happiness was short lived, for the baby boy died.

When she saw her dead child, Kisagotami was stricken with grief. She could not accept that her son was dead. She was used to getting what she wanted, and had no experience of disappointment. Desperate in her grief, she wandered the streets carrying the dead body of her son.

Kisagotami would approach each person she met, asking if they had a medicine that would restore her son to life. People began to think that she had gone mad. As her search became more desperate, they drew away from her. She wandered, crying out to whoever she saw for help, but to no avail.

Eventually, however, someone told Kisagotami that the Buddha was teaching nearby and might be able to help. Weeping with joy and anticipation, she went to the Buddha to beg him to help her. When the Buddha saw Kisagotami, he immediately recognised the depth of her distress and saw that she was beyond listening to sense. Instead of trying to reason with her, therefore, he told her that in order to save her child she must go into the surrounding villages and get some mustard seeds from a house where there had not been any death.

So, carrying her dead child close against her, Kisagotami went from house to house begging for the mustard seeds. Everywhere she went, she found people willing to help her, but when she explained that the mustard seeds must come from a house where there had been no deaths, they sadly shook their heads. There was not a single house where a death had not occurred.

At this point, Kisagotami realised that she was far from being the only mother to have lost a child. Not only had every family had to face the deaths of numerous loved ones, but many had suffered far greater losses than she had. Death was everywhere. As she understood this, Kisagotami realised that she would have to accept that her son had died. There was no magic that could revive him. No medicine could bring back the dead. She was ready now to let his body go.

Burying her child's corpse by the roadside, Kisagotami went back to the Buddha and told him that she could not find the mustard seeds. She had learned the reality of impermanence and was ready to listen to his teachings. Soon afterwards, Kisagotami ordained as a nun in the women's sangha.

Transforming bereavement

When we look at the stories of Patacara and Kisagotami, we see two examples of the Buddha responding to situations of extreme grieving. Both women had suffered tragic losses. Both were incapacitated by their misery and were unable to come to terms with their situations. Both were overcome by their grief.

In modern circumstances each woman might have found herself coming under the support of mental health services, possibly hospitalised, and almost certainly receiving professional psychological support. In the Buddha's time, they wandered through society, finding diverse reactions from others, seeking answers, and despairing of hope.

Yet each of these women was to become a well respected member of the early Buddhist community, the *sangha*. Each was later viewed as a saint and became an inspiration to others. The Buddha's response to them, and their subsequent recovery to mental health and effective participation in the *sangha* is of interest not only because their stories are so compelling, but also because they maybe give us a sense of what a Buddhist response might be to those whose grief is overwhelming. It may show us ways that we might best be of help to others in such circumstances.

Grief and loss are part of the human predicament, and we are all likely to experience a number of major bereavements in a lifetime. Yet this is not something we get used to. The loss of a loved one can challenge us to our depths. Some losses are particularly painful and may throw us into despair and distraction to the point where we feel crazy. Loss is *dukkha* at its most raw. The experience of grief can take us into that heart splitting place where the psyche fights for breath beneath the weight of what has happened. The impetus is to escape, to hide, to create barriers to knowledge of what has occurred. Habitual defences and respites crumble and we grasp at new sources of relief. We look to others for support and yet often feel unheard because the enormity of our feelings seems unutterably unique.

Different societies respond in different ways to the grieving person.

Some bring the person into the heart of their social network for support. Others leave the bereaved person in a position that is more isolated. In modern Western society awareness of the processes of grief have become more psychologically orientated and, although, for many, friends and relatives still offer day to day support, when a person is severely distressed the responsibility for providing more intensive support is often seen as lying with professionals. The professionals involved may come from a variety of disciplines. Many professions have an interest in grief work: the priest or spiritual carer, the bereavement counsellor, the social worker, the funeral director, the legal advisors to name but a few. Each has their role in the aftermath of a death and each interacts with the bereaved relative or friend.

Responses will include practical and psychological elements, depending on the profession concerned. Practicalities and emotional support will, of course, be inter-woven, since no professional can ignore the impact of the death on the mental state of the bereaved, nor, indeed, the psychological implication of the practical changes a death can bring about. The funeral director and the lawyer have often learned a range of skills in offering emotional support as well as functional services. The bereavement counsellor will often check that their client is getting financial advice and is eating regularly.

As far as the emotional and psychological needs of the bereaved person are concerned, person to person concern is always paramount, although it may be expressed in different ways. The establishment of an empathic, supportive relationship is likely to be the basis for any bereavement counselling and can be immensely helpful in all relationships around this difficult time. When Irene died, the supportive presence of community health services prior to her death, and the local funeral directors afterwards gave us immense comfort. Such people provide an anchor when the normal activities of life are thrown into turmoil.

The time of bereavement is a time when the need for human warmth and concern is paramount. Beyond this basic need for the presence of another, however, depending on the understanding of the psychology of loss and grief which is held, the counsellor may see different priorities in their approach to work with the bereaved. It is therefore useful to look at the examples given above and see if we can identify some specific points which might guide us in helping those who are grieving. What might a distinctively Buddhist approach to bereavement look like? Can we study the Buddha's responses in these and other stories from the sutras, and also look at the implications of his teachings for situations of loss, and thereby gain insight that is useful to modern situations of grief?

Impermanence rushes upon us

When we read the stories of Kisagotami and Patacara, the extremity of the women's grief hits us. Each faced sadness that was terrible and frightening. Each woman was apparently driven mad by her loss. Each lost touch with reality in the depths of her grief.

Even in a world where many children died and such losses might be expected, for Kisagotami and for Patacara the pain of bereavement was overwhelming. Patacara was so caught up by her loss that she no longer noticed that her clothes had fallen from her body. Kisagotami believed that her child could be cured even though he lay dead in her arms. The reality of the situation was too painful for each to bear and each sank into delusional thoughts. It is hardly surprising.

As we have already seen, the teaching of the *Four Noble Truths* suggests that when we experience affliction (*dukkha*), as when we are bereaved, the common response is to grasp onto things. This grasping is the primary factor in the creation of our state of delusion. Feelings of grief arise (*samudaya*) and we have an immediate impulse to escape from them.

Unbearable sadness overcomes us and we try to assuage it through things that we find comforting. We look for distractions, often initially through something that engages our senses. Sometimes we even find physical pain preferable to the mental pain of grief. We search around, compulsively grasping at anything that will bring relief, whether this is through venting the feelings in weeping and wailing or through burying them in mundane activity. These are the roots of craving and attachment. In acute grief, there is an impulse to find something, anything, which will mask the intensity of emotion.

The teaching of the Four Noble Truths outlines three levels of clinging (*trishna*). Our first impulse is to bury our feelings in sensory experiences, distracting ourselves with things that will fully occupy our attention. Sensory distraction can take many forms. We may indulge the senses through food, sex, entertainment or other compulsive consumption, or seeking sensory modification through alcohol or drugs, keeping the attention occupied with distractions so that it does not wander back to the painful areas of life that would otherwise concern it. Pleasant distractions can hold our attention when the concern is not too great, but when we are experiencing acute emotional pain, they are rarely sufficient. In situations of severe grief the special meal or the light weight television show are simply an irritant. They are not compelling enough to be a distraction.

When pleasurable sensory experiences are not sufficient, sometimes a person will instinctively turn to unpleasant sensations as a means of distraction. Unpleasant sensations have the capacity to mask painful emotion, partly because they also express some of the pain involved. In some societies it is, or has been, seen as a normal part of mourning to inflict injury on oneself. Beating the breast, tearing the hair and face, and even more extreme forms of self-mutilation are seen as an appropriate expression of grief. How much such behaviours express the extremity of feelings of grief and how much they provide distraction is hard to say, but their importance in the process of grieving in some societies is evident.

Our society does not generally encourage such behaviours, yet the instinct to mask emotional pain with physical pain is still there. Not infrequently, people find themselves physically hurting themselves at such times. Biting the hand, hitting the head, pulling on the hair are all common gestures of sudden grief. Somehow the physical pain gives comfort when a soft embrace does not.

At a more dysfunctional level, emotional pain commonly lies at the roots of self-harming behaviours. Many people who self-harm, whether cutting themselves deliberately, burning themselves, or inflicting physical damage through drugs, food abuse, induced vomiting or other behaviours, have in their background early losses. Grief can persist, a deep sad note in the psyche.

Sensory distractions are immediate. They are acute responses to an acute situation. They can create powerful defences against the full impact of a loss. They can allow expression of grief in indirect ways, or they may even provide a more direct way to express what cannot be put into words. It can be easier to express such feelings through physical enactment. Behaviours become a metaphor for the unspeakable. At the same time, the activity of sensory engagement distracts the bereaved person from their pain.

When sensory distractions are repeated over a period of time, however, eventually the distraction fails to hold the distressed person's attention sufficiently. The immediacy of the initial response is softened and the sense-pain no longer impacts in the same way. Human senses habituate quickly. Our sense organs are built to recognise changes in our environment. We stop seeing or hearing the familiar and let the repeating stimuli sink into the background of our awareness. New focuses of attention are needed to create the same effect.

Also, with the continued repetition of the behavioural pattern of sensory distraction, other processes start to happen. The repetition of the behaviour ceases to be new, different and distracting, but rather becomes part of the fabric of our experience. It moves from stimulus to ground in our attention. It stops being our focus and becomes part of what we take for granted.

This process of habituation to particular behaviours, stimuli and objects of attention, moves us into the second level of escape described in the teaching on *samudaya*. At this point a person starts to identify with the habit energy associated with the activity of distraction. They think "this is me, I do things this way", and, in identifying, they draw comfort.

The phase of identity formation is central to a Buddhist understanding of psychology. It is the phase of *bhava*, becoming. As we have already seen, many of the key teachings of Buddhism relate to the way that experience is subverted and the delusion of a permanent self is created. Repeating habitual patterns of behaviour and perception, we create a sense of persistent identity. This sense provides us with a feeling of security. The experience of *dukkha* faces us with the reality of impermanence. The repetition of behavioural patterns creates an illusion of personal permanence. It gives an illusion of immortality.

The self cannot envisage its own end and thinks of itself as a special case, so thus, in small everyday madness, we imagine that we will not die. This is the *bombu* mind. We inhabit a world viewed through our conditioned perceptions, which are in turn conditioned by our self-invested mentality. We re-write the story of our lives and create a mythology to justify and hold our self-image.

Sometimes, however, this sense of self breaks down. The created view is not enough to ward off the experience of profound grief. Sometimes our sense of self crumbles when we face extremes of pain, and we fall into even deeper withdrawal from life. In the last stage of samudaya, non-becoming (*abhava*), when clinging to identity no longer works, we move into the final phase of attachment, and cling to self-destruction and oblivion.

The experience of loss: identity under threat

Our sense of identity protects us from the pain of everyday life. It may be a refuge at times of loss and bereavement, but it is also at times of great loss that our identity is most under threat. At the time when we might cling most strongly to anything that could offer a sense of permanence, the roots of our sense of identity are also most threatened. This is because the sense of identity is not only an internal psychological construction. It is also supported by external factors in our lives. The things that we do on a daily basis that form the ground of our experience create the sense of stability on which this sense of self is based. With a major bereavement the fabric of our daily lives is torn apart and the external supports to our sense of self disappear with it.

For Kisagotami, a sense of her own identity was already important before she experienced the loss of her child. It is said that she was very conscious of the status which her good marriage had brought her. As a woman she lived in the reflected honour of her husband's social position. Recently she had also achieved new status by becoming a mother, something of great import for an Indian wife. Being the mother of a son was particularly important in the culture of her time. As a mother she gained new respect and took on new social duties, cementing the role as a compelling source for identification. She was a mother first and foremost. This was her identity.

Kisagotami's sense of self thus depended upon her child. It depended on the continuation of his life. Without her child, she ceased to exist as a mother. When her baby died, her identity would also inevitably have died. Clinging to the illusion that her dead baby would live again, perhaps she also clung to the image that she could still remain a mother. Accepting his death would have meant a return to the insignificance and uncertain status of the childless. Thus, she carried on acting as if her child was not dead.

For a mother to let go her dead child is to let go the foundations of her identity as mother. Part of the grief of returning home after a still birth or after the death of a child is that sudden, unwanted return to childless days. The labour ward, the paediatric intensive care unit, the hospital emergency department; all have their dramas in which the mother is a central player. Painful as the process may be, during the crisis that surrounds the death of a child, there is no shortage of role. Returning home, the house is suddenly very quiet. The empty cot becomes a vulgar reminder of the child who is no longer there. The toys in the playroom become pointless objects that evoke painful memories. The breast, full of milk, swells in engorged futility. The former mother feels hollow and groundless. Being a mother depends on having a child. The two identities are mutually conditioning. No mother, no child. No child, no mother.

Some women form new identities out of their grief. A life halts at the moment of the loss and with it the old identity dies too. They become the bereaved mother, continually, as Patacara, living in the misery of their loss, as Kisagotami clinging to the dead child as an indicator of their identity. Sometimes this is extreme enough to create madness, but such identification with the bereavement is not always an unhealthy process. Bereaved mothers have often transformed their role to positive ends, becoming campaigners or fundraisers, fighting for a better world for other children or adopting new causes to love and nurture. Such transformation of the energy of grief has brought much good to the world down the years.

For others the loss gapes like a hole and life feels pointless, echoing with memories that become thinner with the years.

In this way, losing identity is, ironically, an aspect of bereavement. Ironically, for it is at just such a time of loss that we are most likely to seek comfort in our sense of who we are. For Kisagotami, letting go her child had this unconsciously driven double edge. She lost her child and with him she was bound to lose her identity. Bereavement is like that – a loss not only of our loved one, but also of our place in the world. With the death everything is changed beyond recognition. In her grief Kisagotami unwittingly clung to her last link with motherhood. The processes of clinging are, for the most part, beyond our knowledge and control. In her madness she clung to her identity, even though its ground was gone. Her delusion extended to preserving her child as a support to that identity.

Grief and oblivion

Whilst Kisagotami, in her bereavement, clung to her identity as a mother, for Patacara there was no such illusion. She had not just experienced the loss of one child, but had lost all the significant others in her life. When a mother loses a child, she generally still has husband or partner or other children, parents, friends or siblings. There are other relationships that hold parts of her identity and other familiar companions to support the process of grieving. For Patacara the loss was so great that she could not hold on to any part of her previous life or identity. Her world was completely destroyed. She had nothing to preserve her sense of who she was. Without the defence which her sense of identity gave her and without a feeling of her place in the world, her psychological state fell into the lowest level of *samudaya*. The oblivion of madness overwhelmed her.

In the state of sensory distraction, the object world creates distractions for the senses. The things that surround us fight for our grasping attention. As we become habituated to this process, the objects that have held our attention fall into the ground of our awareness. They become the furniture of our world, supporting our sense of identity. Our attention compulsively seeks out further objects to reinforce and elaborate our sense of self. We are held in the grip of this process.

When self-building fails, interest in the object world fades and we sink into a dark, and often featureless space where the only comfort is oblivion. Just as the giant star implodes into a black hole, sucking all around it into its impenetrable centre, so too, the ego eventually reaches a point of implosion where external comfort and communication no longer provides solace, and we fall into silence and dark isolation.

Most grieving people need to withdraw a bit. Grief is like that. The lioness licks her wounds in a dark area of the forest and howls for her lost cub. The swan whose mate was killed by hunters hides in the reeds, no longer interested in foraging for food. Such withdrawal is often transitory, a pulling back of life for healing to occur. At such times our sense of identity no longer matters. Only the grief pervades. Gradually we will return to the world and rebuild a life, but not yet.

The loss of identity that occurs in the state of *abhava* is a process of closing down and backing away from life. As such it is very different from the process of release that might accompany the relinquishment of self structures. If self-structures could be released, one would embrace life in a complete and joyous way. The depth of despair that characterises the state of *abhava* is, rather, a state of disconnection from life.

The state of *abhava* is the state of abject misery: the drug user who simply seeks oblivion, the suicide who really wants to die, the depressed woman who cannot bring herself to leave her bed in the morning. In this state, a person reaches the bottom of the psychological slide. They have given up the will even to create identity. For some psychosis is also a retreat into *abhava*.

Not all psychotic states are so. Some are still more grounded in the area of identity formation. Grandiosity and the fascination with distorted worlds which many people in psychotic states fall into all speak of self-based delusion.

The person trapped in the psychosis of *abhava* wanders disconnected from the world or huddles in corners without communication. Like Patacara, they become oblivious. They cut off completely.

All the significant people in Patacara's life had gone and with them she had lost her ability to connect with the world. She had also lost all the others who she loved and who loved her. She had lost those who supported her sense of identity. She had nothing left to hold onto and so let go of her hold on reality. She lost faith.

The bombu grieves

Grief is common to human life. As Kisagotami discovered, there is no family in which death does not visit. *Dukkha* is everywhere. The Buddha recognised this truth. He saw how inevitably we fall into fruitless attempts to escape from the pain these losses bring. He saw that the whole process whereby we create mental structures to ward off suffering creates a relentless accumulation of attachments that in turn cause us misery. We try to escape, but in doing so we simply compound our suffering.

These responses are not pathological. They are just the ordinary, unenlightened state. They are not to be overcome through some clever psychological manoeuvre. Nor are they to be resisted. They are part of what it is to be human, reflections of our nature as loving animals. If we do not love others, we do not experience loss. As ordinary beings we live betwixt the joys of community with others and the sadness of its breaking. Life is bitter sweet.

When disaster strikes, the public outcry is often for counsellors. Victims of rail crashes or earthquakes, house fires or bomb attacks are offered psychological support. This may be helpful to some, but it does not take away the need to grieve. To read some newspapers, it sometimes seems that in the vogue for crisis management, by offering counselling, the professionals will cure all distress. It almost seems as if the public believes that counselling will somehow undo the trauma that has occurred. If counselling can just be offered quickly enough, often enough, the pain will somehow disappear.

Human support can help, but not by diminishing the pain of loss. Rather such support can help us go through the experience, facing the grief more completely and crying the tears in company. Through contact with another, the bereaved person does not slip quite so far into the pit of withdrawal, but nevertheless, they will unwind their own process of gradual accommodation to the new situation.

Thus is our *bombu* nature. Life holds us, torn between our pain and our escape. Longing for others, yet fearing the loss of their love, we try to connect and then pull back into familiar self-deceptions. Fragile and vulnerable, as humans, we seek to bury our knowledge of impermanence with the fruit of distraction. We seek to cover our naked grief and fear with the clothes of identity. We are seduced by the dark spaces of oblivion. This is what it is to be human.

CONCEPTS INTRODUCED IN THIS CHAPTER

- A review of Buddhist teachings on the experience of grief and loss
- The stories of Patacara and Kisagotami and examples of women struggling with grief
- Levels of grieving: sensory distraction, self creation and oblivion

CHAPTER TEN

ENCOUNTERING OTHER: LIFE BEFORE DEATH

Today the sun shone
And something inside me cried
Not a loud, screaming, desperate cry
Such as brings help
But quiet, almost unnoticed

It is our bombu nature to withdraw. Our karmic history and our psychological defences lock us into the ordinary mindset. We are ordinary beings.

It is usually frightening to face death. No matter how prepared we think we are, we don't know how it will actually be when we are told that we are terminally ill. Nor do we know how we will react when we hear news of the imminent death of a loved one. Nor do we know how we will grieve when they die. Each death is different. Each piece of news hits us in a different way. As time goes on, it seems that more and more people around me are dying. I suppose it is obvious. Sickness, old age and death are ever present. This is *dukkha*. But even in middle age, several of my close friends have already got sick and died. They were still young women; young to die.

Each time, the process has been unique. Yet each time, there have been familiar stages in the emotional unfolding, both for my friends and for me. An emotional rollercoaster, we have swung through hope and hopelessness, fear and tenderness, bravery and grief. There have been times of profound honesty and other times when we have hung onto impossible hopes. Things to be said, and things left unsaid deliberately. The struggle with death and bereavement is probably the rawest experience we have as humans.

One way and another, loss and death inevitably hit us. We try to avoid them, craving for permanence and stability. We fear the inevitable traumas of life. We try to avoid knowing this, and deceive ourselves so that we can pull back into a safe world of predictable phenomena, predictable because they are under our control. But deaths still come.

The process of everyday living involves many small experiences of grief. Greater losses happen too. Unskilled in facing such bereavements we flounder round in our misery, searching for ways to be with it, or hiding ourselves in all the processes of delusion.

In the previous chapter we recalled the stories of Patacara and Kisagotami. These two women faced terrible tragedies. They also went on to become important members of the Buddha's following. What changed them and helped them to transform their grief into a source of strength? How, as people in the Buddha's company, did they cope? How did he help them?

This chapter will look again at these two stories and look at how the Buddha responded to the two women. What was it about his response that changed them? How did the meetings transform their grief into the ground from which they grew spiritual strength and insight?

Grief and religious life

When we reflect on the lives of Patacara and Kisagotami, we are impressed by the ways that they turned around experiences of profound grief and became significant members of the sangha. Their situations had been so painful as to be unbearable, their mental states deranged. How was it that they came to be leading members of the women's sangha, looked up to by others?

Most people feel that, if they experienced losses of the scale which Patacara experienced, they would never really get over the grief. For some people this is true. Some people do stay locked in grief, their lives blighted.

For some people, however, grief can be the soil from which a new life grows. People who have been through terrible traumas can subsequently create lives which are far more worthwhile than they might otherwise have been. Grounded in the knowledge of life's fragility, touched by the pathos of death, the person often becomes more dedicated to living well. The encounter with death stirs up existential questions that may lead to religious or spiritual searching. The tenderness of caring for the dying leads people to devote the same tenderness to others, and to find new expressions for the welling up of love that is so often released in those last weeks and days.

Early encounters with death seem a common feature the lives of many great saints and teachers. The Buddha's mother died after his birth. Honen's father died when he was a young boy, and it is likely that Honen's decision to enter the religious life arose out of this experience. According to one account, it was his father's dying injunction that he should not pursue revenge but seek the Dharma. Shinran also was orphaned at an early age and it seems likely that his experiences of loss turned him towards the a Buddhist life. More recently, the Chinese Zen master Xu Yun, who lived from 1840 - 1959 dedicated much of the first half of his 119 year lifespan to a pilgrimage in atonement for his mother's death, she having died in giving birth to him (Luk 1988).

Such examples, and there are many more, underline the significance of an encounter with grief and bereavement in the spiritual path. Indeed, it is probably rare to find a person who has dedicated their life to a religious path who has not some experience of loss among the motivating factors in their search. Karen Armstrong (Armstrong 1981) speaks of the still birth of a younger sister, and of her other sister's near death a few years later as significant steps in her decision to enter a convent.

Not everyone who experiences loss, however, turns that experience to positive ends. As we saw in the last chapter, the first impulse most commonly felt is to retreat. Grief is *dukkha* and our most immediate reaction to dukkha is to seek comfort in familiar distractions and in creating the sense of permanency which can put at bay the feelings, at least for a while. What makes the difference? Let us return again to the stories of Patacara and Kisagotami.

Encounter and grief:

For both Patacara and Kisagotami, meeting with the Buddha brought a profound change of heart. The Buddha was someone who, by all accounts, had tremendous presence. He was able to form a deep connection with people, and to relate on a level which made an immediate, profound impact. For both Patacara and Kisagotami, meeting the Buddha was an experience of a special kind of personal contact. This contact brought back a sense of reality. Up until the point at which they met him, each woman had been lost in mental anguish. They had been unable to relate to other people because their grief had held them in a personal trap. The Buddha's intense attention was able to break through this. He was able to reach them.

The personal world insulates us from others. Our psychological defences are walls against those intrusive communications that might destroy our mental configuration. When we are raw with the misery of grief, we are not usually ready to let others reach us psychologically. Only when we feel safe in another's presence do we start to open up. The Buddha made people feel safe. He could be challenging, and indeed, with both Kisagotami and Patacara he did not hide in pleasantries. Nevertheless, he offered a solid encounter which they must have sensed was trustworthy. In this he provided a stable reality with which they could relate. He himself was the reality outside their self-world which they could not resist and did not need to hide from.

The man, trapped in the avalanche, catches the rope that has been thrown to him by the rescuer, and thereby escapes. The lifeline thrown from the higher ground beyond the snow drift creates the possibility of release. Embedded in snow, the trapped man cannot easily achieve escape through his own effort. He has no firm ground on which to stand. He stands on slippery ice. Nothing is there to hold him while he struggles to create his own salvation. Only the man on firmer ground can offer the rope.

Through the Buddha's intervention, each woman experienced human warmth from beyond the morass of her pain. It was that personal connection with the Buddha which pulled them out of their misery. The Buddha established real psychological contact, helping each woman to see beyond the limits of her grief and to experience relationship. Instead of remaining focused on the objects of the past, they found themselves relating to another person in a direct, meaningful way which could not be subverted into the grief story. The Buddha's direct approach encouraged them to re-engage with the world.

Being open to others is not easy when we are grieving. It is probably not even something we can do as an act of will. It was the Buddha's special presence which broke through. Just as Shinran describes Amida breaking into a person's heart at the moment of *shinjin*, so too it is the gift of others' presence that brings us back into the light.

Changing the behavioural patterns of grief

When we are stuck in the extremes of withdrawal, getting out of that state is not easy. The self-structure is not simply maintained by distortions of views. It is maintained by our behaviour. The process is dynamic whereby we construct our sense of reality. Action and perception inform one another. We act in particular ways in response to our circumstances and it is our actions that create our mental structures or *samskaras,* the fabrications of the mind. These mental structures create the sense of reality we inhabit. They shape our view and our choices, our responses to other people, and hence influence their responses to us. Thus we go round the circle. It is because we repeat the same behaviours that we continue to build self.

Once we have become stuck in particular behavioural patterns, we tend to play out those same patterns repeatedly and to create the circumstances so that we can go on doing so. Repetition has a strange way of comforting. The small child rocks itself to sleep, and asks for the familiar nursery tale. The young adult seeks out comfort foods that remind him of childhood treats and winter evenings as he returns to his student lodgings. The explorer whistles a familiar tune as he steps out into new territory.

But, comforting as it is, too much repetition can limit us. At times it can become problematic. We are all *bombu.* That is unchangeable. Sometimes, less often than we like to think, there are specific behaviours that can be changed. Breaking the pattern is not easy though. Sometimes behaviours get out of control. The compulsive hand washing of the person who suffers obsessive compulsive disorder, or the food daily rituals of the young anorexic girl, are patterns of repetition that have got out of hand. When a person is locked into habitual patterns of behaviour, breaking the compulsion is difficult. It is rarely something that can be addressed simply by an act of will.

Rather change may come about through a change of circumstances. The circumstances of our lives are conditions that support the patterns of behaviour in which we engage and the mental processes that underlie them. A change of circumstances can therefore indirectly produce change in those processes. Since the habit patterns depend on certain conditions remaining constant, these conditions can be disrupted.

The Buddha's direct manner and special presence enabled him to create authentic relationship with the women in spite of their level of withdrawal and craziness. This ability to achieve encounter, even when the other person was severely withdrawn, disrupted the habitual patterns of relating of each woman. Patacara and Kisagotami each lived in a mental confusion. This was in part supported by the conditions which the other people around them provided. People around them unwittingly contributed to the continuation of their madness. They did this in different ways. Typically, people responded by ignoring the crazy women. Sometimes they responded by treating them as mad. If they spoke with them, they tried to reason, but to the women their arguments seemed unconvincing.

It is easy for someone who is already locked into a crazy view of the world to subvert such responses into supporting conditions and to continue seeing things from that viewpoint. Part of the nature of psychosis is that the self-story has become so compelling that everything can be woven back into it. Whatever happens, it can be viewed in some way that reinforces the story rather than challenging it. It takes something very special to disrupt this process.

So, if one is stuck in paranoid thoughts, those who reason will be perceived as trying to trick and to deceive. The thought will follow that such reactions should be resisted. The speaker will be ignored. So the paranoid thoughts continue to re-produce themselves.

If one is stuck in grandiose thoughts, then if somebody tries to argue, the thought arises that the critic lacks true perception and cannot understand the situation properly. Here the reaction might be to feel that the other person should be pitied. Again, the thought patterns reinforce themselves.

Thus the fantasy world remains intact and is supported. Breaking into it requires a different kind of relating. It requires real psychological contact.

On the occasions when the Buddha met Patacara and Kisagotami he managed to engage with them. His response to them was different from that which they had encountered elsewhere. His tremendous presence related to them. His response was not tinged with personal agendas. It got through to them in a way others had not. It did not play into their expectations.

Such patterns are not confined to severe mental states, however. We all fall into these patterns. Whilst the person with whom we are talking accords with our expectations, there is a sense in which we don't really see them. We relate in ways that are programmed, behaving in line with our habitual and automatic reactions. Such responses come easily. We do not really engage. It is only when somebody surprises us by not responding as we had expected that we might be jolted into reassessing what we are saying, but in most cases when this happens we retreat. We terminate the engagement and shift our attention to other things so that we do not have to unsettle our sense of how things are. In the normal course of things our habits are not challenged. We can guard our sense of identity.

Counter-part roles and real others

When we are caught in a strong personal story, it is not just the sense of self that is distorted. In practice, the sense of self mostly falls into the background of our awareness. We do not spend our time thinking "I am this sort of person". Rather we find that what in Buddhism is referred to as the *self* manifests in the perceptual world which we inhabit and in our behaviour. Perception is conditioned by the mental structures. The conditioned, *bombu* mind sees things through a frame of habitual and self-invested view. This distorted world fulfils expectations because it is seen in a selective way.

The effect of the conditioning process is that we see things in ways that support the status quo of our minds. Our sense of the world is relatively constant because perception conditions our mental state and that mental state in turn conditions perception. It is a circular process and remarkably stable. We can maintain the same world view for years, and many of us do.

This distortion can even happen to the degree that the person feels no sense of self at all. Locked in a world of distorted perceptions, she may feel completely empty. This kind of loss of identity is not a loss of self, however. It simply means that the self is only manifest in the self-world it has created.

Whilst we are locked in a self-world of this kind, we are not divorced from our surroundings however. Our behaviour and life choices affect our environment so that real changes happen around us. Thus we create the conditions for the real world to actually respond to us in accordance with our self-image. This happens in a number of ways. Firstly, we create practical circumstances around us. We go to places that we identify with, we buy certain artefacts: books, furnishings, pictures. We cultivate a lifestyle. We surround ourselves with all sorts of paraphernalia that speaks to our self-image.

Secondly we invite other people to support our self-image. We subtly invite them to treat us as we perceive ourselves to be. This does not necessarily mean we get treated the way we want to be treated. It is more likely that we will be treated the way we expect to be treated. If we feel lonely, we may want people to be friendly, but our behaviour may prompt them to keep us at a distance. If we are frightened of people, we may want them to be kind, but our behaviour may lead them to take advantage of us. We reject people whom we expect will dislike us and seduce others whom we anticipate may take advantage of us. We are not usually aware that we are doing this.

Each of us lives in a world populated by our preconceptions. We have experienced certain patterns of relating with others through formative relationships and this informs our relationships with friends, acquaintances, those in authority. All our relationships have elements of habit. We feel comfortable with people whose style is familiar to us, whether because they are similar to us or because they are similar to other people we have known. To "not know how to relate to someone" causes us anxiety. There is a need to have some sort of blue-print.

One aspect of this is that our sense of identity is tied into roles that have counter-parts in the roles of others. We feel comfortable where there is a good fit. Just as the mother needs the child in order to maintain her identity, the teacher needs a student and the bully a victim. Counter-part roles are part of our psychological environment. They support our sense of self. We therefore spend much psychic energy in seeking out others who can play them out. We feel our way into relationships that mirror our expectations and we subtly invite others to adjust to fit our needs, in the nuances of interaction as well as in the gross interpretation of the role.

While we subtly invite others to conform to our needs, at the same time, without realising it, we adjust to fit the other's self-needs. All this happens mostly below the level of awareness, but it drives our relationship decisions and shapes our interactions. It also limits our capacity to really engage with the other person in a direct way. In the extreme it may lead us to have completely false views of the person with whom we are interacting. We may only see the expectations which we are projecting onto the other and, in doing so, mistake these projections for reality. One day we may say "I never really knew him."

While we view others in distorted ways, those others help us to perpetuate our delusions by playing out the roles which they have been ascribed. The unspoken, unconscious bargain that happens in human communications tends to assist us in maintaining our preconceptions and habits of relationship. As we seek out people who can play complimentary roles to ours, we invite others to take on our counter-parts.

Patacara and the counter-part relationship

For the person who is as strongly caught up in a deluded world as Patacara was, the process of withdrawal from real psychological contact with others is completely beyond awareness. Patacara had become mad, and in doing so had gradually developed a mad identity. In as much as she had any self-view, she probably even saw herself as mad. She became "Patacara the madwoman". People around her saw her that way. They responded by shunning or abusing her. Through their words and behaviour they told her she was mad. These responses kept her mad identity in place.

Patacara's behaviour invited particular responses, which then held her "mad" identity in tact. Her crazed behaviour persisted. Her identity was never challenged and she remained locked in her disturbing self-world. Her situation was so awful, the grief so painful, that only by such a drastic withdrawal from reality could she carry on living at all. Her madness came as a relief. In it she lived without facing the real circumstances of her life. Maybe for a time this was for the best.

When someone is severely ill, it is sometimes necessary to induce a state of coma so that the body can be cared for in intensive care through artificial means until it has healed enough to cope once more with ordinary life processes. A temporary state of madness cuts off the normal functions of living, giving space for the mind to heal. Perhaps this is what Patacara needed.

Once in the state of madness, however, conditions occur that tend to maintain the state, perhaps beyond its usefulness. In falling into such a state, Patacara created the conditions for it to be perpetuated through other people's responses. Her madness persisted.

When the Buddha refused to allow his followers to send her on her way, Patacara's sense of herself as a madwoman was challenged. The Buddha, a great teacher, was treating her as a sane person. He took her seriously.

Commonly, Patacara was rejected. This is what she expected. If the Buddha had sent her away and thrown abuse, Patacara would have gone, still cocooned in her mad identity. Instead, the Buddha called her to him and spoke in a gentle but firm tone. He did not play the counter-part role as others had. She had to listen, and she had to listen from her sane part. His unexpected concern broke her out of her crazy world and into contact with another human.

This story in itself gives us pause for thought. How far do modern ways of relating to the mentally ill hold them in their non-functioning role? There are always some ways of responding that will maintain the status quo and other ways that cut across it. Playing the counter-part role to another person's script may provide a feeling of support and normality to the troubled person, and in some circumstances this can be helpful. It does not, however, necessarily allow real psychological contact to be established.

For the person who has been mentally ill for a long time there is a danger that "being mentally ill" has itself has become an identity. This means that the therapist or support worker, as people associated with that illness, become part of the scenery of the person's personal world. They become counter-part roles to the person's illness, tending to maintain that mental state rather than challenging it. This means that if the support worker or therapist responds in predictable ways, maybe, for example, using predictable text-book therapeutic responses, the sick person is likely to stay locked in their habitual world. The stereotyped response prevents real communication from happening because it is predictable. It may seem more caring, but it feeds into the expectations just as much as a hostile or rejecting response might.

Creating conditions for encountering otherness

When a person feels overwhelmed by the loneliness and tragedy of their loss, it can feel as if the whole world died with the loved one. Life loses its meaning and the bereaved person inhabits a world of shades, drifting between life and death and longing for the oblivion of death to take them away too.

At such times, human contact is of great importance, but it is not always easy to establish. The person is locked in isolation, their whole being disconnected from life by all the mental processes that arise in response to the pain of loss. As we have seen in the last chapter, these processes can take different forms and may involve the defensive construction of a personal world which attempts to preserve something of the old life in tact, or they may be simply a withdrawal from life, an unvoiced wish to follow the one who has died. Encounter with something outside the personal world can break through the misery of isolation that has grown around the rawness of the loss.

Then, if someone is able to establish a relationship in which engaging deeply is possible, this can be a reminder that there is still a world of the living to be connected with. Human relationships can still be meaningful and the possibility of loving again has not died with the death of the beloved. When grief is overwhelming, the feeling of loss pervades awareness, and the person may lose touch with the ongoing presence of life. They cannot feel the joy of daily experience and see only the pain of what is not there.

When the Buddha spoke to Patacara, his presence and lack of personal agenda meant that he was able to meet her on a level that is rarely present in human conversation. His deep authenticity offered to Patacara a lifeline out of her personal hell.

Encountering the loss

People respond to deaths in very different ways. The same person may feel quite differently about different losses. Reactions are unpredictable and can be disturbing. It can be just as distressing to feel nothing when a close relative dies as it is to feel overwhelmed by grief. The loss can feel very raw, or it can seem completely unreal. This unreality is common in the early stages of grief and may sometimes continue indefinitely. The experience of grief may be blurred by fantasies that the person has not really gone for good. The bereaved person may continue in ordinary life, getting on with the day to day tasks, and keeping cheerful, as if nothing has happened.

The Buddhist teachings suggest that it is our nature to try to avoid knowledge of *dukkha*. As *bombu* we tend to disperse feelings that arise in distractions and attachment to mundane sources of support. These attachments become compelling for us. If we can experience the loss in a more authentic way, this may help to break the isolation we have created. But facing the reality of the loss is not easy.

The Buddha's response to Kisagotami helped her face the reality of death and the permanence of her loss. He invited her to search for the mustard seed, knowing that she would fail to find a house in which death had not occurred. Others had tried to reason with her, but he did not. He sent her out with a practical task to do. In this response, the Buddha behaved in an unexpected way. He broke the pattern by not giving the kind of response that Kisagotami expected. Others tried to argue and she had learned well how to resist them. The Buddha's response caught her off guard, maybe even called her bluff a little.

The fascinating part of the account of the Buddha's conversation with Kisagotami is that apparently he was inauthentic. Certainly, his intention was for her good. His response can be interpreted as skilful means (*upaya*), but this, as we will see, seems to miss the point a little. The Buddha was willing to be inauthentic in order to help Kisagotami to see the reality of her situation. He created a situation in which Kisagotami directly experienced the impact of death on many people. This created the conditions for her to discover for herself that *dukkha* is everywhere. He knew her search would fail.

Not attacking defence structures

When he failed to respond to Kisagotami as others had done, the Buddha was not playing into her script. Kisagotami clung to her dead child while everyone around her tried to take the child away. She clung to motherhood even though the child was no longer alive to be cared for.

When others tried to persuade her to give up the dead baby, Kisagotami felt threatened to the depth of her being. Her identity as a mother was under siege on all sides. People begged her to let the child's body go and this compounded her distress. Her identity as a mother, which was after all the only source of comfort she had, was endangered. This happened at just the time when she felt least able to cope with further changes. Although it was irrational, she clung on to her forlorn hope that the child might live, or at least that she might go on being a mother to it. People saw the futility of her position, as, at some level she must have herself, and chided her, begging her to see sense, but this in itself made her cling more strongly. We are rarely willingly loose our hold on that which is being wrenched from our arms.

How often does our very attempt to change someone result in them clinging even more desperately to the behaviour we would have them let go of? How often does the former wife lament that her ex-husband, who infuriated her with his idleness in the house, is now an enthusiastic cook? Or the former husband curse his mouse-like ex-wife's newly found confidence? Such is human nature.

In the well known story of the competition between the sun and the wind, the wind tries with all his might to blow the traveller's coat from off his back. Buffeting the traveller from every side, he grows increasingly frustrated as the man simply buttons his coat more firmly. The sun in his turn shines benignly on the traveller, warming him. Only then does the man smile and take off his coat to enjoy the summer afternoon. Direct attack is not always effective. Gentleness may outweigh strength. People do not relinquish their defences easily.

The Buddha did not respond to Kisagotami in the same way as the other people she met. He did not force her to continue to defend her role as mother. Instead of confronting Kisagotami with the reality of her situation immediately, he put her into a situation in which she let go defences spontaneously. By showing love and not directly challenging her distorted world, he, paradoxically, undermined its foundations. No longer needing to justify her motherhood to herself, Kisagotami became open to whatever experiences befell her. Of course, she may also have found a new role for herself as the comforter of others. Often the recovery from grief involves rebuilding our sense of identity in a new way that matches our new situation more appropriately. Whatever, when she found herself surrounded by the reality of other people's losses, Kisagotami was open to seeing them.

To Patacara, the Buddha's response was a direct challenge. He told her that he could not take her grief away. To Kisagotami, the Buddha's response was one that challenged her defences. He did not, however, do this by a direct attack. This would have been counter-productive. The truth came to her naturally as she found herself in situation after situation where the universality of loss became real.

Inspiration and learning to trust again

The story of Kisagotami is often explained in terms of the Buddha using skilful means (*upaya*). His intervention, which at one level was to draw her into a deception, is perceived as a wise move, intended to show Kisagotami the folly of her position. There are further dimensions to this initial

encounter, however. So far Kisagotami had found only rejection and disbe-
lief. People tried to reason with her or send her on her way. Understandably,
they felt powerless to deal with her deluded hopes. They could not manage
to get through to her.

When Kisagotami met the Buddha, he did not play the counter-part
position to hers. More than this, firstly, he took her seriously. Secondly,
gave her hope. At one level this hope was false, but at another level he had
real hope for her. In his response, the Buddha deeply manifested his love
and concern for her. This caring response to Kisagotami *was* authentic. The
Buddha felt a great deal of hope for Kisagotami. This hope later proved
sound, as she became an important member of the women's sangha. But the
Buddha knew Kisagotami would not understand this hope if he expressed
it verbally to her. He did, however, convey it in his manner. His actions
spoke the truth even though his words seemed to offer false hope.

When someone else has confidence in us, we feel it and are deeply
affected by it. No doubt Kisagotami initially believed that the Buddha was
confident because he knew her baby would be cured. Otherwise she would
not have set out on her search. As it became evident that she would not find
the mustard seed, however, her faith in the Buddha did not diminish.
Something in his manner inspired her with confidence in him, which was
deeper than simply in his instruction. This confidence reflected his
confidence in her. He had confidence that she had the capacity to face the
grief. He also had confidence in a benevolence which transcended even life
and death. She caught that feeling of confidence and grew in faith.

What the Buddha offered to Kisagotami was love. What the Buddha
offered to Patacara was love. His ability to love completely without
personal taint was remarkable. What he offered was true unconditionality.
Such love touches deeply. It inspires. It teaches us to trust again.

A real person to person meeting may be what a person who is in the depths of grief most needs, but such a meeting can be painful to engage in for both the bereaved person and the person who is supporting them. When we open ourselves to the bereaved, we open ourselves to the universality of grief. With the pain of one loss, we feel the pain of all losses. Loving completely is like embracing a thousand knives. The Buddha loved in such a way. As *bombu* we can only love imperfectly. Yet we can still offer others something precious. We can offer the best contact we are able.

Taking a wider perspective

The experience of loss often leads us to withdraw from others. Our world becomes centred round the feelings of grief, and sadness pervades everything. Life becomes short and feels lacking in meaning. Our world becomes small. We feel self-preoccupied and lose interest in things beyond our immediate orbit.

For Patacara and Kisagotami, the Buddha helped them to step back into the world. Both women saw the experience of personal loss within a wider context. This shift of perspective came as a result of their encounter with the Buddha. Each woman was able to let go the sense of isolation and at the same time moved beyond her sense of individualistic entitlement to grief. Loss is universal, the Buddha told Patacara. Loss is universal, Kisagotami discovered as she went from house to house. Each woman discovered that she was no longer a special case.

So both women experienced the shock of discovering the reality of their losses. Their experience brought them face to face with their bereavements. This was an experience of encounter. It was an encounter with loss. It was an encounter with the Buddha. It was an encounter with the love he expressed in his words and actions. It was also an encounter with the wider world, with the universality and finality of death and with the afflictions of others.

The meeting between the Buddha and each of the women was both inspirational and shocking. It was certainly transformative. Encountering reality created a crisis for each woman in which she had to let go of her previous patterns of relating. She had to break out of her defensive strategies and change her habitual responses. In doing this, each was able to find a more authentic relationship with the world. Both women had to live what was true. All this became clear in their encounters with the Buddha.

The role of faith

Facing grief is an act of faith. It involves moving out of defensive ways of thinking and behaving, and being open to the real situation. When Kisagotami and Patacara met the Buddha, each of them changed in their own way. Each faced the reality of their situation. They stopped relying on their old defences and put faith in the Buddha.

The teachings on *samudaya* suggest that we need to unhook from the objects of our attachments. Unhooking from these, a person reaches out into the unknown. This act of letting go is an act of faith. It is therefore not an act we can pre-determine. We cannot plan to have faith. Faith comes as a gift. We cannot receive a gift if we are trying to control its nature. Faith is a response to an encounter with something beyond our self-world. For Patacara and for Kisagotami faith came from their meeting with the Buddha. Who embodied those special qualities of love, reliability and compassion that inspire faith. He inspired them to let go of their grief.

No longer clinging to unreality, the two women gave up the defensive patterns of behaviour which they had built up around their grief. Kisagotami buried her dead child. Patacara let go of her crazed grief. This process of letting go happened through their faith in the Buddha. In taking this step of faith, both women stepped onto the spiritual path, and through this new found faith, they found the energy of their grief naturally became reinvested in new outlets. They both ordained and became important figures in the Buddhist sangha, and themselves became inspirational to others. No doubt this was a reflection of their experiences.

A personal account

Of the period following Irene's death, my husband David writes:

> *My mother's death was an unwelcome and profound shock. A week after diagnosis, early one mid-May morning, she was gone. Cancer took her. That week was extremely intense. The death itself was blessedly peaceful and somehow intensely full of life and love. She squeezed my hand and went away into the silent land. I wept profusely then and afterwards and as that fierce storm blew itself out a cloud settled over me. Though tears came less frequently, gloom prevailed and it was hard to find a spark of joy in the everyday things of life or even in those occurrences one knew, but somehow could no longer feel, to be of special beauty or delight. The cloud persisted through all the summer, autumn and winter, the closing seasons providing a touch of camouflage but nothing really disguising the fact that the whole experience had been overwhelming. I continued to function, but I was not fun to be with. Grief enclosed me. When I did feel a surge of energy, it was anger with fate or at the human lot which is mortality. Through Christmas it persisted. I observed enjoyment but did not participate in it and on her early January birthday wept again. A desolate winter.*
>
> *When I reflect upon this now what impresses is how vulnerable we are. What did I have from all my years of religious training to provision me for such a pass? Certainly I had no immunity. The pain of grief may even have been more acute. Is it not at such times that our convictions are tested and the efficacy of what we have practised is put on trial? If*

I can claim anything from my years of exposure to Zen and so forth, then it is not any ability to ensure that suffering not arise, but rather the underlying faith that enables one to bear it. Gloomy I remained. And, again, there is another test. What is it that finally lifts such gloom? Is it the application of technique of prayer or meditation, mindfulness or precept? I cannot affirm so from my experience. What shifted me from my place of melancholy was rather an exposure to the new grief of others. Asked to perform the funeral of an old friend, I met with all his relatives and though I did not realise it at the time, with hindsight I can see that this somehow changed me. It was as though it was their turn now to weep and mine to stand aside and yield place to them.

In one sense the change was abrupt; in another not. I still weep from time to time. The cloud has not totally forsaken me even now two years on, but the capacity of joy returned that day. Looking into the eyes of those others and meeting recognition through the shared circumstance of loss was half the remedy. Knowing that their loss was theirs and mine was mine and that, despite the parallel and recognition, a difference and mystery remained, was the other half.

My mother's death has changed me in a manner that it is impossible to imagine ever reversed. Not only do I suffer the visits of that cloud from time to time, but I appreciate how it is for others in a different way, especially the elderly, the frail and the sick. I am, as yet, none of these things, but accompanying Mother through her passage at life's end has been a dreadful yet also irreplaceably wonderful gift.

CONCEPTS INTRODUCED IN THIS CHAPTER

- Encounter as a way beyond grief
- Counter-part roles and real encounter
- Faith and inspiration in encounter

CHAPTER ELEVEN

NEMBUTSU IN A GRIEVING WORLD

And, in the wide-eyed half-sleep of a nightmare I wonder
When you are grown, children,
Will you still go and find deserted woods?
(from *Blackberry Week*, poem written1985)

The world is struggling. No book on religion or psychology should ignore the context in which we are now writing. The loss of a loved one brings grief, but the prospect of the loss of human life as we know it brings grief beyond knowing. Our planet is probably facing changes over the coming decades that it has not faced for billions of years. The human race is facing challenges that go beyond any we have known to date. I do not write this lightly.

Maybe we are in the dark days at the end of a civilisation that has cracked itself open with over-consumption. As the Romans and Mayans before us, our degenerating society grows fat while barbarian forces muster on the surrounding heights. Maybe our cities and our technologies will stand as lonely memorials, crumbling in the desert sand, like Ozymandias' fallen image. Or maybe less dramatically, life will simply fade into an increasingly difficult adaptation to harsh conditions.

In his most recent book, *Revenge of Gaia*, James Lovelock adds his voice to the growing circle of scientists and environmentalists who paint a picture of a grim future. Climatic changes are now almost universally acknowledged, and in the last few weeks the Intergovernmental Panel on Climate Change has concluded unequivocally that these changes are the result of human activity. We can no longer hide and procrastinate in scientific debate. Yet humans show little real inclination to change their ways. Although we now re-cycle cans and buy lead free petrol, we do not make the scale of changes that would really make a difference. Optimistic mythologies suggest that in the face of impending disaster, humankind may at last learn to pull together and share resources, but already wars are breaking out that seem to have their roots in a struggle to control diminishing oil reserves. On past record, it seems more likely that we will go down fighting each other to the last man. Such is our folly.

Technology advances. Wisdom, as always, is often lagging behind. With new resources, our potential to destroy is awesome.

When I was sixteen, in the early nineteen seventies, a programme was broadcast on television called *Due to Lack of Interest Tomorrow Has Been Cancelled.* I remember, incidentally, that it was broadcast on BBC 2, and that our family did not possess a television that could receive the signal properly. Our set, the first the family had owned, was not designed to operate on the new channel. How much broadcasting and technology has advanced in what feel to be so few years! I sat by the crackling screen, its picture broken into fragmented images and listened in tears of frustration and anxiety as a catalogue of pollutants and environmental threats was outlined. In thirty years, the message seemed to be, our planet would be uninhabitable.

The following day, my friends and I, who had all watched the programme, met in the school-yard, horrified by the picture it painted of the situation we were inheriting. Feeling a need to do something, we sought some means to speak out, to influence others, to cry out for our planet and our futures. A school project gave us the license to do this in a practical way. We began a survey.

"Do you believe that in thirty years we will all be dead from pollution," we asked person after person, first within the school, then in the high street. Many responded "yes".

I'm glad to say that thirty years have passed since then, and life continues. Indeed, it does not feel so different. Change is more subtle than I naively imagined. When I was twenty, we read that breast cancer was common, so we should be vigilant and check our bodies regularly, since one in twelve of us were likely to suffer from it at some point in our lives. The other day, I received a leaflet that told me that one in nine women can now expect to discover the same disease. Despite the many advances in treatment and health monitoring, new problems arise and old ones exacerbate. The causes of increasing cancer rates are not, for the most part, identified. Some of the increases that are reflected in the current statistics may be put down to better detection rates of early tumours, but, although these account for some of the improvements in survival rates (early detection means a better chance of survival) these changes do not explain the real increases in overall numbers of cancer diagnoses. There are many possible factors and causal links in a disease that develops over time in the population at large are notoriously difficult to prove. We are all immersed in an environmental soup, subjected to chemicals and radiation, climatic factors and patterns of lifestyle, any of which may cause tissue damage.

Despite our ongoing faith in progress and in scientific discovery, we find ourselves constantly overtaken by events. Prediction is difficult, and sorting the valid from the plethora of concerns that are raised rarely seems possible except in hindsight. Global issues vie for prominence. Will the inevitable tragedy come through nuclear war or global warming, through pandemic diseases or exhaustion of resources, chemical poisoning or eradication of natural environment? Over the years, concerns have risen and fallen on the scale of perceived probabilities. We are still here despite my adolescent fears. Things do not necessarily unfold as we imagine.

Relating to the planet

For religion and psychology, then, the challenge is to find a mode of discourse that addresses the reality of our situation. It is not enough to simply explore the imagery and experiences of our planetary relationships as tools for enhancing our own psychic structures. For centuries humans have used the natural world as a metaphor to explore the mind and its workings. Religion has used the imagery of nature to reflect the human experience of the divine. We have seen many examples in this book. Now we must see it for real, as something that is not ourselves, but that exists in all its own fragile beauty and horror. We must appreciate its otherness, and its existence in and of itself, independent of our will.

The bombu nature of humans is such that we keep pulling things back into our personal psychic orbit, making them objects that support our self-structures. Unless we recognise this tendency and make allowance for it, we will approach the abyss still squabbling over our personal entitlements and virtues. Human-centricity is hard to eradicate. One problem is that we all share an interest in maintaining it, so we hardly notice as it becomes the theme of our discourse.

How we view our environment is of great importance to our ability to bring about change, or indeed to survive as a species. Our view is conditioned by the stories we cling to, and it in turn conditions our actions. The human-centric view has been particularly pervasive in the West, since the Judeo-Christian tradition gave man husbandry over all the earth. It made him the farmer, the keeper of animals and tender of crops. It gave him the harvest and the right to determine land use. It gave him authority to proclaim God's will. This view of man's relationship to the planet is not itself necessarily contrary to the needs of environmental preservation. As God's vassals, we are called to offer responsible management of the dominions entrusted to us. Sadly, modern man seems to have forgotten the responsibility whilst, like a wayward child, gorging himself on the fruits of the garden.

Other models offer different perspectives. In her book, *World as Lover, World as Self* (Macy 1991), Joanna Macy examines a number of models which have been implicit in the thinking of different religions. These models reflect some of the different attitudes which people have taken, which create different responses to our habitation of the planet.

In particular, Macy identifies four types of relationship to our world. These images are: *World as battlefield, World as trap, World as lover, World as self.* In the remainder of this chapter, we will look at these models and at how they offer mirrors for the Pureland perspective. We will look at how these models offer approaches that can contribute to our understanding of the environmental challenges that face us, and how we might go beyond them in finding a response to the impending crisis.

World as battlefield

Macy's first image is that of the world as a battleground. This battlefield can take a number of forms as it is a well used image. One way in which the metaphor is used is in describing the world as a place in which the battle of good and evil, of right and wrong, is fought. People take the side of good and attempt to defeat the bad. It is not a great step from this to the all too common situation in which divine right is attributed to certain views or peoples. Sometimes it has led people into striving for a better world, but more often to the justification of religiously rooted conflicts. Since Macy wrote in 1991, the idea of divine right as a justification for war seems only to have grown. Democracies are even more certain of their divine status than monarchies. Having been appointed not only by God but also the populace, they add moral high ground to their credentials. Religious wars have been with us through most of history, but current events once more underline the folly of so many human religions. As human artefacts, religions have *bombu* nature. Religious strife is part of our heritage in the West.

The idea of the battlefield is not always taken literally. The image can also be used to describe an internal process in which the practitioner experiences opposing forces within his or her own psyche. A religious devotee's strength and integrity may be tested against the trials and tribulations of daily life in a world filled with temptations and obstacles. He *fights the good fight* and defeats the spiritual foe. Such imagery can be supportive of spiritual accomplishment. It can rally the person's energy and focus their intention, but it can also lead to a feeling of personal authorisation, which can in turn create an arrogant and one-sided approach to tricky situations. It plays into the ideal of personal perfection and creates a sense of needing to vanquish others in its pursuit.

I was recently talking with a Christian activist about the concept of human rights. We were discussing the difficulty which some Buddhists feel with this concept. This was a strange idea to the Christian, who saw justice and rights as appropriate religious concepts. The problem from a Buddhist point of view is that the idea of *rights* is embedded in a way of thinking that uses non-Buddhist concepts. It is rooted in a set of ideas in which there is a supreme judge of right and wrong. Together with the associated idea of *justice,* it comes with an implicit assumption of a supra-human system of reward and punishment meted out by an ultimate authority.

This is not to say that Buddhists do not believe in the kind of actions that others would associate with upholding people's rights or maintaining justice, but the concepts themselves are not Buddhist. The distinction is partly linguistic but is not meaningless. The concepts used in any debate introduce an extra layer of meaning that subtly influences the process. In this case, they bring the discourse into the arena of the battlefield model. The terminology of *rights* and *justice* is rooted in a way of thinking that includes fighting for rights and overcoming wrong (evil). Fighting for people's rights is perceived as a worthy cause. Indeed, to my Christian colleague, the idea of rights was firmly associated with conflict

Of course, many Buddhists use such concepts without thinking about the implications. They can be useful in dialogue. Really, though, they belong to the Western Judeo-Christian tradition and they bring with them certain aspects of that way of thinking which may cloud our understanding of the issues involved. For Buddhists, thinking in these terms muddies our philosophical base, and, importantly, leads us into ways of viewing the world and others which are inconsistent with the central values of our tradition. Most Buddhists in the West have grown up in the Judeo-Christian tradition and it is all too easy to import ways of thinking and seeing the world, translating Western attitudes into Buddhist language but failing to make the leap into a truly Buddhist understanding.

Talking with the Christian activist this became apparent. "I think it's important that people get angry" she said, "it's only when they get angry that they get out and do something."

This gave me some pause for thought. Indeed, how many Buddhists do get out to protest against the things which are wrong with society? When they do turn out to give witness to atrocities and oppression, what motivates that action? Do most Buddhists subscribe to a mode of thought that leads to inactivity and withdrawal? Perhaps Buddhists should get more angry. What about those who do get out and voice concerns? Do those who do take a more activist stance simply revert to their Western roots to find their motivation through anger and righteousness?

I was recently in Florida in a week when two executions were scheduled to happen in that state. As it happened, one of the people with whom we were staying was a defence attorney for prisoners on death row. It was one of the prisoners that she was representing who was scheduled to die.

During that week, I witnessed the dreadful and complex process unfolding. The death penalty and the processes surrounding it raise many questions and as a non-American I had the privilege of being somewhat outside the system. I also had the privilege of not having grown up in a country where capital punishment is part of the collective mindset.

Others involved in the situation had a variety of views. My friends and most of those I met were actively opposed to the death penalty. They felt shame, anger and helplessness faced with their nation's policies. Others living in the state clearly had different views. They supported the death penalty as part of the system of justice. Many were vocal and cited their religious affiliations as justification for this view. Each group felt right to be on their side.

The execution itself was, of course, the state carrying out its own version of justice. The men had been tried and sentenced in accordance with the law. Their sentence was, according to that system, a just outcome of the crimes committed. In the view of many, it was the conduct of God's will. God and the law are on the same side.

The judicial process is, of course, open to challenge. One line of response to the situation was to try to operate within the law and to demonstrate that *in this case*, execution would be unjust. As a defence attorney, my friend's main task was to look for chinks in the prosecution case, whether in the original judgement, the evidence presented or not presented, or in the technicalities of the legal process itself.

Another line of defence was to question the rights and wrongs of the execution process. In the event, one execution was delayed on a plea that the means of execution was inhumane because the drug currently used to kill the person in executions was believed to cause unnecessary pain. This verdict threw ripples right across the country as every defence lawyer looked to see whether a similar plea might be made for their clients. The last minute stay was not, however, without cruelty. The message to stop the process came through at the point when the man was already strapped to the execution table with a line inserted in his arm through which the poison would be administered. I could not help feeling that this timing itself was intended to inflict maximum suffering on the prisoner. This view seemed to be confirmed when the second prisoner experienced a similar last minute hold in his execution. In such events, it seems apparent that the veneer of justice overlies more aggressive motivations which give rise to acts of bitterness and revenge.

During the period before the scheduled execution date, I joined a group of people assembled before the state capitol buildings. This was to be a press conference, in which the lawyers and families of the men on death-row made their cases. The situation felt almost surreal to me as an outsider. I listened to the daughters of one condemned man; young women who seemed like any other ordinary good-hearted Americans, begging for clemency for their father. The situation seemed to echo the televised pleas of hostage families in far away places. It was hard to believe that in a Western democracy citizens would need to implore their own government for mercy in this way. Was this justice in action?

Among the crowd, a number of Buddhists gathered. This group, I was told, assembled at the capitol building whenever there was an execution. Sometimes their presence was framed as a silent vigil, marking respect for the person whose death had just been administered. Other times, as on this occasion, it provided silent support for those fighting to save the condemned person. I stood with them, observing and adding my presence to the group opposed to the killing.

Was this a fight for justice? What motivated us? Was anger the force that encouraged us to stand against the state's decision? Looking into my own heart, I cannot say. Certainly anger and frustration arose. I am, after all, *bombu*. Predominately though, I felt deeply saddened and touched in ways that stay with me. I recall the sight of the prisoner's daughters, one strong and calm in her statements to the cameras, warm in her manner as she shook my hand and thanked me for coming, the other distraught and weeping quietly in the background. Beside their grief, I felt almost intrusive on their situation. I also felt compellingly involved in their lives.

And yet, life is complex. If I had met the victim's family, heard their distress, might I have understood in my heart their longing for revenge and justice? Might I have felt it too? In a more recent case, where a man, who had been on death row for three years, was released because the evidence against him proved to be false, the family of the man he had been falsely accused of murdering were full of anger. They wanted someone to die in return for their loved one's death. Having a man in jail, any man it seemed, was better than knowing there was an empty cell and no release from their grief. Who could say that in their place we would feel otherwise?

The human mind longs for certainty. It creates gods who can pronounce and distinguish right from wrong, good from evil. Having an angry god on ones side gives justification for righteous anger. A god who judges can be a tyrant but if this is the price for certainty of salvation, it is often deemed worth paying.

The battlefield model is not particularly compatible with a Buddhist perspective. Buddhism does not think in terms of justice and human rights, but rather in terms of causes and conditions, karma and skilful means, *bombu* nature and universal compassion. Recognising we are *bombu* means accepting the confusion that our minds create, as well as their nature to judge and condemn others and to mete out punishment.

If we adopt a value system based on notions of justice and rights, this holds implicit within it an idea of a higher source of validation and retribution. Embodied in the image of God, these values suggest a source of ultimate accountability, which is then mirrored in the ways we approach one another. In the service of such a god, we feel entitled to discriminate between good and evil, to condemn certain acts and seek justice from the perpetrators. We have a sense of right on our side and on the side of those we view as wronged. We take the power to inflict punishment or to forgive.

A Pureland perspective, on the other hand, is grounded in recognition of our own fallibility. We see others' mistakes and wrong doing in the light of our own wayward nature. We may speak out and criticise, and we may demand changes, but we do so in knowledge of our own weak moral position. Our basic attitude is one of fellow feeling, not superiority. Even when we condemn a situation or activity, the Pureland position suggests that on reflection we should recognise that this too is *bombu*. Our judgements come out of our simplistic perception and our human fears and they probably lack wisdom.

There are many difficulties in the battlefield model when we look at it in the context of planetary disaster. At worst it leads to complacency and even anticipation. God will save His own. The destruction of the planet is part of the prophesied Armageddon. On a lesser scale it can invite attitudes of blame and self-righteousness, entitlement and superiority. On the other hand, the passionate pursuit of justice has led to great social reform, the liberation theology movement and many other benefits.

Above all, though, change must require co-operation, and national boundaries no longer offer any protection against the kinds of difficulty we are facing. Climate change and pollutants do not discriminate. Righteous or villains, we are in the situation together, and only together is there any hope of change.

World as trap

Whilst some religious perspectives see the world as a place where good and evil struggle in a perpetual battle, other views locate good outside the worldly realm altogether. The world is to be escaped and its temptations rejected. Salvation lies in the mortification of the earthly body and withdrawal into spiritual concentration.

Such a view suggests a hierarchical arrangement in which the spiritual realm is placed above the earthly state. The spiritual task is to transcend the physical realm and enter the higher state that is separate from earthly existence. This view is very common in Western thinking. It is quite pervasive. God is perceived as inhabiting a higher realm. The Eternal and the spiritual are seen as *not of this world.*

Among Buddhists it is not uncommon to find attitudes that are world denying. Fear of attachment is often is feature of this attitude. The temptations of worldly satisfactions are seen as pernicious and liable to lead the practitioner to abandon his practice. Worldly troubles are distractions that will unsettle the calm mind and draw out angry or distressing thoughts. I have met Buddhists who do not read the newspapers or watch the news because they fear it will disturb their peace of mind. I have met Buddhists who prefer to live in remote places and limit their company to avoid the temptations of city life.

The other-worldly focus of such Buddhists is often justified on the basis that the practitioner believes that practicing non-attachment involves withdrawing from everything. This is a mistake. As Macy says, it is based on a misunderstanding of the teachings.

Some of my fellow Buddhists seem to understand detachment as becoming free from the world and indifferent to its fate. They forget that what the Buddha taught was detachment from ego, not detachment from the world. In fact the Buddha was suspicious of those who tried to detach themselves from the realm of matter. (Macy 1991,p7)

As we have already seen, in the Buddhist understanding, attachment or clinging arises from our fear of the inevitable afflictions of life, of *dukkha*. It arises from the compulsive need to create stability, to build the self and the self-world. It is an attempt to make life controllable and permanent. Such attachment itself stops us from really engaging with the other.

If we look on the spiritual realm as above and outside daily life, our spirituality will probably be other-worldly and detached from engagement. If we perceive it as enmeshed with our daily activity we are more likely to see engagement with the world and its troubles as a potentially spiritual activity. Just as in all religions, some Buddhists are other-worldly in their orientation, whilst others are more orientated towards this world. The hermit tradition is rich and valuable, but in the present age there may not be time for the luxury of withdrawing into the hills. There is urgent need for action. Finding a spirituality that embraces the world is vital if we are concerned to work for the needs of others and of the planet.

The hierarchical view of the spiritual is very widesread. Sometimes it takes a form in which the deity sits above the world in judgement. Other times the practitioners themselves aspire towards a higher realm. In the West hierarchical spiritual models predominate and these bring with them a set of assumptions that are very pervasive. I only realised just how conditioned to this point of view I was myself when I was asked to read a few paragraphs from a soon to be published manuscript by Professor Takamaro Shigaraki in our Sunday service. In this piece, the Japanese Pureland priest and academic outlined the difference between the worldly view of things and the spiritual perspective. In his view, the worldly perspective places phenomena (and particularly people) in a vertical, hierarchical relationship to one another, whereas the spiritual position, in his view, places them in a horizontal relationship; in a relationship of equality. Thus the vertical axis of human intent intersects with the horizontal axis of Amida's world. Amida meets us on an even playing field.

I read the passage aloud. After I had finished, however, I was corrected by David, who was leading the service. Without realising it, I had accidentally switched the concepts round, attributing the horizontal axis to the earthly, human level, and vertical axis, to the spiritual dimension. This is the way our Western minds are conditioned to think. All too easily we fall back into thinking of God in Heaven above and mankind on earth below.

In the Pureland perspective, Amida is not perceived as "on high". Although there are pictures and images that place Amida above the practitioner, a figure appearing in the sky, the true position of Amida according to the iconography is *far away to the West* in the Pureland. Amida is on a level with us.

Traditionally, Amida is the source of our support, alongside us, but in the writings of Gisho Saiko sensei, who was also a Pureland priest, and an academic, we find Amida placed beneath us. Besides being a priest, Gisho Saiko was also a psychologist, deeply influenced by the ideas of Carl Rogers. I had the honour to meet him a couple of weeks before his death in 2004, when I visited Japan with my husband, David. He was very keen to meet us and arranged a series of events around our visit. A delightful man, he embodied the quiet, self-effacing respectfulness of a great teacher.

Saiko's contribution to psychological theory includes a model for the helping relationship, which sees the therapist providing the core conditions for therapeutic change, derived from Rogers' model, within an ambiance of his or her own faith in Amida (or, for non-Pureland therapists, one might say in the greater power). In this model, the presence of Amida, as the healing force behind the therapy, lies beneath the two human participants. The therapist, having faith, is aware of being held by Amida's power. This presence supports both therapist and client. Gradually, through that faith, the client too begins to open up to the healing presence.

What is interesting here is that in Saiko's conception, Amida is not a power above the participants looking down and bestowing spiritual aid, but rather a ground in which they can grow; a sea in which they float. In this, his view is not so different to Rogers' faith in the core conditions and in the self-actualising tendency, but Saiko's model, based on his Pureland faith, locates the source of strength in Amida not inside the self, but outside the two participants and supporting them from beneath.

The image of being held by Amida, supported from beneath by the personification of altruistic love, is also seen in the poetry of one of Pureland's *myokonin*, a man called Saichi. The *myokonin* is a person who is greatly treasured in Pureland tradition. He or she is perceived as the ideal example of the practitioner. Literally "shiny people", *myokonins* are lay people of simple faith. Theravada places as its ideal the arahat, or enlightened person, Mahayana focuses on the bodhisattva, or infinitely compassionate one, Pureland on the other hand looks to the myokonin as the embodiment of its practice. (One can note here that in Pureland both the bodhisattva path and the path to enlightenment are seen to follow from birth in the Pureland, so they are not ultimately excluded, but they are not seen as attainable by ordinary practitioners in this life)

Saichi was a carpenter who lived in the first half of the twentieth century. He wrote many poems inspired by his faith in Amida, writing them on shavings of wood that fell from his plane as he worked. Many of these expressions of faith were found and collected. In one of them (quoted by Rev Taira Sato in his paper on Saichi's work which he presented at the Eleventh European Shin Buddhist conference in August 2004), Saichi writes:

The sea is just full of water;
there is the seabed that sustains it.

Saichi is just full of evil karma;

there is Amida that sustains it.

How happy I am!

Namu-amida-butsu, Namu-amida-butsu.

(MYOKONIN SAICHI NO UTA VOL.1, P.188)

This delightful poem expresses Saichi's great joy at recognising his bombu nature and realising that his salvation is not dependant on eliminating it. The poem illustrates beautifully the Pureland view of contrition and salvation. We recognise our ever-present layers of delusion and wrong-doing and through knowing our nature, we feel great release. We do not need to struggle to be something we are not. With all our failings, we still know that we are held.

In this poem, as in Saiko's model, we can observe that the Pureland imagery places Amida not just alongside, but actually beneath the practitioner. As the sea-bed supports the ocean, so too, we are supported by Amida. In as much as we are humble in our self-assessment, so too, Amida is not the figure of high authority who looks down on us.

Pureland offers an imagery and methodology that cuts through our pretence, allowing us to let go of some layers of aggrandisement. We do not need it. We develop faith that we are held regardless of our actions. If our actions improve it is out of gratitude and our letting go of fear and competition. Because we are not judged we do not have to put on a performance. We do not have to fear the world and its temptations. We can tread a middle path between compulsive indulgence and ascetic withdrawal. We can embrace the world in all her beauty.

World as lover

If the world is not to be avoided or escaped, perhaps it is to be embraced.

In identifying a third common religious position, Macy explores the image of the world as a lover.

Many religious writings describe the religious experience as a relationship of great intimacy and sensual richness. In some writing, the expression is specifically directed towards the earth itself. Macy cites a number of examples of religious writing of this kind that are quite erotic in their tone. Many of these are from Hinduism but some come from other religions and from non-aligned spiritual writings. Sensual aspects of religion, often expressed in ecstatic and mystical religious experience, are found in many traditions, including Christianity, Sufism and some Jewish traditions.

In Buddhism, the erotic strand of spiritual experience is commonly rejected, as in many traditional branches of the religion, sensuality and sexual desire are seen as a distraction from practice and a manifestation of attachment. There is an exception to this, although Macy does not refer to it, as we do find the erotic expressed in the imagery, and sometimes practice, of *tantra*. In *tantric* Buddhism the power of negative forces is harnessed in spiritual practice. What is otherwise eschewed, becomes the focus for religious activity. Through the symbolism of *tantra*, the coupling of deities and celestial beings comes to represent the union of great forces that act upon our lives. In practices that invoke such imagery, the power of these cosmic couplings is brought into the spiritual practice and used to fuel spiritual transformation.

The ecstatic or eroticised physicality which is found in religious experience of these kinds can take different focuses. Sometimes it is directed towards the deity. Other times it is turned toward the relationship with the earth itself. In relating to the *world as lover*, we may experience a deeply emotional enjoyment of majestic scenery, a passionate involvement with the forces of weather and oceans, and an intimate entrancement with the mysteries that surround the unfolding of life itself. Feelings of awe arise in response to the grandeur of scale on which cosmic changes occur. We tenderly wonder at the fragility life in all its tiny forms. We honour and celebrate our environment, and weep for its destruction with the pain of the bereft partner abandoned by the beloved one.

Although the image of the lover is erotic, other ways of relating to the earth seem to hold similar levels of personal intimacy. To Macy's categories, I think we could add the idea of *world as mother*. This image is widespread, has something in common with that of the lover, for it evokes feelings of human closeness and points to a special, personalised relationship. The idea of Mother Earth occurs in many different societies and cultures. Intimate to a point that closely approaches the erotic without ever, except in circumstances where the nature of the relationship is deeply betrayed, crossing the boundary into sexuality. The processes of gestation and birth draw the energies of sexual expression into a generative process, the act of creation. The generous sensuality of motherhood, the intimacy of nurturing the child, the pride of relinquishing the offspring to adulthood and independence, the joy of watching future generations going forth into life, all reflect in microcosm the human relationship to the planet. But what wayward children has mother earth conceived!

Motherhood provides a window to our nature as humans, but also to the greater processes of life itself. For many it brings a sense of having participated in something that transcended the ordinary realm and having been taken into a different space where the greater picture could be glimpsed. To experience pregnancy and birth can be to experience the spiritual dimension. In a short article I wrote in 2002 for an online journal, I described my own experience of motherhood in the light of spiritual experience.

Giving birth to my first child, it was perhaps the most profound spiritual experiences of my life so far. Reaching down and grasping in my hands that slippery, taut little form as it emerged between my legs, I made contact with life in a way I had never before. No one needed to tell me of immortality. Here was the miracle of life sucking at my breast, the link to past generations and to the future, another small vessel in the process of unfolding evolution. No airy concept, this was the reality of life passing through my body, of my body and yet beyond my body, linking me into the greater, the process that has unfolded from time begun, and will unfold till time done. (Brazier 2002)

Pureland Buddhism is perhaps more able than many forms of Buddhist thought to embrace the image of world as lover, or indeed as mother. A relational religious experience, the Pureland practice expresses our feeling of intimacy and relationship with the measureless mystery behind the universe. This sense of a measureless, beneficent force is personified in Amida. It can be experienced both through our relationship to the ordinary and the natural, as in the work of poets such as Saigyo, and in our sense of an ultimate loving presence behind its existence. In Amida we experience the embodiment of those life energies which deeply move us. In religious terms, Amida is the manifestation of Buddha-ness, the quality Shakyamuni, the historic Buddha, brought to this world. Through the practice of calling on Amida, we experience relationship with the enlightened presence in the world, with the universality of love.

But all forms of religion are bombu; human attempts to frame our relationship to the mystery. Whether our expression takes the language of Pureland Buddhism or Christianity, Hinduism or nature worship, these are just poetic forms, like Saigyo's snipes rising up from the reed beds, they point the way towards an experience more universal and more mysterious than human mind can fully hold or express. Finding expression for that experience that hovers at the edge of our awareness is, however, of vital importance to our integrity and survival. The human, without respect for the divine, courts *hubris*.

In Pureland, the *nembutsu* practice calls out towards the distance. It is the song of longing, the cry of the lover, the call for the mother's embrace. It is the heartfelt search for connection between our smallness of being and the great forces of life and what is beyond life. Nembutsu creates a bridge, a link, which brings us into an intimacy with both the phenomenal world and the glimpsed ultimate. In nembutsu we dance with Amida. In our religious experience we embrace the great Otherness of the world and the universe beyond it. When we enter into nembutsu deeply, we feel the deep intimacy of that act. We feel ourselves to be held.

World as self

Macy's final category of religious experience identifies the experience of world as self. This way of seeing things falls into a tradition of thinking evolved by Arne Naess and others. Naess, writing in the mid 1970s, considered that much of the thinking around ecological and conservation issues at that time treated the environment as something detached from people, to be fixed in various ways where it became problematic to human needs. This view did not address the root of the problems which, even then, were becoming evident. He felt that for us to really address these problems, we needed a shift of consciousness and a move from seeing the world as an object for our use, to feeling it as something with which we were intimately connected. His movement, called the deep ecology movement, views this intimate connection as the route that can offer a chance for our planets survival.

The level of involvement that is necessary for us to arrive at this view the world is one in which we cease to regard the world as something separate from ourselves. Rather than seeing the world as a loved one, according to Macy, we need to let go of the grandiosity that manifests in our longing for union with something greater than ourselves, we need to break open our small egos and become one with the cosmos. Having reached this point, we will experience a shift of awareness. We will feel the grief of the planet as our grief. From this perspective, the dying trees where acid rain has fallen, the polar bears, cut off from winter feeding grounds by drifting ice floes, the withering crop dying on arid, cracked soil when rains have failed, are not just sad occurrences, they become personal injuries. We feel the *Great Grief* as personal grief. We weep for the daughters of planet earth as for our own children.

In elaborating the image of *world as self* Macy draws on the image of *Indra's Net*. This image, which was developed particularly in Chinese Buddhism, represents the universe as a net, with jewels at every knot, each of which reflects all the others, creating an infinitely interconnected system of reflections. *Indra's net* has become a symbol for many Buddhists representing the inter-connection of life. It has been widely used by Buddhist environmentalists to illustrate the inter-dependency between eco-systems. The idea has been popularised further by Thich Naht Hanh's concept of *interbeing* (Hanh 1988), also adopted by the environmentalist groups, which suggests that, beyond even inter-connection, we inter-exist with one another and with all the elements in the world.

Doctrinally, this concept poses certain problems, which have been discussed at length in my husband's book, The New Buddhism (Brazier 2001), but as a metaphor, the idea of inter-being offers a powerful image which can be used in ways that are both inspirational and thought provoking.

From a Pureland perspective, on the other hand, the idea of identification with the world seems problematic. Implicit within it seems to be a notion that the source of salvation is within us. This view is common in certain sections of the Buddhist world, but it is quite out of line with the

Pureland view of the practitioner as *bombu*, reliant on Amida's grace for salvation.

Pureland offers a relational approach to religion and to life, and, as such, more naturally adopts the idea of intimate relationship than of merger with the other. Such ideas as that of world as lover or as mother; as confidante or as provider; sit more comfortably with the nembutsu life.

All ideas offer perspectives on the truth, and none offer the last word, since reality is infinitely complex and unknowable. To feel the pain that destructive acts inflict upon planet, whether through empathy or identification, however, provides a deeper motivation for action than a more functional pragmatic approach. In our *bombu* state, we are helplessly attached to notions of self, so creating identification with the planet as a motivation for activists may provide the skilful means whereby more people are moved to seek changes for the earth.

Awakening Interest

Due to lack of interest, tomorrow has been cancelled. Among the thoughts and images that have shaped my life, that message has had powerful impact. As time passed, my anxieties for the planet did not diminish, but eventually I set them aside. It was not lack of interest that led me to take other directions in life, but a feeling of impotence and fear. The more I read on the disasters that might lie ahead, the less I felt able to do anything to contribute to the situation.

A few years later, I met people who told me to live for the moment and focus on the present, and I breathed a sigh of relief, letting the burden of anxiety go. But messages work on us unbidden. The seed once sown has grown over the years, and now motivates me to write.

How do we address the despair that arises from our knowledge of impending troubles? How do we act effectively? How do we avoid the pitfalls of self-righteousness or spiritual withdrawal? How do we avoid excesses of dependency or egotism? How to we find light in these dark times?

The questions clamour. Answers do not come easily.

CONCEPTS INTRODUCED IN THIS CHAPTER

- Religion and psychology in a planet facing ecological collapse
- Joanna Macy's four models of relationship with the world
- Justice and rights are not Buddhist concepts
- Gisho Saiko's model of the therapeutic relationship
- The myokonin as a Pureland ideal

CHAPTER TWELVE

DANCING IN THE LIGHT

> But leap still!
> And yet dance!
> My heart's colt –
> Joyful to hear Amida's teaching
> (Ippen *in Hirota, 1986*)

August comes. Today Susthama is sparkling. As my little Dharma sister prepares the meditation hall for service, she is bright with joy and her movements seem to dance. She doesn't just smile, her face is full and open with happiness. Later when we have sharing time, she says that she feels as if her heart has split open.

"I am getting smaller and smaller" she says and as she says it the sun seems to shine out of her.

The world grows. We grow small. Like violets on an old path, the world fills the cracks of our being. We are invaded by life in all its complex beauty and weather into relationship with the elemental world. We soften. Just as old bricks lose their hard edges, their constituents crumbling back into soft clay and tiny stones, so too, we find our resting place in the greater processes of life. No need to defend now. We are surrounded by the light of life, and in it we dance.

Nembutsu: the spirit of dance:

Ippen, a Japanese Pureland monk and hijiri who lived 1239 – 1289, is known for having developed dancing nembutsu practice. Hijiri were wandering teachers, who followed a religious life by walking from place to place, living close to the natural world and to ordinary people. They taught in popular ways, drawing crowds in the market places, and expressed their faith in ecstatic practices and in arts and poetry. They lived in the country-side, often sleeping rough, in spaces open to the elements. It was not an easy life.

Ippen spent the first ten years of his spiritual life studying under a teacher in the monastic system of thirteenth century Japan. He spent time in Zenkoji temple, one of the big temples in Nagano, where he followed the strict practices of temple life. Towards the end of this period, and following various religious revelations, he entered solitary retreat as a hermit. Ippen later came to look back on these early years as a time in which he had been mainly driven by self-will, but he did, towards the end of the period at Zenkoji, and while in his hermitage, have profound religious experiences, some of which he expressed through painting. It was the visionary experiences that brought the religious life alive for him. Also, during his time at Zenkoji, he would have met the many hijiri for whom the temple was a place of pilgrimage. Perhaps these encounters encouraged him to take up the wandering life himself.

Having left the temple to wander the countryside, Ippen's early ministry involved a fervent search for converts. In this search, whenever he encounter people on the road, he persuaded them to recite the nembutsu. In return he gave them *fuda*. *Fuda* were pieces of paper on which were block-printed nembutsu texts. *Fuda* were seen as evidence of a person's salvation, but were also treasured as sacred, and sometimes even quasi-magical objects, by the recipients, representing their place in the Pure Land. During this time Ippen kept meticulous records of his achievements, which involved distributing hundreds of thousands of *fuda*.

Whilst Ippen was enthusiastically collecting converts, he had come to believe that the recitation of the nembutsu was all that was necessary to achieve birth in the Pure Land. He was excited by this simple message and set out to save the whole of Japan on the strength of it. This period of fervour, however, came to an end when Ippen was brought to question the efficacy of his method. In conversation with another monk, whom he encountered on his travels, the issue arose of whether the recitation of nembutsu was really sufficient to ensure birth in the Pure Land, or whether the mind state of the person reciting it was important. Could faith be assumed in the person making the recitation, or did the person need to have a more active faith in order to be saved. In other words, was there a mind state to be achieved, upon which the receipt of Amida's grace depended? This question was one that had been much debated by nembutsu practitioners of Ippen's time. For Ippen, it challenged the worth of his activity. If a particular attitude of mind were necessary, or perfect faith were a prerequisite to birth in the Pure Land, his ministry might be leading people to a false belief in their own salvation.

Troubled by this realisation, Ippen left his early ministry, and went to the shrine at Kumano. There in intensive practice, he experienced a revelatory vision which was to change the direction of his teaching and set him on a new direction for the final sixteen years of his life. This vision convinced Ippen that there was no requirement upon the practitioner, and that birth in the Pure Land did not rest on any state of mind or personal achievement. Saying the nembutsu was enough. This revelation emphasised the *other-power* nature of the practice.

Following his inspiration, he once again took up the wandering life, this time setting out alone, with only minimal possessions, he spent four years in the countryside, walking the hills and meadows and sleeping under the stars. During this time, he devoted himself to the nembutsu, placing his faith only in that practice. It was a turning point in his ministry. After several years alone, Ippen gradually again began to attract a following. A small group of disciples joined him, sharing in sessions of continuous nembutsu practice.

Ippen began to introduce dancing to his practice in 1279, ten years before his death. His inspiration for this practice in all probability came from Kuya, a very well known hijiri, who had lived in the tenth century, and who had long been a great source of inspiration to Ippen. Kuya appears to have introduced ecstatic dancing as part of his expression of the nembutsu, and, as with Ippen's own use of dance, it may have evolved from the practice of circumambulation and reciting the nembutsu, which was done with the accompaniment of drum beats and stamping. Thus initially Kuya's dancing practice was probably a natural occurrence, arising out of the joyful chanting of the nembutsu. Later it became more formalised, and special platforms were erected in the village centres for its performance.

The history of Ippen's dancing nembutsu, however, remains uncertain. Historically the practice of dance as an aspect of religious expression in Japan may have had some of its roots in funeral practices. Dancing had been a part of old Japanese religion, a rite that brought peace to the dead. In the scroll paintings of Ippen's life, the first dancing is shown in the vicinity of a grave, but no explanation is given of its significance. This may offer some additional explanation for its early origins. It is not difficult to imagine, though, that dance would have simply emerged as a spontaneous expression of the nembutsu. Ippen and his followers lived the nembutsu with great faith and energy, their faith inspiring joy and fervour. To express this in dance would seem like a natural extension of the vocalisation.

The dancing nembutsu is not the only type of dance to have existed in Buddhist contexts. Dancing had also been associated with the bakti tradition in India, which had offered ecstatic dancing practices. This tradition, though later taken up by Hindu groups, was originally Buddhist. Tibetan Buddhism also has its dance traditions, in all likelihood imported from its pre-Buddhist roots. There is no obvious link between the Bakti tradition or the dances of Tibet and Ippen's dancing nembutsu, but all of these dance traditions seem to be independent examples of ways in which the ecstatic spirit has emerged in Buddhism, offering an alternative path to the quieter and often more ascetic paths offered by other practices.

Earlier this year at our centre in England, as part of our winter retreat, we undertook a twenty four hour period of continuous nembutsu practice. Alternating sessions of walking and sitting, we kept the chanting going without a break from mid-day on one day to mid-day the following day. This practice was a powerful experience, generating great energy in the group. It was indeed a practice that relied upon the group for its success. Each person needed from time to time to leave the room for natural breaks, but as a whole the chanting was not broken. Even in the minute by minute chanting, the fact that we were a group was important for the chant's continuity. By having the group divided in two teams, we used an interlinking pattern of four sung nembutsu with two silent ones so that each person could draw breath or move between the sitting and standing phases or relieve the dryness of mouth with a quick sip of water, without disturbing the rhythm.

As the process unfolded and darkness fell, and as we continued to walk and chant and chant and walk through the dark hours of the night, the practice began to work its own patterns upon us. Steps that had been even and measured took on slight changes of rhythm as limbs stiffened, and the notes of the chant began to vary as voices exhausted their original tone. Into these changes, new rhythms emerged and tonal variation led to wonderful symphonies of chords and dissonances. Sometimes our steps became earthy as tribal dancing, our movements connecting heavily with the ground and with the dark energies of body and voice. Other times they seemed to dance lightly with jaunty sweep of hips and shoulders, expressing the joy of heart that the practice embodies. Yet other times they seemed to glide in a serene flowing movement reminiscent of the religious passing silently down the ancient corridors of some cathedral cloister.

It is not difficult to imagine how the practitioners of Ippen's following, fired with the fervour of the nembutsu, would spontaneously in their circumambulations break into dance. Dance is a natural and common expression of religious experience, though sadly lost from modern religion until very recently. Dance opens the heart and invites the body to participate in the act of devotion. It inspires us. It enthuses us.

We can note here that the word *enthusiasm* comes from the ancient Greek *en-theos* or god-entering. The term was used of oracles, such as the oracle of Delphi. The priestess of the Delphic oracle would enter a trance-like state in which the sun god, Apollo would enter her body and speak through her. This embodiment of the divine was often linked with sacred dancing. Dance opens us up to the spirit of divine energy.

Embodying the nembutsu we are moved. The joy of Amida enters the heart. We leap with joy, as Ippen's heart leaps, a colt, bounding across a spring field. Opening to the greater power of the immeasurable, we let go the inhibitions of self-nature and dance free.

Dancing in the world

The sun shines and we feel joy. The sky is blue and somehow our bodies become lighter. It is easy to feel connected with life and with the love in the universe when the sun is shining. Yet days of rain and grey skies are also a gift if we can find the appreciation to hold them. So much of the time we do not notice what we have. There is a human tendency to allow the ordinary things of life to fall into the background of our awareness and for our focus of attention to be monopolised by the surprising, the intrusive and the irritating.

We do not notice that the cashier smiles as she hands us change, or the dustbin man puts the bins neatly together on our drive. We do not notice the pavement has been swept this morning and flowers have been planted in the hanging baskets along the street, nor do we see that they are watered daily in hot weather.

Far less, for it would seem ridiculously sentimental, do we notice that the sun has risen in the morning or that we have air to breathe and water in our taps. We do not see the plants that grow in the pavement cracks, and, if we do, we regard them as interlopers to be eradicated.

Depression and anxiety have become the tyrannies of our age, inextricably bound with, on the one hand, our existential powerlessness, our ever-present dukkha, and, on the other, with our seemingly endless sense of lack (Loy 1996) and craving for material comforts. These roots perpetuate those processes which bind us into a dulled mentality. They ground our spirit. Like a tethered horse we pull the heavy mill wheel, grinding the life out of our existence. We shape the world to fit our imagined needs but feel dissatisfaction with the results. These are the roots of mental ill health, and the source of our distress.

A return to life involves reversing this process. Instead of trying to impose our reality upon the world, it involves inviting the world's reality to speak to and enthuse us.

Beyond a human-centred view

The human-centric view is pervasive. It is pervasive in the collective mentality, just as the sense of self in an individual. Like spoilt children, we feel entitled and then become disappointed and sulky when our expectations are not met.

This position runs deep. Our societies are built on human interests and human concerns. Our laws, for the most part, protect human life and interests. Our planning is for human environments and needs. Our industry and agriculture is centred on human welfare.

It is true that there are laws to protect animals from gross abuse, and owners will be prosecuted for abusing their pets. Such behaviour offends our sensibilities, our image of ourselves as civilised, caring people. Experimenters are regulated and unnecessary suffering is officially outlawed in laboratories which use animals for research. What is defined as unnecessary, however, is largely a function of human needs and concerns. Those experiments which can be shown to bring benefit to humans are sanctioned, even if they involve horrific mutilation and misery for the animals involved. The assumption that the ultimate good involves extending or preserving human life, even if it is at the expense of the deaths of many other creatures, is rarely questioned.

Even matters that seem quite trivial are seen as justification for such work if they are perceived as bringing human benefit. Vast numbers of small rodents are sacrificed to conduct tests in line with new regulations, which demand that even products which have been used for years are demonstrated to meet current toxicity levels.

Such activities have their critics, and, indeed, the field of animal ethics has become a sadly embattled arena. There is much literature which addresses the issues of animal testing and experimentation, which brings into question the efficacy of such work and the transferability of conclusions arising from animal testing to the human arena. Even in such literature, however, the human-centric position is often, though not always, used as the basis for argument. Drugs that are tested on animals may not be suitable for human tissue, it is argued. Eating a vegetarian or vegan diet is healthier. Cows should not be give hormones and antibiotics routinely because these show up in the milk we drink. Compassionate farming leads to happy animals which give better, conscience-free meat.

Some such attitudes to animals arise from our Judeo-Christian roots. These convey attitudes of human centricity such as that found in the idea that man has been given husbandry over all the earth. This view, which is used by Christians to promote environmental concern, suggests that it is the human responsibility to tend the earth and care for all creatures in it. It is a way of thinking that places animals in an inferior and dependant relationship to humans, which parallels that of humans to God. We are in turn invited to treat animals with caring and responsibility, in the way that reflects the way that God cares for his chosen people, the human race. This system of thought gives humans a duty of care towards those lesser creatures that share this living space. Humans remain the species of highest status. As those made in the image of God, their special position was always determined. The tree of knowledge offered its fruit, and devouring it, they came to believe in this privileged situation. Such was the fall.

To think in other terms seems unthinkable.

Yet as the planet moves towards the brink of ecological collapse we are faced with stark choices. The life style that has become the logical outcome of our sense of species entitlement is clearly unsustainable.

World as Other

The environmentalist and writer, James Lovelock, is well known for developing the idea of the earth as a living organism. Known as the Gaia theory (originally the Gaia hypothesis), he has presented his ideas in a number of books, the most recent being *The Revenge of Gaia* (Lovelock 2006). In this work, Lovelock reviews the current global situation and concludes that not only is climate change happening, but also that its effects are irreversible.

Lovelock supports his ideas with a plethora of data and climatic modelling, which make compelling reading. There is plenty of evidence to be found. Whether or not a particular prediction comes to effect, the general trend is hard to dispute. More than that, chillingly, Lovelock plots our current situation against predictions made in 1988 (Lovelock 2006 p50) and concludes that we are, on current assessment, hitting the graph somewhere not far below the worst scenario envisaged eighteen years ago. With the addition of a number of factors which he sees as potentially contributing to a positive feedback scenario (the loss of reflective surface in polar regions to deflect sun's radiation; the death of plankton in the oceans diminishing carbon-dioxide removal; the release of the greenhouse gas, methane, from tundra as it unfreezes; and the loss from the atmosphere of aerosol gases that lower temperatures artificially, as industry is reduced, to name just a few) the future looks bleak.

Plenty has been written on climate change, and there is no need here to go into great detail, save to illustrate the seriousness of our situation. Particular pieces of evidence can be questioned but the overall trend seems indisputable. We hear regularly of extremes of weather, and experience with almost every season the hottest, the driest, the wettest or sometimes even the coldest conditions in recorded history. Weather systems respond to temperature changes with dramatic effect. Hurricanes and typhoons break records for ferocity and frequency. Drought causes crop failures in many areas of the globe, while floods caused by sudden storms and the effects of poor water management take many lives. Climate related disasters have always happened, but their frequency is increasing. Each year the polar ice freezes later and thaws earlier and its summer extent grows steadily less. With each revision of this manuscript, new climatic catastrophes have occurred that might be included.

Lovelock's contribution to theory, however, has not simply been to catalogue and explore the ramifications of climatic factors and to speculate about future scenarios. His central thesis, the Gaia theory, offers a particular way of viewing our planetary system.

It is interesting to compare Lovelock's theory of Gaia with the four models of world-view offered by Macy. While Macy's view presents four options that can broadly be seen as dependent on the human perceiver for their existence, Lovelock's Gaia is an independent lady. According to Gaia theory, the earth is a self-regulating system, which functions rather as an organism, regulating its processes so that the conditions of life are maintained. According to Lovelock, Gaia's health is suffering as a result of human activity over the last century or two. Her overheating can, according to Lovelock's analogy, be seen as a feverishness, which will eliminate the disease which is invading her – us.

This view of the world could, in Macy's style, be viewed as a fifth possibility: *World as Other.* Gaia is not a function of either our needs for an authority or temptress, passionate involvement or mystical oneness. It is a system that has existed since long before human life arrived and one which may well outlive us. Our relationship, if it is to survive, must be one of gratitude and respect. The image of Gaia is a subject of wonder, full of complexity, and the epitome of otherness. Gaia does not need us, but we need Gaia. We are not inter-dependant, we are simply dependant.

Such a view perhaps offers us an image that reflects something of the Pureland perspective. As small beings, we inhabit a system that is far, far greater and more complex than we can really conceive. The understanding which humankind is accumulating grows ever more rich, and yet, as any scientist will tell you, every discovery reveals new questions and every "truth" is provisional. Faced with the living system of our planet, we encounter something immeasurable. Faced by the cosmos beyond, we look out into Amida's face. The Buddha of infinite light reflects in a myriad galaxies and stars.

Foolish beings, our foolishness may be our end. Despite her sickness, Lovelock believes that Gaia will survive our selfish behaviour, even if the human species is greatly diminished or perishes in the process. Gaia does not have Amida's heart.

Despair work:

In the previous chapter we looked at the way that Joanna Macy (Macy 1991) offered models for exploring the conceptualisations that different religious perspectives offer for viewing the world. We also looked at how these different perspectives affect our attitudes to our planet. Central to her understanding, however, has been her view of the way that so many people experience the impending difficulties as a source of feelings of hopelessness and despair.

Faced with the enormity of difficulties which threaten not just our nations but the whole biosphere of the planet, answers do not come easily. Even if we cycle to work and refuse to buy heavily packaged produce from distant lands, this will have little impact when our neighbours are driving high consumption cars and flying to far away places for holidays several times a year. Even if we can lobby our politicians for reforms in industrial and transport policy, it will do little to turn the tide as China and other East Asian countries enjoy a financial boom that is accelerating building programmes, car ownership and all the other attributes of Western life-style.

It is hard to know where to act in order to have impact. We oscillate between feelings of futility and driven attempts to create change, between a sense of desperate urgency and withdrawal into distraction and denial. Consumerism is rampant as ever, fuelled perhaps by the need to forget. Behind it all, we despair.

A dread of what is happening to our future stays on the fringes of awareness, too deep to name, too fearsome to face.(Macy, 1991 p15)

Much of Macy's work has been to help people to explore their feelings of despair. Of course, this reflects a Buddhist perspective since Buddhism is fundamentally concerned with the way we respond to affliction (*dukkha*). So often in experiencing *dukkha* we retreat into the creation of distraction and defensive self-structures, and yet what we need to do is to gain the faith to face *dukkha* as it arises. In facing the future, the outcomes will depend to a large degree on how much our solutions are grounded in projects that are basically attempts to control and assert dominion over the situation; that are basically concerned with our identities and self-building; and how much they really engage with the situation itself. Honest reflection and encounter with the truth brings us back to sanity. Despite our grief, somehow, at a planetary level, we need to stop hiding in madness and face reality. It is not easy.

As Macy describes her work, she shows how, going into the experience of despair, people often experience a profound transformation. In talking of this work, firstly she describes how it is grounded in encouraging people to find a personal link to the global situation. What is to be engaged with is not a theoretical creation, but a real, impactful, experience of the environmental changes that are happening in the real and familiar world of each one of us. The link might be a personal experience of seeing a piece of land change under the impact of industrial or urban development. It might be an experience of looking at one's child and wondering what sort of world they might inherit. It might be walking along the shoreline on a beautiful piece of coast and seeing washed up debris and detergent scum. Whatever the scene, it encapsulates for the speaker the effects of big processes in the landscape of their own environment.

The following description is one I wrote in autumn 2003 for *Dharma Life* magazine, describing my own response to the extreme hot weather and drought that hit France that year.

This summer the trees in our retreat centre in France were turning brown by early August. When the wind blew, sucked up by soaring thermals in the searing heat, leaves scattered across the field in a whirling mass. Temperatures rose steadily till they peaked at 42 degrees in the shade and stayed there for two weeks. Everywhere the landscape was shrivelled and bleached. Trees stood, branches bare. The drought had lasted all spring and the countryside was feeling its effects.

Watching the slow decay of woodlands and hedgerows in the surrounding countryside, the reality of climate change hit me in a way it hadn't before. If this weather pattern were to continue, great swathes of forest would simply die. Agriculture would struggle and in many cases fail. The countryside as we knew it would change beyond recognition. As I looked up into the blue sky, criss-crossed by plane tracks, and knew the interconnectedness of increasing fossil fuel consumption and environmental change, I felt.... What did I feel? Was it anger? Was it despair? Was it grief? A sensation in my chest, tears pressing into my eyes, thoughts circling, my reaction was visceral and poignant. Thoughts tore at me. This had to stop. Someone had to listen now. (Dharma Life magazine, Spring 2004)

As we explore the reality of a situation or the impact of an image of this kind upon us, we are likely to feel strong emotion. In as much as we can allow the situation to engage with us, we allow ourselves to feel the dukkha. Of course, the impulse to escape is always arising, and even the dramatic emotional outpouring can be a form of sensory distraction and clinging to self. This said, we still may indeed be put in contact with our real grief through such routes, and through it, the *Great Grief* that embraces all of humanity.

The expression of such grief often brings with it despair. For Macy, this

is important because at the point of despair we realise our individual powerlessness. Contacting our powerlessness allows us to let go of ego based
"fix-it" solutions. It brings us to the ground of reality. Such messages are
not always popular. *Despair is tenaciously resisted because it represents a
loss of control, an admission of powerlessness. Our culture dodges it by
asking for instant solutions when problems are raised. (Macy, 1991 p18)*

Macy's identification of powerlessness as the key to change equates
well with the principles of Pureland Buddhism. Recognising our bombu
nature we connect with Amida. Realising our small, limited existence, we
open to the immeasurable. Whilst enmeshed in self-creating projects, we
are too focused on individual agendas. As we saw in chapter two, despairing of the self-project brings us into relationship with what is other. Letting
go of our belief that we can find solutions alone, we see the bigger picture.
As we struggle to face these big issues, we gain a sense of the presence of
something greater than ourselves, something that might be represented by
Amida. In her writing, although her Buddhist background is in other traditions, Joanna Macy sometimes strays very close to a Pureland position:
*There is the sense sometimes of being sustained by something beyond one's
own individual power, a sense of being acted "through". It is close to the
religious concept of grace. (ibid p34)* Her own interpretation of this feeling
is rooted in the images of inter-connection and inter-dependency, which she
describes with the image of *indra's net* and the notion of *inter-being* discussed in the previous chapter. However, her conclusion that we are not the
sole authors of our actions and nor do we individually have the capacity to
achieve the solution, accords well with the *other-power* position.

In Macy's work, the individual despair gives way to collective vision.
From exploring the images of grief, new roots of action emerge. It is only
by facing dukkha, that we can also open up to the wonderful things in the
world. *Until we can grieve for our planet and its future inhabitants, we can-*

not fully feel or enact our love for them (ibid p20)

Thus Macy invokes grief and despair as the motivating source for her activism and encourages others to do likewise. Her work provides an interesting counter-part to that of the Christian activist with whom I discussed anger (described in the previous chapter). Motivated not by anger, but by the sadness and pain that arises from our direct experience of the situation in which we collectively find ourselves, we discover within that very pain the energising force to go forward.

This realisation is, of course, that which we find given in the teaching of the Four Noble Truths. Experiencing *dukkha* our reactions create energy *(samudaya)* which can be harnessed *(nirodha)* for the path of social action *(marga)*. Not anger, but the force of sorrow releases us. Unhooking from the processes of attachment and self-building, and recognising our *bombu* nature, our powerlessness, we engage with the task through the grace of greater forces.

Reconnecting with the world

A recent edition of the Journal of the British Association for Counselling and Psychotherapy, *Therapy Today* (December 2005 edition) was devoted to the use of environmental approaches in counselling. It is on the one hand, a sign of current preoccupation with environmental concerns that a journal which caters for members of the counselling profession, the majority of whom work in main-stream settings, using traditional therapeutic models, devoted a whole issue to this matter. On the other hand, it was a reflection of the predominating human-centric view that most of these articles spoke of the opportunity to use the natural world as a therapeutic arena or as a source of metaphors for the human psyche, to be used for the improvement of mental health. The real effects on mental health of living in a planet which is rapidly being overtaken by changes that may well threaten our species' existence were not discussed. Therapeutic work that uses the natural world as a mirror may have some impact on global issues if it enables us to identify with the world, to see it as self, and therefore care for its preservation, but they do not really tackle the basic problem of human self-interest.

This said, the impact of environmentally based work on individuals who participate can be profound, and the outcomes can include a shift of consciousness which not only leads to changes in mental health, but also connects the person to a spiritual and sometimes religious sense. In the edition of *Therapy Today* referred to above, there appeared an anonymous account given by a woman who was working with a therapist to explore unresolved feelings of grief dating back to the death of her five year old daughter seventeen years earlier. Her therapist, who used contact with the natural world as part of his counselling approach, encouraged her to explore her grief through immersion in that world.

Nick (her therapist) gently guided me towards using my love of walking as a metaphor for my grief, and encouraged me to find solitude and privacy to sob and howl my grief out. I found the thought at first quite scary – to walk alone to a private spot and think about the little girl I had lost and grieve for the future she had never seen. But the natural woodland, bracken and heather and quietness of my chosen place absorbed my grief, sobs, anger and frustration at how cruel life can be. It engulfed me, it was dense and scary – but in some way it was also a comfort. I realised my smog had been an internal comfort blanket to prevent my grief being felt, and the beautiful surroundings held me gently, naturally and softly. Somehow it was fitting, as I still believe no other person could have enabled me to express my vast feelings of pain. Motherhood is portrayed as the natural role for women and the connec-

tion with the forest was powerful and very real in allowing me to give back to nature my grief and anger. (First Person, article in Therapy Today, December 2005)

In this very moving account, we can, I think, see some progression from the use of the environment as a tool, towards a more intimate relationship with the natural world. At the beginning of the passage, the use of environmental imagery is seen as a metaphor. In other words, the unexpressed grief was paramount, and the idea of walking provided concepts and images that might help in this process. At this point, the thought feels frightening. Both the grief and the situation feel unfamiliar and overwhelming.

In contact with the natural world, however, a process of change starts to unfold. The woman first becomes aware of her internal *smog*, the dulling of feelings that had been protecting her from her grief. It is interesting that here she is already talking of her experience in terms of an environmental phenomenon. The metaphor of smog, the polluted, heavy blanket of fog that obliterates everything, creates an image of something that has entered her being. It is not an image of self, although we could analyse it in those terms, but of an invasive clouding of her mind.

The surroundings of her chosen spot, however, break through this fog. They hold her grief and allow its expression. The details of bracken and heather, forest and moorland become vivid. They bring her back to life from the shadows of her sorrow. As a grieving mother, she feels herself held in a way that no human presence could offer. This holding is, she says, gentle, natural and soft, qualities that seems to echo the theme of motherhood.

Dancing in the light: a message for the dark times

This book began, as the last one ended, with a death; the loss of a loved one. It began also with a mystery.

The bees still buzz around the window under the branches of the lime tree, although the room now has a new occupant. The flowers in the garden still bloom and squirrels run across the line on which containers of peanuts hang for the birds. Life goes on. It is greater and far more wonderful than we can ever describe.

In these pages we have touched joy and sadness. We have explored the longing of the heart, the *yugen* quality that reaches out into the unknown with hope and wistfulness. We have heard the bitter-sweetness of grief and motherhood. We have glimpsed briefly the lives of some of the many figures who down the years have developed and passed on the teachings of this particular form of Buddhism. We have also looked at its meaning today, and its contribution to the fields of Buddhist psychological understanding and of applied spirituality. And in these latter chapters, we have looked further. From personal grief and personal joy, we have moved on to view a wider picture.

People live in a context of their times, and now, no less than any other, our psyches and our spiritual thinking are forged on the anvil of world events. We cannot separate the personal from the political nor can we prise the individual's psychology from global events.

Standing in the early years of the new millennium, it is hard to gaze into the future with confidence. Looking back at the great expanse of history, I feel great sadness. If this is to be the end, the decline and fall, what will preserve the heritage of Shakespeare, of Classical Greece, of Indian philosophy, of Arabic scholarship? Who will recite the poetry of Wordsworth or sing the songs of Africa? Who will dance to the tunes of the world? How have we betrayed our forefathers in such a short space of time?

But there have been dark ages before. Times when one did not venture out without a sword beneath ones cloak. Times when wolves and owls inhabited the ruins of cities, and people hid in their squalid hovels around small fires.

On those occasions, humans survived.

The Kamakura period in Japan was in many ways such a time. And yet, it was also the time of great religious growth. Whilst plagues and fighting beset the land, teachers such as Honen and Shinran were developing their understanding and taking their message out to the ordinary people.

In such times, in the past, it has been the monasteries which have carried the teachings and the knowledge forward. In these dark times, religion itself must look deeply into its heart and understand its follies. Whilst current trends toward fundamentalism and religious divisiveness underlie conflicts and oppression, there is a need for a message that takes a different direction. The world has suffered too long from the pomposity of religions. The time has now come for them to show more humility.

So what is our role, what our mission? How do we pass on the message in the dark times to come? If humans hang on by any means, the future will be bleak. Just as dark age monasteries carried the religion of their day, preserving the knowledge for the ages to come, so too, those of us who practice with faith now need to prepare to carry a message on to future generations. That message should be complex. It should be radiant with all the voices of the world. But more, it should be humble; a quiet nembutsu, linking these poor bombu beings to the indefinable presence that holds us still.

For we are bombu. Our bombu nature has brought us to the brink. Not recognising our limitations, we have forgotten how to sing in gratitude. We have lost our connection to the great, the wonderful and the immeasurable. Let us remember before it is too late.

So in the dark times, will we dance in the light
Namo Amida Bu.

GLOSSARY

Abhava: non-becoming; destructiveness (the last stage of samudaya)

Abhidharma: one of the sections of the tipataka, or early Buddhist texts. This material is the distillation of theory and thus psychology. There are more than one versions of the Abhidharma, since different traditions preserved and developed it in their own form.

Amida: measureless. The Buddha who is measureless. Japanese amalgamation of Amitayus (Buddha of Infinite Life) and Amitabha (Buddha of Infinite Light)

Amitabha: the Buddha of infinite light, one aspect of Amida Buddha

Amitayus: the Buddha of infinite life, an aspect of Amida Buddha

Bhava: becoming, being born, becoming a self (the second stage of samudaya)

Bhikshu: Buddhist monk

Bhikshuni: Buddhist nun

Bodhi Tree: the tree under which the Buddha was enlightened. Bodhi means enlightenment.

Bombu: (Ch &Jp; sometimes written *bompu, bonbu* or *bonpu*) Ordinary person, foolish person. This term is used to describe the sincere practitioner of Pureland Buddhism.

Buddha-nature: the potential for Buddhahood

Dependent Origination: a central teaching of Buddhism. This theory says that all things depend upon causes and conditions; The narrow version of the theory involves the *twelve links* which are a series of twelve steps forming a chain. This can be interpreted as the stages in building the self. The theory of twelve links has many interpretations, so the reader may wish to read more widely

Dharma: the Buddhist teachings, reality, truth.

Dukkha: affliction; the first Noble Truth

Fathomless blind passion: according to Pureland doctrine, ordinary people are *bombu*, and thus filled with *fathomless blind passions*

Fellow feeling: the feeling of recognition we have for others troubles when we are aware of our own *bombu* nature.

Fully Functioning Person: a concept developed by Carl Rogers to describe the optimal state a person might reach

Fuda: pieces of paper on which were block-printed nembutsu texts. These papers were regarded as having religious and sometimes magical significance in medieval Japan

Great Grief: the grief of all living beings. The bodhisattva, having deep insight, feels the Great Grief and weeps for the world.

Hierarchy of needs: theory developed by Abraham Maslow which suggests that humans have a variety of needs that are met in a particular order, physical needs being the first priority. This theory suggests that it is only when a person's basic needs for physical safety and nourishment are satisfied that higher needs on the social and spiritual planes are met

Hubris: the ancient Greek term that expressed an act where humans overreached themselves and usurped the role of the gods. Such acts inevitably brought disaster.

Indra's Net: an image, originating from Chinese Buddhism, represents the universe as a net, with jewels at every knot, which each reflects the others, creating an infinitely interconnected system in which each element reflects every other.

Inter-being: a term coined by Thich Naht Hanh to describe the inter-connection of phenomena; our inter-connectedness with one another and with the universe.

Kama: sense pleasures

Karma: actions; the theory that our actions condition future actions. What we do leaves a potentiality for us to repeat the same activity. Actions sow karmic seeds that ripen when similar circumstances arise.

Lakshana: a sign or indicator; specifically a indicator of self

Mahayana: Buddhist schools, mainly of the East Asian and Tibetan traditions which follow a broader interpretation of the Buddha's teachings. Buddhist schools are traditionally divided into Mahayana and Hinayana (*Theravada* specifically; the word hinayana is often seen as somewhat derogatory meaning *narrow path*)

Manovijnana: the mind sense, mind's eye. Mano-vijnana is seen as one of the senses in the Buddhist mind models, alongside sight, smell, taste, touch and hearing.

Mara: the figure of death, a sort of tempter, tempting us to worldly ways and spiritual death

Marga; the spiritual path; Fourth *Noble Truth*

Middle Way: the Buddha is said to have taught the middle way. Sometimes taken as the way of moderation, it can also have the implication of centredness or full application.

Myokonin: a Pureland ideal, the person of simple faith. Often a person of simple means, whose life exemplifies trust in Amida.

Naga Serpen: the mythical snake-like creature representing the spiritual energy

Naikan, Nei Quan: inward enquiry: a method of life review developed by Yoshimoto Ishin (1916-1988) who was a Pureland Buddhist

Nirodha: containment, restraint (sometimes translated cessation); *dukkha nirodha* is the third Noble Truth

Pratyayas: conditions; twenty four *pratyayas* are listed in the seventh book of the Abhidharma. These describe the types of relationship which lead to the creation of particular mind states.

Projection: a term commonly used in Western psychodynamic psychology to describe the unconscious attribution of personal characteristics, not perceived in the self, to another. For example, a person who is suppressing their own anger may (wrongly) perceive another person as angry.

Quan: insight meditation; *Quan* is the Chinese word for *Vipasshyana* style meditation, but, in the tradition described in this book, usually involved a personal enquiry into life experience.

Rupa: image; object of perception; an object in which power is invested. The quality of rupa generally refers to the perception of an object conditioned by self (as in the skandha process) but the term is also used of religious objects, which are viewed as representations of the spiritual dimension.

Samadhi: a high meditative state, a visionary experience achieved in meditation.

Samsara: the worldly cycle of delusion.

Samskara: mental structures; one of the skandhas; samskaras are the fabrications of the mind.

Samudaya: that which arises, the second Noble Truth

Sangha: the Buddhist community, traditionally referring to the monastic community, the term *sangha* is often now used of any group of practitioners who feel affinity with one another.

Shakyamuni Buddha: the historical Buddha

Shikantasa: meditation that combines sitting quietening the mind and insight. Referred to as just sitting it is likened to sitting on the river bank, watching the stream of water.

Shunyata (Sunyata): emptiness; the teachings on *Shunyata* are complex and open to different interpretations. One way of understanding them is as meaning that all things are "empty of self" ie non-self.

Skandhas: the five elements that make up the person, ie the self. These five elements form a cyclical process

Sutra: a Buddhist text, teaching.

Tantra: esoteric Buddhist practice, mainly Tibetan in origin, in which all energies are transformed into the path.

Three Poisons, The: the three elements which are at the root of all deluded states. All human fallibility is seen, in Buddhism, to be reducible to some combination of the three elements, greed, hate and delusion. These three states are basically positive, negative or ambivalent manifestations of clinging (trishna).

Transference: a term commonly used in Western psychodynamic psychology to describe the unconscious attribution of characteristics of one person, often a parent, to someone in the present, often the therapist. In its strict usage, the term transference was originally intended to imply the transfer of specific characteristics of the real parent rather than generalised ones, however later theorists such as Kelly have identified more generalised, idealising transference, linked to the person's narcissistic needs.

Trishna: craving, clinging. The tendency of humans to grasp at things in order to avoid reality.

Tulkus: reincarnated Tibetan lamas

Upaya: skilful means; using a method of teaching that will convey the point that may in itself not be completely transparent.

Vipasshyana: insight meditation; meditation that involves reflection on processes of mind and body with a aim of achieving insight. (Pali: *Vipassana*)

Wheel of Life: a Tibetan image depicting the different teachings on samsara and the human position.

BIBLIOGRAPHY

Armstrong, K 1981 *Through the Narrow Gate* Macmillan UK (republished Flamingo 1997)

Atone, J and Hayash, Y (trans) 1998 *An Anthology of the Teachings of Honen Shonin* Bukkyo University, Los Angles extension. USA

Brazier, C 2002 *Buddhism and the Feminine* paper written for Butterfly Online journal (discontinued)

Brazier, C 2003 *Buddhist Psychology* Constable & Robinson UK

Brazier, D 1995 *Zen Therapy* Constable & Robinson UK

Brazier, D 1997 *The Feeling Buddha* Constable & Robinson UK

Brazier, D 2001 *The New Buddhism* Constable & Robinson UK

Epstein M. 1996 *Thoughts Without A Thinker* Duckworth, UK

Fisher, R 1993 *Buddhist Art and Literature* Thames & Hudson, UK

Fitzgerald, J(ed) 2006 *Honen the Buddhist Saint* World Wisdom Inc, USA

Gendlin, E.T. 1981 *Focusing.* Bantam, London & New York

Hanh, T N 1988 *The Sun My Heart* Parallex Press, Berkeley, USA

Hirota, D1986 *No Abode; the record of Ippen* University of Hawaii Press, USA

Inagaki, H 1994 *The Three Pure Land Sutras* Ryukoku University, Japan

Kashiwara, Y 994 *Shapers of Japanese Buddhism* Kosei Publications, Japan

Krech, G 2002 *Naikan: Gratitude, Grace and the Japanese Art of Self-Reflection* Stone Bridge Press USA

Lovelock, J 2006 *The Revenge of Gaia* Penguin, UK

Loy, D, 1996 *Lack and Transcendence: The problem of death and life in psychotherapy, existentialism and Buddhism,* Humanities press, New Jersey USA

Loy, D.R. 2002. *A Buddhist History of the West : studies in lack.* New York, Suny.

Luk C (trans)1988 *Empty Cloud, the autobiography of the Chinese Zen Master* Xu Yun Element Books, UK

Macy, J 1991 *World as lover, World as Self.* Parallax Press. Berkeley USA

Masson, J 1989 *Against Therapy,* Fontana, UK

Maslow, A 1954 *Motivation and Personality* Harper & Brothers New York

Mitchell, D 2002 *Buddhism: Introducing the Buddhist Experience* Oxford University Press, UK

Murcott S. 1991. *The First Buddhist Women : Translations and commentary on the Therigata.* Parallax

Press. Berkeley USA

O'Reilly M 2000 *The Barn at the End of the World: The Apprenticeship of a Quaker, Buddhist Shepherd* Milkweed Editions USA

Proctor, G 2002, The *Dynamics of Power in Counselling and Psychotherapy,* PCCS Books, UK

Reat, R 1951 *Buddhism: A History* Asian Humanities Press, California USA

Reynolds, D 1980 *The Quiet Therapies* University of Hawaii, Press, USA

Rogers, C.R. 1951 *Client-Centred Therapy.* Constable, London

Rogers, C.R. 1961 *On Becoming a Person.* Constable, London

Rogers, C.R. 1983 *Freedom to Learn.* Merrill, New York

Rhys, Davids, M.A (1909). *Poems of the Early Buddhist Nuns, Therigata.* Pali Text Society, Oxford.

Sanford J, LaFleur, W and Nagatomi, M 1992 *Flowing Traces: Buddhism in the literary and visual arts of Japan* Princetown University Press, USA

Unno, T 1998 *River of Water, River of Fire: An introduction to the Pure Land tradition of Shin Buddhism,* Doubleday, New York

Watson (trans) 1991 *Saigyo: Poems of a Mountain Home* Columbia University Press, USA

Buddhist texts

Some references in this book originate in the Pali texts. These are the scriptures recognised by all Buddhist schools but particularly associated with Theravada. They offer accounts of the Buddha's mission, describing in detail the places and contents of his various teaching encounters. One of the volumes on which I have drawn extensively is the *Majjhima Nikaya* (MN) but there are quotations from other Pali Suttas too. These are referenced in the text of this book and for the most part full translations of the material quoted can be easily traced on the internet.

Other materials quoted are more specific to the Pureland schools. *The Three Pure Land Sutras* are Mahayana sutras which are widely recognised by Mahayana Buddhists but have particular relevance to Pureland for obvious reasons. In these I have sometimes used translations which we have developed in Amida-shu. I have also used the excellent translation and commentary on these sutras by Hisao Inagaki, (published 1994 by Ryukoku University, Japan)

Other texts include the writings of the Pureland masters Honen and Shinran. These are:

Honen *Senchakushu,* (published 1998) Kurona Institute Books, University of Hawaii Press, Hawaii & Japan

The Collected Works of Shinran in two volumes (published 1997); Shin Buddhism Translation Series; Jodoshinshu Hongwanji-ha, Kyoto, Japan

Papers and other materials from web sites

Since relatively few books on Pureland exist in English, and those which there are can be hard to track down, the internet is a major source of good material on Pureland. Both Jodo-shu (http://www.jsri.jp/) and Jodo-shinshu, (http://www2.hongwanji.or.jp/english/), the two largest Pureland schools in Japan have English language sites. Many other sites exist, run by universities and individual temples.

Bloom, A 1968 *The Life of Shinran Shonin: The Journey to Self Acceptance (*Reprinted from Nvmen, XV, I, 1968, with the permission of E.J.Brill, Leiden, Netherlands © 1968, E.J. Brill)

Electronic edition, 1999, Institute of Buddhist Studies, Berkeley, California

http://www.shin-ibs.edu/pdfs/BloomLS.pdf

Sato, T 2004 *Faith as Inner Peace* an earlier version of this paper presented at the 2004 European Shin Buddhist Conference can be found at http://www.wheelswithinwheels.net/dharma/innerpeace.htm

Shigaraki, T *What is Shin Buddhism: 24 Lessons by, retired President of Ryukoku University, Kyoto, Japan http://web.mit.edu/stclair/www/whatis-shin.html*

http://www.jsri.jp/English/Honen/life.html, provides a good account of Honen's life at and his site of the Jodoshu Research Institute is a mine of information on Pureland from the Jodo school.

Our own organisation, Amida-shu, has a number of materials on its web sites at www.amidatrust.com and www.buddhistpsychology.info. These include an on-line Introduction to Pureland Buddhism course which is free to anyone paying a small membership subscription.

INDEX

BOOKS

O books
O is a symbol of the world, of oneness and unity. In different cultures it also means the "eye", symbolizing knowledge and insight, and in Old English it means "place of love or home". O books explores the many paths of understanding which different traditions have developed down the ages, particularly those today that express respect for the planet and all of life. In philosophy, metaphysics and aesthetics O as zero relates to infinity, indivisibility and fate. In Zero Books we are developing a list of provocative shorter titles that cross different specializations and challenge conventional academic or majority opinion.

For more information on the full list of over 300 titles please visit our website
www.O-books.net

myspiritradio is an exciting web, internet, podcast and mobile phone global broadcast network for all those interested in teaching and learning in the fields of body, mind, spirit and self development. Listeners can  hear the show online via computer or mobile phone, and even download their favourite shows to listen to on MP3 players whilst driving, working, or relaxing.

Feed your mind, change your life with O Books,
The O Books radio programme carries interviews with most authors, sharing their wisdom on life, the universe and everything...e mail questions and co-create the show with O Books and myspiritradio.

Just visit **www.myspiritradio.com** for more information.